THE FUTURE OF BANGALORE'S COSMOPOLITAN PASTS

THE FUTURE OF BANGALORE'S COSMOPOLITAN PASTS

Civility and Difference in a Global City

Andrew C. Willford

University of Hawai'i Press

Honolulu

Library of Congress Cataloging-in-Publication Data

Names: Willford, Andrew C. (Andrew Clinton), author.
Title: The future of Bangalore's cosmopolitan pasts : civility and difference
   in a global city / Andrew C. Willford.
Description: Honolulu : University of Hawai'i Press, [2018] | Includes
   bibliographical references and index.
Identifiers: LCCN 2017040689 | ISBN 9780824872908 (cloth alk. paper)
Subjects: LCSH: Bangalore (India)—History. |
   Sociolinguistics—India—Bangalore. | Cultural
   pluralism—India—Bangalore. | Tamil (Indic
   people)—India—Bangalore—Ethnic identity.
Classification: LCC DS486.B362 W55 2018 | DDC 954/.87—dc23
LC record available at https://lccn.loc.gov/2017040689

University of Hawai'i Press books are printed on acid-free
paper and meet the guidelines for permanence and
durability of the Council on Library Resources.

All photos by author

Cover image: An ancient structure reflecting Bangalore's plural past, Someswara Temple has
long served as a shared space traversing linguistic and political divides.

For my father

Contents

Acknowledgments

This project began about a quarter of a century ago. There are far too many individuals and groups that helped me along the way at various stages to list here. Rather than try to recount all those who helped and encouraged, I will mention only a very select few who were quite important at critical stages. First, my advisors at the University of California at San Diego, F. G. Bailey, Suzanne Brenner, and Tanya Luhrmann, were encouraging and careful readers who helped me see the value of comparisons. At UC Berkeley, George and Kausalya Hart taught me both Tamil and a deep appreciation of south Indian literary and religious traditions. Eugene Irschick, Christian Ghassarian, and Lawrence Cohen offered timely advice and encouragement that I will always be grateful for. In Bangalore, I was kindly hosted by the National Institute of Advanced Study (NIAS) in the summer of 2009. At NIAS, I am grateful to A. R. Vasavi, Narendar Pani, Solomon Benjamin, and Carol Upadhya, in particular, for their stimulating conversation and ideas. Vasavi has also been a wonderful interlocutor and colleague for many years. For valuable research assistance and friendship throughout the past twenty-five years, I thank S. Carlos, Linda Carlos, and Cohan Sujay Carlos. At the National Institute of Mental Health and Neuro Sciences (NIMHANS), I thank Drs. Sanjeev Jain and Mathew Varghese.

The Einaudi Center for International Research at Cornell University, Fulbright-CIES, and the American Institute of Indian Studies all provided fellowship funding for parts of this research.

I wish to thank the anonymous reviewers for the University of Hawai'i Press for their generous and extremely helpful suggestions. Pamela Kelley has been a patient, wonderfully supportive, and sagacious editor throughout the entire process. Her sensibilities have always proven to be correct, despite my occasional resistance to good advice.

Finally, I wish to thank my wonderful family for their love and support over the years. Vasantha has been not only my best friend but an amazing mother and partner throughout this long odyssey. Rabin and Anisha have come to know Bangalore quite well, though I suspect their love for this city has, quite understandably, more limits than my own. I thank them for their tolerance of my Bangalore obsession.

Introduction
Identity in the Modern, Postcolonial World

Dravidian University is just outside of Kuppam, Andhra Pradesh, a small town about one hour's drive from Bangalore. This university is dedicated to the study and promotion of Dravidian literatures, cultures, and history. Its strategic location at the borders of Tamil Nadu, Andhra Pradesh, and Karnataka belies its sleepy Deccan landscape of rocky hills and dry groves. I was there to attend a conference on Tamil literature, though I was myself speaking on the topic of the Tamil communities in Malaysia.

One night a senior colleague from Russia and I decided to explore some local villages. Hailing an "auto" (autorickshaw), we sped off at dusk into the dusty countryside on a partly paved but very bumpy road. Our brisk departure was soon halted several times to pick up passengers along the way. At one point, we counted ten passengers in our auto—three in the front, straddling the driver, four in the backseat, where we were seated, and three standing behind and alongside, somehow hanging onto the auto. By then we were moving at a slow crawl. My colleague looked at me and said, with a big grin on his face, "I love adventure."

After about four or five painfully slow kilometers uphill, we entered a village that had a large, attractive temple that looked old. We decided to get down here and explore. Greeting us in the village were lots of children playing in the streets. A few elders looked curiously at us but left us to walk about. After a few minutes of light conversation with the children—mainly in English as they did not know Tamil and we did not know Telugu—an elderly Brahmin priest from the temple came out to greet us. He, like many Iyengar (Vaishnava) priests in the region, spoke an elegant and fluent Tamil, offering to show us around the village and temple. We gladly accepted his offer.

Walking through the various sections of the village by cell phone light, with the exception of the well-lit *agraharam* (area where Brahmins lived), he told us of his village's history and present challenges (water being a principle one in this arid climate). Finally, we stood within the temple (a lovely structure dating from the 1800s, he explained), learning about the annual festival that approached in a few months. He mentioned that the children no longer speak anything but Telugu, the official state language, and would gradually learn English. His children still understood Tamil and Kannada but were not necessarily literate in it. But his grandchildren were increasingly monolingual, he lamented, despite the close proximity to Dravidian University, an institution dedicated to the study of all four principle Dravidian languages: Tamil, Telugu, Kannada, and Malayalam. As a border town where at least three of these languages were widely shared, Kuppam was an ideal location for this multilingual institution. Yet, being in Andhra Pradesh made the teaching of the state language paramount at the expense, evidently, of the other two local languages. The elder priest would have grown up before the linguistic states were drawn, and thus he was conversant in all three local languages. His concern about language and culture loss as a consequence of modern language-based statecraft was made palpable when he said that the children would no longer understand the *devaram* (sacred hymns sung in Tamil) or prayers that he conducted in Tamil.

This little vignette opens this study to introduce the idea of language loss, and by extension, identity attenuation in contemporary India. This is occurring in response to statecraft and, in particular, the creation of linguistic states.

Bangalore has come to signify "progress" and economic possibility, both within India and to the outside world, to which it turns for investment. As the capital of the linguistically drawn state of Karnataka, it has become increasingly charged by movements to make the city more monocultural and monolinguistic. The very ambiguous but materially powerful forces of globalization that produce inward migration, material development, and landscape transformations, coupled with the redrawing of political maps within a postcolonial context, enable and generate monocultural fantasies of the nation. These in turn contradict the densely textured forms of pre- and early modern cosmopolitanism that have been inscribed onto the landscape of the Deccan and in the Bangalore region in particular. How this tension and paradox are resolved is the central question in this book.

More generally, I take this case study to examine the processes by which postcolonial technologies of statecraft create modern forms of identification that suppress alternative possibilities. These other possibilities subsist in the layered cultural practices and idioms that mark what might be called "cosmopolitan" pasts. The question, then, is to what extent older forms and modalities of pluralism can survive the onslaught of modernity, allowing for what Ashis Nandy (2002) has called an incorporation of the Other myths as one's own.

Inspired by Ashis Nandy's discussion of plural selves in Cochin, Kerala, this book ultimately points to sites of cultural practice that work against the monocultural imaginaries that threaten the older fabrics of cosmopolitanism that have continuously existed within the greater Bangalore region. I argue that it is only in the postcolonial rendering of linguistic states that a linear history has demanded territorial linguistic nationalism, and with it, an impossible disentangling of entangled and complex linguistic and cultural pasts (Nair 2005; Srinivas 2001). While many scholars point towards the maritime interconnections that linked specific Asian locales within wider circuits of circulation (Tagliacozzo, Siu, and Perdue 2015), I call attention to South Asia's Deccan as a historical crossroads and suggest that it was a zone of contact between several overlapping empires and a wider world (Rao, Shulman, and Subrahmanyam 2003; Stein 1994).

With the birth of the modern Indian state, the more fluid and protean identities that emerged within the Deccan became increasingly ossified due to the measurement of language affiliation. That is, there has been, at the level of statecraft and regional politics, a disentangling of more pluralistic identities. Ironically, these "modern" parochialisms have emerged at the very moment when Bangalore has become, arguably, India's most cosmopolitan and global city. Moreover, as Rao, Shulman, and Subrahmanyam (2003) suggest, different modalities of temporality and historicity in south India encourage the pluralisms and multiple narratives that complicate the bounded notions of identity produced by modern statecraft (Gottschalk 2000; Kaviraj 1992; Mayaram 1997, 2003). It is in these vestiges of pluralism and fluidity within religious and linguistic practices of the region that both mitigate against and, paradoxically, simultaneously provoke fantasies of ethnic, linguistic, or religious nationalism.

I suggest that 1956 is the watershed moment in this narrative, as this was the year in which Bangalore became the undivided capital of a linguistic state. Given the "serial" imagination that ensued from this legal designation, a new possibility for imagining differences came into being. As Benedict Anderson (1998) has argued, the processes by which both "bound" (e.g., forged by census) and "unbound" (facilitated by newspapers, novels, and film) forms of serialized identities are produced can generate phantasms. Unbound seriality, Anderson argues, is "open-to-the-world" (1998, 30) and expansive, arriving after the advent of newspapers and novels, allowing for sensations of simultaneity across time and space. While Anderson notes its progressive and exciting qualities, it is also phantasmic in the sense that the hypostasized identity of, say, being "Indian" or "Indonesian" involves a forgetting of locality, context, and political control. It allows for "imagined communities" (Anderson 1991) to take shape out of different cultural contexts under the umbrella of cosmopolitanism and/or nationalism. Bound seriality is yet more volatile, perhaps, as it emerges through measurements that can seem arbitrary and narrow. As realized through the technology of the census as, wedded to a legal order, categories reduce a more variegated group of people under a common denominator that is, quite simply, defined in opposition to an imagined other. It is, according to Anderson, the creation of a "finite series like Asian Americans, *beurs*, and Tutsis. It is the seriality that makes a United Ethnicities or a United Identities unthinkable" (1998, 30). That is, types and categories can silence the fractal, porous, or fluid nature of identities (Deleuze and Guattari 1987).[1] I suggest that these suppressed differences, when enshrined in bureaucratic legality, have become the basis for institutionalizing political divisions in colonial and postcolonial statecraft.

But given the impossibility of these modern or serial identities to exist without a suppression of more complex multiplicities raises a question of rationalization. While it could be argued that a cynical and tactical implementation of new forms of identification can be worn like a coat, it is more plausible that the positive investment in an identity claim occurs following its first institutionalized iteration rather than emerging from primordial sentiments. Grounding identity in conventions, enabled by serial measurements and imaginaries, provides an aura of retroactive historicity to the violence of the state and law in enacting and demarcating ethnic difference.

I aim to demonstrate in the ethnographic case material that follows that a plural modality of being still exists in Bangalore and the wider region, bearing the imprint of an ability to incorporate multiple selves into the self (Nandy 2002; Schönbeck 2012). Ultimately, I hope to show what makes civility possible and, conversely, what factors exacerbate tensions within communities and between groups, be they real or imagined to exist. This, I hope, will serve as a model case through which to investigate mitigating and worsening factors in the civility of everyday life in complex cultural and linguistic spaces.

While my own thesis draws upon the work of Benedict Anderson, Arjun Appadurai, Thomas Hansen, Ashis Nandy, and Jacques Derrida, among others, analytically speaking I aim in this work to provide a broader overview of the relative strengths and weaknesses of the anthropology of nationalism, ethnicity, and identity. As such, this study avoids polemics and instead aims to be a critical reflection upon theories of what might be called "excessive" and violent forms of identification versus the conditions that contribute to civility. Thus, this book is in part written with pedagogy in mind, particularly for the anthropology of postcolonial nationalism and identity. At the same time, it is also an ethnography of contemporary Bangalore, albeit one with a somewhat narrow focus upon sites of intensified contestation and/or resilient pluralism over a roughly twenty-year period of on-and-off-again observations and conversations. Here I have also benefited enormously from utilizing the historical and ethnographic work of Janaki

Nair and Smriti Srinivas, respectively, two eminent scholars of Bangalore's past and present.

But the present book is not a comprehensive ethnohistory or ethnography of the city (see especially Nair 2005; S. Srinivas 2001); rather, this is a more limited window into the forces that challenge and sustain civility between linguistic and religious groups. To be more specific, I focus mainly upon the sizeable Tamil-speaking community within Bangalore, examining their minority experience. Secondly, I examine how linguistic serialization and religious serialization interact and overlap by looking at the tensions that emerged during the Ayodhya-related violence that swept Indian cities in 1993. While religion, like language, became a wedge issue affecting intercommunal harmony, it is also a powerful site of pluralism, particularly as the traces of past practices continue to exert their presence within daily life, confounding more singular or serial imaginaries (Thiranagama 2011). A kind of "fuzzy" or permeable boundary remains between religious and linguistic groups, built upon ontologies of belonging and faith that survive modern forms of enumeration (Kaviraj 1992; Mayaram 1997).

This book explicates the forces that are driving cultural identification in exclusive, noncosmopolitan and monocultural directions at the precise moment when globalization and regional implosion through economic development and migration are stretching the symbolic boundaries of the Bangalorean "locality" (Appadurai 1996). In order to understand the extent to which complex and textured histories are being forgotten or disaggregated in the politics of identification, I describe different foci within the symbolic practices in urban space.

First, I discuss those sites of cultural production that have particular conscious symbolic resonance for the members of cultural and linguistic organizations. For example, the production of symbolic imagery surrounding Rajyosatva Day (the founding of Karnataka Day), the proliferation of an urban iconography of the mythic founder of the Bangalore, Kempegowda, the cult status of recently deceased Kannadiga film icon Rajkumar, and the refused "unveiling" of the Thiruvalluvar (Tamil poet and philosopher) statue in the city have all become focal points of struggle, metonymizing a singular imaginary of cultural and linguistic unity (Nair 1996, 2000, 2005; Niranjana 2000; Prasad 2000; Vasavi 2007). Disaggregating the complexity of the Deccan cosmopolitan past, at least temporarily, is aided through these points of symbolic convergence upon focal icons, which in turn appear to have great, if not excessive, symbolic resonance. But in tracing the semantic genealogies of these symbols of ethnic or linguistic pride, icons of authentic identity appear to be very modern renderings (Hobsbawn 1983; Anderson 1991; Thapar 2005). These, I argue, are born out of a way of apprehending history in typographical or "serial" (Anderson 1998) forms that works against the performative genres, textures, and temporal modalities of South Asian life (Rao, Shulman, and Subrahmanyam 2003; Mayaram 1997; Gold 2014). Though the historicity of the Bangalore case is unique, the theoretical implications of this study will be of interest to scholars working on similar problems of excessive and volatile identifications in postcolonial contexts elsewhere.

A second and even more critical dimension of this book comes in its ethnographic focus upon sites of cultural practice that *work against* the monocultural imaginaries that threaten the older fabrics of cosmopolitanism that have continuously existed within the greater Bangalore region. Srinivas (2001) calls these enduring pluralistic cultural practices "landscapes of urban memory." She describes pilgrimage rituals, such as the *karaga jatre,* that incorporate various Tamil, Kannada, and Telugu communities into a performative religious tradition that also crosscuts religious divides (Hindu, Muslim, and Christian). Building upon this notion, I describe shrines and temples in and around Bangalore that are dedicated to Kumaraswamy (Murugan) or to varied forms of Amman, the goddess, have a large following of Tamils, and yet are increasingly popular to Kannadigas and Telugus as well. Moreover, the rituals, such as the carrying of *kavadi, karaga,* or *timithi,* that are often associated with Tamil culture are also practiced by Kannadigas and Telugus. In short, a fluid linguistic and ethnic line exists within these shrines, as many priests and devotees are of mixed ancestry— not surprisingly, as these shrines and temples lie at the borderlands of history, where the Gangas, Cholas, Chalukyas, Vijayanegarans, Hoysalas, Hyder Ali, Tipu Sultan, Wodeyars, and British all ruled *without* linguistic homogeneity or hegemony. Rather, it is only in the postcolonial rendering of linguistic states that a linear history has demanded territorial linguistic nationalism and an impossible disentangling of entangled and complex linguistic and cultural pasts. Amid the gloom of many increasingly communal conflicts, Bangalore still retains a fabric of civility against the modern and serial markings of difference (Nandy 2002). Thus, I argue that the past is a living resource for the negotiation of identity in the present.

Investigating the growth and even revival of these multicultural and multilinguistic rituals and shrines in the greater Bangalore region is extremely significant for at least three reasons. First, as Smriti Srinivas (2001) has noted, the "urban memory" enacted through the ritual performances in these shrines works to reconstitute and reinvigorate patterns of syncretism and cosmopolitanism that have a long history in the region (Pollock 2006; Stein 1994; Rao, Shulman, and Subrahmanyam 2003). Second, the fact that certain shrines are growing in popularity with a working-class constituency perhaps works to reconstitute a "locality," as Appadurai (1996) argues, in contradistinction to the cultural- and linguistic-purifying discourses that mark the petit bourgeois–dominated populist politics of the Karnataka state. Third, as development—and particularly, in Bangalore's case, high-tech development—brings transnational capital, and with it a growing affluence among the middle class, the working-class areas of the city feel the encroachment of urban transformations upon the fabric of old neighborhoods and communities. In this sense, the reconstituting of ritual space through a revival of temple festivals is related to the literal sense of threat and encroachment many neighborhoods and shrines experience in the face of globalization. Moreover, the populist fantasies of cultural and linguistic singularity that, as mentioned above, have been gaining currency and are symbolically condensed upon certain key figures and themes are also fueled by the economic transformations of the landscape, and with it the threat of cultural displacement that it may bring as a new cosmopolitan elite supplants existing patterns of power and culture in the urban space. By focusing upon these predominantly working-class sites of ritual production, we view the effects of globalization as being greatly differentiated by class; and the forms of cosmopolitanism that are being silenced at one level continue to reassert themselves at another.

The book is organized as a series of interlinked thematic essays. The first half of the book focuses upon sites of contestation within Bangalore's linguistic and religious landscape, considering the ways in which modern forms of political identification produce internal others (Appadurai 2006). After a brief introduction to the history of Bangalore and the region, I focus on the battles over linguistic identity through two key events: the abduction of Kannada film icon, Rajkumar, by the bandit-turned-Tamil nationalist, Veerapan, and the fallout from the Cauvery riots, years earlier. I then turn to the rise of the pro-Kannada movement and its specific struggle with the enduring presence of Tamil speakers within Bangalore. Next I shift to the question of Hindu nationalism and show how the struggles for language became conjoined to questions of religious identity. The figure of the Tamil and Muslim, as metonymizing a potential "antinational" presence, is illuminated through a discussion of the symbolic struggles over the nationalist and religious hero, Swami Vivekananda.

The latter part of the book points to sites of enduring pluralism and civility within the metropolis and regional Deccan culture. These sites of plural religious and linguistic practice provide, in Srinivas's felicitous terms, a "landscape of urban memory" mitigating and countering the serialized imaginaries that have arisen as a result of structural, cultural, and political pressures. This enduring pluralism, reinscribing a Deccan "texture" and historicity (Rao, Shulman, and Subrahmanyam 2003), is suggestive of the kind of modality that Nandy (2002) observes for Cochin, whereby selfhood and identity remain nonexclusive and open to multiple historical and linguistic pasts. But it is also suggested that an emergent focus on symbolic struggles over identity within both political and social worlds contributes to a desire to simplify, standardize, and ultimately expel or mark otherness from one's imagined community and self-identity. This can be manifested in xenophobic statements about the threat of the foreigner, figured as minorities, buttressed by the valorization of symbolic icons, creating, in Vasavi's (2007) words, a gradual process of "Political Darshan" for heroic defenders of identity. I argue in a late chapter, too, that discourses surrounding a mental health-care crisis parallel and overlap with the political assertions of identity described earlier. In examining a clinical, psychiatric context in Bangalore, we will see how psychopathology and excessive identity assertions might share a common provenance: the demand for singularity within modern life, be it as a political subject, modern IT worker, or a good Muslim or Hindu.

In laying out the case for both a threat to an enduring cosmopolitanism and a resilient civility that counters it, I also revisit several classic theories of the nation and ethnicity, attempting to demonstrate their continued utility and vitality within more recent and sometimes amnesiac analytical framings of identity and political sovereignty.

On a more personal level, this set of ethnographic essays, reflections, and observations also marks a more than twenty-year love affair with Bangalore. Though not a sustained ethnography of the city, I feel that the cases provided here offer ample material for the illustration and analysis of the forces that push identity in monocultural or serial directions versus those that open up spaces of permeability, fluidity, and, ultimately, civility.

The remainder of this introduction maps out the recurring theoretical orientations and literatures that this book draws upon in order to understand the vicissitudes of identity within Bangalore's changing landscape. In so doing, it also provides a somewhat simplified thematic overview of some of the main currents in the anthropology of nationalism and ethnicity (also see Hutchinson and Smith 1996; Eriksen 1993; Willford 2001). I conclude this chapter by reflecting upon both the limits *and* enduring value of instrumental, cultural, and psychological approaches to identity politics and violence. By pointing to fairly recent work that breaks free from these apparently intractable divisions, I illuminate the intervention I hope to make in writing this book, while also considering the enduring salience of older and sometimes forgotten literatures. Lastly, I conclude by assessing attempts by anthropologists to deal directly with the phenomenal forces of identification by fusing macrotheorization of the nation with microstudies of particular communities and social actors, drawing liberally on psychoanalytic and deconstructive theories. I suggest that Bangalore's recent permutations, postindependence, provide an excellent venue for exploring these issues.

Anthropology and Nationalism: Beyond Instrumentalism and Culturalism

Early British structural-functionalism in the 1950s was influenced by the organicism of Emile Durkheim and Herbert Spencer. Radcliffe-Brown, Evans-Pritchard, and their followers at Oxford sought to understand how small-scale societies operated as "systems" in relative equilibrium.[2] Another school of structural-functionalism that is more relevant to this study emerged under the training of Max Gluckman. Gluckman and his students—Victor Turner, F. G. Bailey, Abner Cohen, and others—viewed society as inherently conflictual. Moreover, Gluckman's students had much more of an instrumental view of the social actor. Thus, Gluckman and his students were interested in social conflict and change. This required closer consideration of the forces of change, which naturally led to analysis of outside political pressures upon local communities.

F. G. Bailey's work on social change in Orissa, India, *Tribe, Caste, and Nation* (1960), captured much of the complexity of nation building through an analysis of the emergence of civil bureaucracies, constitutional changes, and capitalism. In two remote villages in highland Orissa, he described changing relationships between tribal (*adivasi*) Konds, "clean caste" Oriyas, and untouchables. Bailey argued that "tribe," "caste," and "nation" were malleable structures within an emerging political arena. Rather than presenting a "traditional" people being forced into change by the modern state, local actors demonstrated agency in their strategic manipulation of the structures available. Anticipating later critiques of "essentialism" (e.g., Tsing 1993; Dirks 1993), Bailey rejected the notion that subjects within traditional social systems were subjectively constituted by collective value systems. Instead he suggested that actors will appropriate ideologies for their own ends whenever possible.[3] For example, certain "untouchable" (*harijan*) individuals were able to make use of civil legal structures inscribed through the Indian constitution in order to transcend traditional injunctions against their participation in certain political, economic, and religious spheres. Most important, Bailey's *Tribe, Caste, and Nation* forced ethnographers to consider how local events were linked to larger structures, and thus nationalism could be fruitfully studied at the village level through the fieldwork method. As Bailey noted, "Events in the village provide a text, in the commentary upon which the wider systems are unfolded" (1960, 269). Bailey's perspective, though located at a historical moment in India's history, allows us to better understand the strategic deployment of cultural categories and discourses within the modern, postcolonial political order in Bangalore.

While Bailey's study opened new doors of inquiry concerning the manipulation of social change, Louis Dumont offered an important dissenting voice. Dumont, in his famous work on the Indian caste system, *Homo Hierarchicus* (1980), argued that Bailey's approach denied the pervasive and socially constitutive power of hierarchy as ideology embedded within Hinduism and the Hindu caste system. Dumont suggested that Hindus in India were fundamentally different from Western social actors because they were ideologically constituted by the all-encompassing cultural logic of hierarchy in Hindu theology and social practice. In Dumont's eyes, the low-caste political maneuvers in Bailey's analysis were either anomalies or an "underestimation" of the ideological power of caste—that is, a misreading of the analyst based upon his own commitment to a sociological analysis of structure devoid of culture (1980, 351–354).[4] For our purposes, it is important to note that Dumont poses a more urgent question for anthropologists: Do cultural differences constitute qualitatively different social actors and communities; and thus, are there unique cultural ontologies to different nationalisms (Kapferer 1988; Price 2013; Sahlins 1994)? We will return to this question of cultural difference throughout this study to question the limits of instrumentalist analysis.

The extent to which ideology—particularly ethnic and nationalist—becomes a socially relevant emblem of allegiance was explored by Fredrik Barth through fieldwork conducted among Swat Pathans in Pakistan. While symbolic interactionists and interpretivists looked towards the production of intersubjectivity and a sense of "primordial" bonding *within* social groups (culture), Barth's work alerted anthropologists to the production and organization of differences or "boundaries" *between* groups (1959; 1969). In Barth's analysis, ethnicity is not the result of primordial bonds (e.g., race, culture, language, and custom) within a group; rather, it is based upon "conventions of difference" that emerge through an interaction between different social groups within a political field. Pathans, Barth observed, might share common cultural features in different regions; however, in some areas they may see themselves as an ethnic group, whereas in other places they do not. Therefore, Barth suggests that the socially relevant boundary is more important to "ethnic allegiance" and categorization than is the "cultural stuff it encloses" (1969, 11–17).[5]

Like Barth, Abner Cohen (1996) saw ethnic identity emerging from "intensive interaction between ethnic groupings" (quoted in Hutchinson and Smith 1996, 83). Cohen suggested that ethnicity was a strategic assertion of identity within a sociopolitical field. The actual cultural content of ethnicity, the so-called primordial bonds, however, could be manipulated in order to serve political inter-ests.[6] Cohen, through his fieldwork in Africa, demonstrated how apparent revivals of "tradition" were in fact creative manipulations of ethnic or tribal categories and symbols—that is, a politicizing of group interests within an idiom or "style" of "tradition" (Bailey 1963, 222–223). Anticipating Hobsbawm's (1983) assertion that "tradition" in political discourse is largely an "invention," as well as Anderson's (1991) discussion of "official nationalism," Cohen argued for an instrumental view of ethnic and nationalist sentiment. Whatever its limitations, which we examine throughout this book, this perspective has proven both useful and necessary when examining various stakeholders and their interests within an ethnic political field.

While I will argue for the continued salience of instrumental analysis, this study asserts that culture and history cut deep into the landscape, producing particular idioms of political expression. Two key anthropologists, Clifford Geertz and Bruce Kapferer, inspire this attention to cultural difference. Geertz, utiliz-ing Weber's social action theory, argued that the significance of particular social actions required understanding the system of meaning in which such actions were deeply embedded. Geertz thus viewed culture as a text—interpretation required the hermeneutic sensitivity to chains of association that only an intimate appre-ciation of a particular social context could convey. In a number of works, Geertz utilized his interpretive approach to address the problems of nation building and nationalist ideology. Nationalist ideology, for Geertz, cannot unequivocally be viewed as a political "weapon" (instrumentalist) or as a "remedy" for social and psychological strain (functionalist). Rather, ideologies have *particular* meanings, emerging from particular historical circumstances and cultural contexts.

Ideology is the product of people making meaning of social experience, and as such its interpretation must be an act of making meaning of the symbolic richness of those meanings. The extent to which an ideology is successful at motivating a large population to support a political agenda is a function of the expressive power that specific symbols carry within a particular historical and cultural con-text (Geertz 1973, 213). From this premise, Geertz suggested, in what became an influential of oft-stated aphorism, that ideologies, insofar as they were motivat-ing, offered coherent models "of" and "for" social reality (see Ortner 1979 for a theoretical elaboration of this formulation). Ideologies are "maps of a *problematic social reality* and matrices for the creation of collective consciousness" (emphasis mine) (1973, 220).[7]

Bruce Kapferer went one step further by suggesting that nationalisms were born of different "cultural logics" or *ontologies,* out of which practices and ideas have been generated over time. His ambitious book, *Legends of People, Myths of State* (1988), attempted to demonstrate how nationalist ideologies were rooted in fundamentally different conceptions of the person, state, and cosmic reality (ontologies) through a comparison of Sri Lankan and Australian nationalist myths. In so doing, he suggested that the universalist and "objectivist" versions of nationalism offered, for example, by Gellner (1983) and Hobsbawm (1983), in which nationalist discourses were reduced to their homogenizing function or used as a tool for elite politicians yet were the "inventions" of their sponsors, were inadequate for their failure to explain the furious passions such ideologies can generate. To answer the latter question, Kapferer argued that the symbolic power of "tradition" is to be found in everyday social practices and their antecedent ontologies.[8]

Kapferer, though obviously sympathetic to Geertz's interpretive approach, argued that his own position was not to be mistaken for idealism. Instead he suggested a dialectical movement between ontology, ideology, and practice. Ideology, he argued, is a conscious reflection and interpretation, or a model "of" and "for" reality (following Geertz). Ontology, on the other hand, "is beneath the level of conscious reflection. . . . While not a conscious reflection, ontology is nonetheless as integral to consciousness as its logic is ingrained in the habituated practices of the everyday realities of human beings" (1988, 84).[9] In the context of this study, the "landscape of memory" (Srinivas 2001) and the ritual space that reproduces it confound the modern political boundaries that attempt to create "bound" identifications, be they territorial and/or ethnic (Deshpande 2000; Price 2013).

Nationalism can "operate at depth"[10] because it draws upon a logic that is pre-conscious—that is to say that the cultural ontology is structured into the minds, selves, and everyday practices of people.[11] In Kapferer's view, the constitutive power of cultural logics explains why nationalisms can inspire or unleash a violent and collective "madness." The "madness," though appearing irrational, is rooted in particular cultural logics.[12] My suggestion, however, is that a cultural logic can also serve as a source of civility, even if it is organized in hierarchical terms. In this sense, civility does not equate to hospitality or equality but to an enduring permeability between community boundaries. Indeed, everyday violence occurring in the form of hierarchical exchange (e.g., caste and gender hierarchy) can persist and thrive within a shared sphere of cultural meaning (Mayaram 2003).

Marxist-inspired anthropologists (to lump a divergent group into one camp), in contrast, voiced a persistent chorus of caution against granting a deeper reality to the primordial. For Marxists, ethnonationalist and/or religious ideologies act as hegemonic forces—particularly upon those not among the ruling classes. While manufacturing consent through institutional powers and disciplines, ideologies act to mask an underlying reality: the nexus of power and class domination.[13] Put crudely, those with the means to "invent" traditions (Hobsbawm 1983) or disseminate "official nationalisms" in a top-down fashion (Anderson 1991) do so in order to protect or gain privileges within the emerging political structure of the state.

Talal Asad, for instance, offered a useful critique of religion and nationalism in his influential *Genealogies of Religion* (1993). In a meticulous deconstruction of Geertz's definition of religion as a "cultural system," Asad suggested that the "essence" of religion (or of any system of symbols) cannot be defined universally, for to do so is to "separate it conceptually from the domain of power" (29). The crucible of Asad's argument was an assertion that Geertz analyzes religious ideas and practices as systems of meaning, artificially separated from the mental and material conditions that produced particular symbolic codes and practices. Asad, drawing on Foucault, asks the reader to consider how religious truths became "natural and authoritative as opposed to others" (31) which were rejected or suppressed.[14] My discussion of modern statecraft and serialization will build on this notion.[15]

As Anderson (1991) demonstrated, nationalism and imperialism had worked hand in hand during the colonial expansion of capitalism (see also Handler and Segal 1992). Elites in the core nations could legitimize their colonial projects in terms of nationalist ideologies, while simultaneously benefiting from the expanding opportunities provided for nonelites through the economic, military, and civic upward mobility afforded in the colonies.[16] That is to say, class conflict was mitigated by creating a national consciousness—but equally important were the economic benefits accrued by the global division of labor and exploitation of workers in the colonies.[17]

Central to the debate (political philosophies notwithstanding) between those sympathetic to Marxist frameworks and those who saw in it a denial of cultural uniqueness and the depth to which symbols operate was a fundamental, ontological issue regarding human nature and culture. The two essential positions can be noted. On the one hand, Sahlins (1976) and other structuralist-influenced anthropologists (e.g., Kapferer 1988; Dumont 1980) saw a cultural code as preexistent to the division of labor (indeed, as its ordering principle). Conversely, those sympathetic to world-systems theory saw culture as ideology within the "superstructure," or more dynamically, as a dialectic of mutually constitutive economic and ideological structures (e.g., Bourdieu 1977).[18]

While we cannot discount the analysis of the strategic deployment of religion and ethnicity for political gain in the ethnographic stories that follow, it is useful to point to a limitation in such critique and therefore of a necessary engagement with and accounting for the phenomenal force of ideology. There exists, we often witness, an excess of identification within particular religious, ethnic, and national causes that seems to confound obvious interests or value systems. Therefore we are compelled to ask: What is it that gives the nation-state or ethnic group its aura or spirit? Moreover, how does the nation-state's apparent modern origin, its "invented" nature, to borrow Hobsbawm's (1983) famous term, produce such passionate and indeed religious zeal among its citizen subjects? Here our theories become more difficult, speculative, and psychological.

Does not the sometimes-asserted nature of nationalist ideology partially expose the state's cultural arbitrariness and cultural inauthenticity—that is, as "clothed" in nationalist ideology? Does not the violence and repression inflicted in the name of "order" reveal the porous, compelling, yet fractal nature of national identity—an identity contingent upon violent suppression, serial techniques of measurement, as well as gendered and ethnic assertions of hierarchy (Agamben 2005; Pemberton 1994; Hansen 2001)? Therefore, while an instrumental critique of ideology fails to explain, phenomenally speaking, the quasireligious nature of the nation-state, it is the fissures and cracks and certainly the absence of cultural unity and authenticity in nationalist discourse that seem to give rise, paradoxically and circularly, to desires for an imaginary unity of community. Nationalism, then, expresses an impossible desire for gemeinschaft (social intimacy) within capitalist modernity, though this desire is itself variegated (and often haunted) by divergent interests and subject positions within the normative hierarchies inscribed in nationalist discourses.

The desire for "spiritual" value that often saturates nationalist discourses—or its negation by those it excludes—is one that not only betrays historical specificity and political contingency but one that often convulsively repeats its message of authenticity and unity in an attempt to silence the specters of doubt that haunt both leaders and led (Derrida 1995). Doubt and belief are often shown to be dialectically constituted in ethnographic studies of nationalism (e.g., Hansen 2001; Ivy 1995; Appadurai 2006). As Arjun Appadurai argues in addressing the potentially violent and corporeal manifestations of identity assertions, we must come to understand the relationship between exacerbated uncertainty of identity and its paradoxical obverse, the violent and fetishistic "dead certainty" that often marks today's ethnonationalist struggles.[19]

Our ethnographies often suggest a "non-discursive"[20] or phantasmic dimension, silenced and submerged within the public sphere, that is uncovered and witnessed through its effects (e.g., Siegel 1997; Morris 2000; Hansen, 2001; Willford 2006; Zizek 1993). Significantly, postcolonial cultural analysis has often been more critical in unmasking cultural pretensions of "value" in colonial discourse. As Homi Bhabha (1994) has succinctly argued, the colonial desire to produce subjects who would recognize their colonial masters—and thus, following Hegel, bestow upon them mastery—betrayed anxieties of colonial rule (Rutherford 2012). These anxieties were rooted in the partial recognition of cultural and moral inauthenticity.

But when the same Hegelian critique of sovereignty is directed towards post-colonial nationalist—let alone spiritual—imaginings, important voices of concern have also been raised. For example, Partha Chatterjee (1993), in critiquing Anderson's analysis of nationalism's modular form, lamented the loss of "difference," rooted in a moment of "spiritual" critique that marked the genesis of nationalist imaginaries.[21] Indeed, Chatterjee sought to locate a moment of cultural authenticity—a retrievable subaltern not constituted in the nation's modular form (Anderson) or in the dialectics of mimesis by colonial masters (Bhabha). Marshall Sahlins, too, lamented the flattening of cultural analysis to an "obsession with power" in his notion of the "double erasure"[22]—that reducing cultural discourse to the operations of power silences the resiliency of cultural difference, even in the face of structural domination (economic and political) produced in tandem by colonialism and global capitalism.[23] Sahlins was, therefore, less convinced of the analytic necessity of theorizing a nondiscursive or "hidden" domain that requires defetishization, deconstruction, or disclosure.[24]

Sahlins's and Chatterjee's concerns notwithstanding, one could argue that the sovereign ideology's (national or colonial) power is produced out of its impossibility to constitute its subjects completely. Through repetition and compulsive iteration, an absence or "lack" is masked and partially mastered, as in the constitution of the subject in Freudian and Lacanian psychoanalysis, or in the logic of the supplement in Derridean thought. This analytic move involves a characteristic sleight of hand in which the individual subject is extended, in isomorphism, with and to the national subject. One might argue, however, that the psychoanalytic models of Freud and Lacan are explicitly social, in that the constitution of the subject involves the fractious internalization of the superego or, in Lacan's terms, a submission unto the Law (the "Symbolic"). That is, Lacan's notion of the subject's entry into language and mediated self-consciousness, via language, is dialectically mediated by the Other's desire, which in turn is inherently social and thus productive of a necessarily divided subject. The subject, partially recognizing the arbitrary Otherness of the internalized Self (as alienating other), faces the "Real" or contradictory emptiness and radical contingency of identity.

Aside from a problem of reification (of the nation or ethnicity as subject), there is the issue of methodology. A nation or ethnic group cannot be put on the couch in order to assess its relative pathology.[25] If there is a structural homology between the nation's impossibility to achieve universal recognition from its subjects and the subject's impossible desire to master what it has lost through its entry into language, signification, and, ultimately, identity through the nation, then we might expect in the function of the superego and the master ideology of the state a similar submission unto the voice of authority that is, on the one hand, unavoidable and on the other, impossible to satisfy. Through the force of repetition and reiteration, the symbolic voice of authority begins to exert its phantasmic presence (Derrida 1995; Siegel 1997, 1998, 2006; Pemberton 1994). The "emperor's new clothes," in other words, though partially perceived as absent, exert a phantasmic presence through a collective suspension of doubt—a doubt that is silenced through a repetition of identity that belies, indeed covers, awareness of its own empty or contingent origins. That is, the apparent ontological unity of the Self, like the nation, lies in its contradictions and contingency, supplemented and necessitated by an archive of differences (Derrida 1995). This point will be developed in conjunction with the notion of "bound serialization" to suggest that repetition and the conjuring of differences work hand in hand to obscure the porousness and permeability between identities within Bangalore, political machinations notwithstanding.

Zizek (1993) has cleverly argued that there exists a homology between the logics of capitalism and the demands of the superego. Just as the excess of capital produces no satiation of desire but instead exacerbates desire, so too the more one serves the internalized master, the more one feels ambivalence and guilt for not heeding the master's call more completely. True belief, involving the constant reiteration of identity, is one possible symptom of an ascribed or serial identity's fragile hold. At the same time, the function of a master ideology, such as a national ideology, is ironically to partially master the alienation and uncertainty that is produced by the Other, which might in turn be produced by the master ideology itself. In this circular reasoning, mastering the wound of an alienating ideology might involve, paradoxically, fixating upon the very source of the wound in an attempt to silence the anxiety produced by this "Real," to extend Lacan's term to address the nation.[26] The dialectical antagonism produced by the superego (the more we obey, the more we feel guilt) can produce in nationalism (or colonialism) an internally divided and necessarily negative and dissonant constitution of the "purity" that marks identity. This is achieved by locating and signifying the source of inner antagonism through symbolic displacement onto imaginary others (e.g., Taussig 1987; Hansen 2001; Kakar 1996).[27]

Ashis Nandy (2002) has similarly observed that sometimes the most rabid forms of xenophobia and ethnic hatred are expressed by those who have personal and intimate ties with the same hated other. That is to suggest that a recognizable double within the subject can, under certain political or social conditions, produce feelings of a monstrous pollution within that in turn are displaced onto an

Other whose wholly "animal" nature in the imaginary of the subject belies a more intimate relationship with this Other, now deemed impossible or undesirable due to political contingency (also see Hansen 2001; Kakar 1996; Willford 2006; Siegel 2006; Gherovici 2003).[28]

The aforementioned necessary criticisms notwithstanding, we can note, albeit only in the broadest terms, that the resonant force of ideology can draw sustenance through the identification of others who can metonymize unacceptable desires as alien or Other[29] (Aretxaga 2009).[30] But the critical question that remains is how one can conjoin the metonymic representation of Otherness with the workings of law and statecraft (Comaroff and Comaroff 2006).

Benedict Anderson provided a critically important thread to a revised Marxian globalization argument, but one that drew on phenomenology. Invoking Walter Benjamin's analysis of photography, Anderson (1991) argued that "new modes of apprehending the world" came about through print capitalism, which in turn suggests the role of markets and standardization; here the Marxian and Gellnerian position can be somewhat reconciled. But the ultimate zeal of nationalism—the willingness to *die and kill for*—is not merely the product of socioeconomic forces but rather assumes phantasmic form in the imagination. However, it was the ability to imagine a simultaneous group identity—the concept of simultaneity—that enabled nationalist consciousness to emerge. The possessive force of ideology, particularly nationalist or ethnoreligious, in his more recent writings and in the writings of James Siegel (1997, 2006) lies in the alienating newness of the ideology itself through techniques of serialization (Anderson 1998; Morris 2000; Pemberton 1994; Hansen 2001; Ivy 1995). That is, it takes hold primarily as a fetish, masking magically its own performative force through the supplemental claims of authenticity that rely on various displacements and repetitions. The more an ideology asserts a truth, be it religious or nationalistic or a combination of the two, the more it compulsively silences the specter of emptiness through a kind of archival process that defines authenticity negatively, vis-à-vis the "dangerous supplement" (Derrida 1976) that threatens it. The question for sociocultural analysis is then, What produces the pathological fetishistic form of identification that has reared its ugly face in Bosnia, Rwanda, South Asia, and elsewhere? Second, What kind of ethnographic critique can open up or deconstruct politically sponsored *disavowals of the Other*?

Arjun Appadurai, a pivotal voice I draw inspiration from in this study, extended Anderson's argument within his influential work on global culture (1996). The possibilities for mass-mediated "scapes" providing new modes of identification is, coupled with migration, the engine of what he calls "culturalism"—the hypostasized expression of difference. Media and migration are the anchors behind the emergence of global *diasporic ethnoscapes*. These transnational cultural formations in turn confound the boundaries of the nation-state and make possible a perpetual multicultural imaginary, enabling groups to resist the pressures to conform or assimilate to national imaginaries that are state driven.

Appadurai also pointed to the dystopic possibilities mass-mediated representations can produce—be they in India, the United States, or elsewhere. Transnational culture flows can produce a swirl of reified and simplified differences all around us—as we see in the Internet and satellite television. While most would not find that this potpourri of cultural forms instigates a clash of culture, it is possible to read recent ethnic and religious imaginaries as being fueled by the uncertainties unleashed by globalization; and particularly how nation-states—or even, in India's case, linguistic states—combat these pressures through discourses of nationalism or regional subnationalisms. Herein lies the greatest risk: If these ideologies of ethnic or religious nationalism involve disavowals of difference through stereotypes of the Other, then the phantasm of the disavowed in turn fuels feverish stereotyping. Indeed, how do we explain the inhumane outbursts of ethnic and religious violence in recent years, Appadurai asks?

Implicitly following the dialectical premises suggested here, Appadurai argued that identity is contingent, malleable, and only fixated upon when a sense of "radical social uncertainty about people, situations, events, norms, and even cosmologies" exists (2000, 305). Appadurai's insight will be deployed throughout this study to draw lines of asserted difference together under a common analytic rubric. That is, as Bangalore's exacerbated uncertainty of identity is generated by its unwieldy growth, new discourses of a more serialized and homogenized identity have taken hold, be they linguistic, ethnic, religious, or even medical.

Ethnic labels are products of state policies and juridical techniques, such as censuses, partitions, allocations, reservations, and constitutions (i.e., religion, caste, ethnicity as vehicles or prohibitions within electoral politics). Naturally, such a view of globalization must trace political technologies to the age of colonialism, when such methods were hardened in practice. But the global present—particularly the advent of mass mediation, migration, and travel—has accelerated this uncertainty to levels unthinkable, according to Appadurai. This uncertainty can even manifest itself through psychological symptoms, as I suggest in a later chapter.

Aside from reanimating the importance of authors mentioned earlier such as Cohen, Bailey, Barth, and Geertz, Appadurai asks us if political violence correlates with the increasing velocity and intensity of hypostasized and bounded identities (e.g., the bound serialization of identity). If so, then an uncanny sense presides whereby the (ethnic, linguistic, religious) Other, prohibited now by political contingency, exists within the realm of the "unimaginable."[31] That is, the phenomenal force of suppression produces concomitant displacements. Is this why "betrayal" is such a common theme in ethnic violence (Malkki 1995; Ghassem-Fachandi 2012; Hansen 2001; Thiranagama 2011; Aretxaga 2009)?

Appadurai returned, somewhat obliquely, to the classical dialectical understanding of self-recognition through the Other: "Purification and clarification appear to be in a dialectical and productive relationship" (2000, 315). As in Hegel's famous master/slave encounter and the struggle for recognition that ensues, recognition is the condition of self-identity, yet in that recognition comes also dependency and intimacy. No identity is sovereign or autonomous. In this dialectic and even in its pathological struggle to silence the Other lie the seeds of potential mutual recognition, and ultimately a form of civility can become possible.

Finally, while I have spoken of anthropological and social scientific approaches to the study of nationalism in this introduction, we will take heart in the knowledge that such critical methods of inquiry—that is, methods for inward and outward reflection and dynamic (re-)interpretation—have always existed. Indeed, what now follows by way of an ethnographic exploration is a study not of ethnic disaster but rather an analysis of *both* frayed and serialized identities in a postcolonial city, *as well as* an enduring civility in which a common "landscape of memory" (Srinivas 2001) crosscuts and counters exclusionary imaginaries of community bound by ethnicity, religion, or language. Moreover, and analogous to the crosscutting and permeability of identities I allude to here, I draw in catholic fashion upon the instrumental, culturalist, Marxist, psychological, and deconstructionist strains of thought outlined in this introduction in order to show that not only can all contribute to our understanding of identity in the modern, postcolonial world, but that in so doing we also can note the limits of any one approach to the subject of civility and difference. I also wish to suggest that the case of the southern Deccan and Bangalore in particular is very felicitous in this regard. While not a port city (as in most studies of plural identities), its situatedness at the borders of empires and states throughout the past two millennia has made it the cosmopolitan place that it is. It is to this earlier cosmopolitan space that I now turn in order to set the stage for the first postindependence stirrings of monoculturalism, with the formation of language-based states in 1956.

CHAPTER 2

Bangalore in History
Empires, States, and Borderlands

Bangalore,[1] the present capital of the state of Karnataka since 1956, lies near the border of Tamil Nadu and Andhra Pradesh in southeastern Karnataka. The city, synonymous globally with high-technology industries, has witnessed a dramatic rise in population during the last thirty years. Immigrants to the city—both from other parts of Karnataka and from elsewhere in India—have made it one of the most prosperous and cosmopolitan of Indian metropolises. Despite an influx of wealth and a relatively peaceful history during the last two hundred years, the city has also witnessed increasing incidents of ethnic and religious violence since the 1990s. Before describing these events, however, a brief history of the city and region provides an understanding of the "traditions" being invoked and imagined by various contestants in the city.

Bangalore is on the cool Deccan plateau directly between Chennai and the tropical Malabar coast. Though the history of the city begins in the sixteenth century CE, the region—comprising many ancient villages, forts, and pilgrimage sites—has been at the crossroads of south Indian history since the seventh century CE, and probably earlier. Even during King Ashoka's Mauryan Empire (fourth century BCE), the region was marked by Buddhist and Jain inscriptions. Roman coins have also been found in Bangalore, suggesting that the region was part of an early trade route between west, east, north, and south (Sastri 1975). During the last two thousand years, the region has been ruled by various southern empires, resulting in the spread of religious ideas, the migrations and mixing of linguistically diverse populations, and the emergence of synthetic local traditions.

Between the sixth and eighth centuries CE, the Chalukya Empire ruled much of the central Deccan from their capital cities of Vatapi and Aihole, in present-day northern Karnataka. At the southeastern border of their empire were tensions with the other great southern empire of this period, the Pallavas. The Pallavas ruled from Kanchipuram and Mahabalipuram (near present-day Chennai). The Bangalore region was to fall under both Chalukya and Pallava rule and cultural influence during this period. Chalukya leaders actively patronized Brahminical traditions and Sanskrit language from the north, while also officially recognizing

Kannada as the local language (Thapar 1966; Sastri 1975). The Pallavas were similarly patrons of Tamil and Sanskrit, and as they conquered stretches of the Deccan, they spread these languages into the region. Kannada itself developed under the influences of both Tamil and Sanskrit. During this period, the distinctive Tamil school of Hinduism known as Saiva Siddhanta developed in the Pallava and Pandyan controlled areas (Pandya was a kingdom in the deep south). This school of thought was popularized by Tamil Saivite saints known as Nayanmars. Their *bhakti* (devotion) towards Shiva, regardless of caste position within the Brahminical system, was seen as an ideal for social reform, as well as offering Dravidian resistance to the "Aryanization" of the south (Thapar 1966; Ramaswamy 1997). This form of Hindu practice—and the development of Tamil poetry and hagiography that emerged from it—also spread to the Deccan, where Kannadigas (Kannada speakers) and Telugus were attracted to the Tamil variety of Shaivism (Ramanujam 1993).

The next empire to exert cultural influence upon the Bangalore region was that of the Cholas (Annaswamy 2003; Sastri 1975). As the Pallavas and Chalukyas declined in power, the Cholas dominated over much of the Deccan and Tamil-speaking areas between the tenth and eleventh centuries.[2] The Cholas ruled from Thanjavur, in present-day Tamil Nadu. Their rule was a golden age for Tamil literature, the arts, and for the development of a classical Dravidian style of temple architecture. By 1024 CE, the Bangalore region was under Chola rule and was called Nikarilacholamandala (M. N. Srinivas 1994). The Cholas, being master temple builders, left a legacy of construction that can still be seen in Karnataka today—in addition to their many architectural achievements in Tamil Nadu (Annaswamy 2003). It was also under Chola rule that Tamil-Hindu cultural influences spread to Southeast Asia through commerce and colonization. In sum, the Chola period was one of Tamil cultural and linguistic hegemony throughout much of south India (Sastri 1975; Stein 2010; Coedes 1968).

By the twelfth century, the Hoysala kingdom, this time based in the Kannada-speaking Deccan, gained ascendancy over the Chola territories near Bangalore (Annaswamy 2003; Sastri 1975; S. Srinivas 2001). While the Cholas and Pandyans continued to dominate most of the Tamil-speaking regions, the Hoysala Empire assumed much of the territory formerly under the Chalukyas. The Hoysalas were great patrons of Hinduism, sponsoring construction of major temples near Mysore and in both Belur and Halebid, all in present-day southern Karnataka. In addition to their military prowess, they were master artists, developing an ornate style of sculpture. As the Cholas were to the Tamils, the Hoysala period—especially during the twelfth and thirteenth centuries—became known as a golden age for art and religious architecture to the Kannadigas. But whereas Saivism flourished among Tamils, Vaishnavism took root within the Hoysala realm. There was an interesting Tamil connection relating to this development.

Vaishnavism was popularized in Karnataka in the eleventh and twelfth centuries by Ramanuja, a Tamil Brahmin who became famous throughout India due to the development of a school of Vedantic philosophy known as Visishtadvaita, which reconciled personal devotion with the more monistic or nondualistic Vedanta philosophy. The Cholas were ardent Saivites and came to resent the growing popularity of Ramanuja and his movement. According to legend, the Cholas banished him from 1098 until 1122 to the Hoysala territories. There he converted the Hoysala king Vishnuvardhana from Jainism and established monasteries and temples dedicated to Vishnu and his avatars.[3]

The influence of Ramanuja and his disciples was also seen in the Kannada language itself. Earlier *bhakti* literature,[4] coupled with the influence of Ramanuja and his followers, brought Tamil devotional practices and poetry into Kannada-speaking areas. Legend has it that many of the present-day Vaishnava Brahmins in Bangalore—known as Iyengars—descend from the Kannada-influenced Tamil speakers who followed Ramanuja. According to one legend, the Hoysala king who was converted to Ramanuja's sect adopted the Tamil language along with his subjects (Bayer 1986). While the Iyengars are usually considered Tamils, the evidence suggests a Tamil-Kannada (and to a degree Sanskrit) regional culture that developed in the Mysore-Bangalore region. The syncretic nature of Iyengar linguistic and cultural identity will be addressed again later.

The last great empire to rise in the south was that of Vijayanagara. This empire, which arose in the mid-fourteenth century, came to dominate much of south India for over three hundred years. Though based in northern Karnataka, it also extended deep into Tamil- and Telugu-speaking areas. Under the protective umbrella of Vijayanagara, the Hindu south maintained freedom from Mughal conquest. For this and for its patronage of Kannada literature, Vijayanagara became a potent symbol of both Hindu (Sastri 1975) and Karnataka (Stein 1994) nationalism. Vijayanagara allowed a degree of local autonomy within Tamil (Chola) territories, operating as a confederation with loyalty to one Hindu-preserving emperor (Sastri 1975). Nevertheless, Tamil rebellions against Vijayanagara rule were not uncommon. Two of the most famous (or infamous, depending on whether one is a Tamil or Kannadiga) were led by Nagama Nayaka and Chellapa Saluva Nayaka, who helped found the Nayaka kingdom in Madurai in opposition to Vijayanagara (Stein 1994).

The city of Bangalore was founded by a Vijayanagara chieftain named Kempegowda I in 1527.[5] Both Kempegowda I and his son Kempegowda II utilized Vijayanagara revenues to build a fort, clear roads, build temples, and erect watchtowers in the city. The Vijayanagara king Krishnadevaraya granted control of the land south of Bangalore (present-day southern Karnataka) to a Tamil Brahman (Iyengar) named Govindaraja. As it was in Ramanuja's time, the region was linguistically cosmopolitan under Vijayanagara rule (Stein 1994).

The seventeenth and eighteenth centuries were politically turbulent after the fall of Vijayanagara. In 1638, Bangalore was captured by the sultan of Bijapur. The city was then sold to Chikkadevaraja Wodeyar, the raja of Mysore in 1687. In 1759, however, the city was surrendered to Hyder Ali, a general in the Mysore army. Hyder Ali and his son Tipu had gradually supplanted the Wodeyars as monarchs in the kingdom after a series of decisive battles against the Magadi kingdom to the north. Under Hyder Ali and Tipu Sultan, Bangalore grew as an important satellite to Srirangapatna, from where the sultan ruled. It was also during this period that the city came to have a large Muslim minority population (Nair 2011). There is evidence that Tipu Sultan promoted a degree of religious pluralism, at the very least, out of political expediency, defending and patronizing important Hindu shrines within his realm. This was true even within his capital, Srirangapatna, the ancient city whose patron deity was Ranganathaswamy, the reclining image of Vishnu.[6]

The British captured Bangalore in 1791 and later killed Tipu Sultan in a battle in Srirangapatna in 1799. Under the British, Bangalore was given back to the Wodeyar rajas from Mysore. This was imagined by some, particularly colonial officers, as a defeat of Islam and the restoration of a Hindu kingdom (Nair 2011). Taking a larger perspective, however, it appears that neither religion nor language were driving political alignments. Urdu had become an important regional language under Hyder Ali and Tipu Sultan, though Kannada, Telugu, and Tamil were also widely spoken. Indeed, the Bangalore area, under the rule of Mysore kings, was, just prior to Hyder Ali's rule, under the control of the Bijapur Sultanate, which in turn resisted the Mughal expansions into the south. Therefore, alliances crosscut religious affiliation and were regional in nature. While Hyder Ali had supplanted the Wodeyar Hindu rajas, he was previously their leading general and had been given Bangalore as a personal revenue grant in 1758 (Heitzman 2004).[7]

With the restoration of Wodeyar rule, the Mysore king allowed the British to build the largest cantonment in south India adjacent to the old city in 1809. The "Cantonment," as it was known, also became the principal British administrative center for the region. Railway links between Madras and the Cantonment allowed for increased trade between the two cities; and more important, the Cantonment section of Bangalore became an administrative and military extension of the Madras Presidency. The Cantonment attracted a large population of immigrants to Bangalore in order to serve the needs of the growing British population. Civil servants, traders, contractors, artisans, laborers, and servants were recruited or attracted to the Cantonment. Most were Tamil speakers—many having been recruited from Madras. At the same time, the Cantonment also produced a stream of working-class immigrants, leading to the haphazard growth of the city:

> Only some parts of Cantonment have wide roads, bungalows set in spacious compounds. . . . Cantonment also contains long narrow lanes in which houses cling to each other, the neighborhood being palpable, noisy and conflict-ridden. . . . Then there are parts of Cantonment which look as though they have been transplanted from a small Tamil town like Villapuram or Vellore: Houses with Tamil-style verandahs in front, massive, carved wooden doors with parts daubed with turmeric or *kumkum* stripes, and the inmates living the same way that their cousins in Tamil Nadu do. There are also slums on the outskirts of Cantonment. (M. N. Srinivas 1994)

In effect, the Cantonment and the old city became two entities (Pani 2010; Nair 2005). One result of this division, as mentioned, was the dramatic growth of the city. Additionally, Bangalore, though always at the crossroads of various empires in the south, became a border town between the Tamil- and Kannada-speaking states. The British departure in 1947, on the other hand, created challenges and problems for a city dichotomized by former Cantonment and non-Cantonment sections. After independence, the Cantonment section of Bangalore remained part of the Madras Presidency until 1956, when state boundaries in India were redrawn along linguistic lines.

With the creation of Karnataka in 1956 and the redrawing of state boundaries, the Tamils in Bangalore found themselves a minority within the capital of a Kannada-speaking state. At the time, there were detractors to imagining the Mysore state in linguistic terms. Some influential figures argued that given the polyglot nature of the city and region, the state should be more inclusively imagined in terms of a regional culture, rather than having an exclusive linguistic identity (Nair 2011). This argument ultimately lost, particularly as linguistic nationalism gained strength in neighboring Tamil- and Telugu-speaking territories within the Madras Presidency and with the creation of the states of Tamil Nadu and Andhra Pradesh. But the multilinguistic legacy of the city made English the initial lingua franca for government and law. Most Bangaloreans grew up speaking many languages, including Kannada, Telugu, Hindi-Urdu, and Tamil, and were thus able to communicate freely with each other. For Tamils, though their numbers were slightly less than the dominant Kannadigas, the proximity of nearby Tamil Nadu made it easy for them to maintain a separate linguistic identity. Moreover, as Pani (2010, 21–22) points out,

> The Tamils in the City were comfortable with Kannada as a language and with the local culture. . . . The Tamils in the Cantonment, on the other hand, had during the colonial period little or no knowledge of Kannada. Instead they had some familiarity with English. In the post-colonial period, when the Cantonment was slowly integrated into a larger Bangalore, the Kannada culture of the City came into direct and daily conflict with the Tamil-dominated culture of the Cantonment. And since the knowledge of Kannada was low, if not non-existent, among the Tamils of the Cantonment, the conflict was based around the role of Kannada as a language.

Postindependence Bangalore has become one of the most developed and prosperous cities in all of India. It has replaced Chennai (Madras) as south India's most important center of industry and commerce. Its favorable climate—above the sweltering tropical heat of south India—has also attracted many expatriates and multinational corporations. Bangalore became an information technology (IT) center and is the home of the Indian-owned companies Wipro and Infosys (Heitzman 2004; Nair 2005). With the emergence of these and other companies, many of them multinationals, located in the southern part of the city and to the east near the township of Whitefields, the vision of a high-tech metropolis took shape. Planners and the high-tech industry combined talents in the form of the Bangalore Development Authority (BDA) (S. Srinivas 2015; Heitzman 2004; Nair 2005).

Central to envisioning the high-tech city was providing infrastructure for greater mobility, as well as abundant housing. On the side of transportation, "Ring Roads" circumambulating the busy city centers were created to allow easier access to high-tech parks. A metro train system was also created, in part to upgrade rapid transit in the city. These projects dramatically altered the city landscape and sparked a growth of housing developments along newly created industrial corridors focused upon the high-tech industries. While in the past, Bangalore grew around the old city and Cantonment, a population boom around the IT estates occurred. As Smriti Srinivas notes, "By the end of the twentieth century, with the liberalization of the Indian economy, Bangalore came to be regarded as 'India's Silicon Valley' with technical, scientific, and professional strata, local and global microelectronics, and information-based industries. Today, the radial system of national highways is linked to the new Ring Roads, and much of the high-tech profile of the city is tied to this regime of mobility" (2015, 125).

But the dramatic growth of the city's infrastructure was insufficient to match the needs of the growing population. Overpopulation, pollution, traffic jams, and strains on electricity and potable water systems became endemic and contributed to the everyday stress of life in the city. A growing sense of crisis during the 1990s over transportation, pollution, and other symptoms of uncontained and poorly planned growth gripped planners and residents alike (Heitzman 2004; Nair 2005).

Beyond the physical discomforts of urban sprawl, the social and cultural transformations also produced anxieties over identity as villages were incorporated into the city limits and thus interconnected with other communities and different social strata (Nair 2005; Pani 2010). With class disparities also widening between the emergent middle class supported by the IT industry and a large working class, insecurities over class position fueled a desire for gated enclaves and suburban lifestyles dependent upon yet separated from the servicing working class. As Appadurai (2013) has argued, this complex relationship between a widening urban class divide is generative of "spectral" presences manifested in fear and displacements of unsavory characteristics onto the poor, the figure of the migrant, or the Muslim and/or Christian. I will return to this spectral presence of the poor or ethnic Other within a middle-class imaginary throughout this study. What can be noted for now is that a new and complex cultural and social mosaic was rapidly introduced in the 1980s, 1990s, and 2000s with the growth of new infrastructure and subsequent population boom. This new mosaic, however, rested upon an old fabric of cultural life that still persists (S. Srinivas 2001; 2015). Srinivas captures this spectrality within new housing developments and, more broadly, among an emergent middle class in a vivid way that is worthy of extended quotation:

> The brochures for dream homes gloss over the existential reality of these highways and the mottled urban fabric that is being constituted here—the density, discomfort, and danger of traffic; the numerous shrines and roadside temples that attract constituencies that travel these roads; the villages engulfed by new road systems; and the complex public signage and politics that seek to make sense of or struggle over these new lifeworlds of work, mobility, and selfhood. These brochures promise an almost autochthonous lifeworld untouched by external phenomena, especially the messy quotidian reality of the streets, the world outside the housing estate, and the irritating tedium of the state and its inefficient services. In this sense, their vision coincides with attempts by the liberalizing state to create a new middle-class version of the beautiful and purified city. However, neither

spatial nor religious history can be made to disappear without a trace and, in the case of the beltways, such elements return to haunt, mark, or orient these spaces. (2015, 131)

In my own experiences living in the enclave of CV Raman Nagar, on the eastern side of the city, for twelve months in 2014–2015, I could witness firsthand how the development that Srinivas describes played out. I stayed within a gated apartment complex with fairly rigorous security. Nobody from the neighboring village could enter in the large and landscaped complex without an invitation from residents living within it. When domestic help arrived or deliveries from local businesses were made from the local, largely working-class area surrounding the gated complexes, they were subject to heavy scrutiny, which among other things meant having bags checked upon exiting the grounds. Within the complex there was a high concentration of IT and other professionals (doctors, engineers, etc.) from various parts of the country. Hindi could be heard as ubiquitously as the Kannada or Tamil spoken outside the complex.

Outside the complex was an older village that had been incorporated into the city limits along the Old Madras Road, where a new Metro line had provided quick access to the city for professionals.[8] Those using the Metro were primarily middle class, as the buses were still the cheapest mode of travel for workers. Walking the now congested village roads was an exercise in alertness, as these narrow roads and alleys had become choked by motorbike and automobile traffic as motorists sought shortcuts from the ever-jammed-up Old Madras Road. Moreover, the various gated communities had mushroomed between these older villages without the planning of artery roads to relieve congestion, making these older villages perpetually clogged by vehicles and the noise of horns. While luxurious cars pushed their way through narrow roads, pedestrians dealt with cracked or nonexistent sidewalks, as well as the busy street life of a south Indian town where vendors sold hot oil-fried snacks, vegetables, and fruits along the roadside and cobblers and bicycle repairmen also plied their trade on the street. Several roadside shrines to various Hindu deities became active in the early evenings and mornings, with prayers being conducted for passing foot traffic or the occasional car that would stop and have a priest conduct a short *puja* (worship) for its driver, all while blocking traffic. Occasionally, one could witness a religious festival, funeral procession, or political rally on the village roads, providing yet more cacophony and congestion. These older villages, in short, were thrust into the pains of modern urban life without the associated infrastructure that would make life more convenient. The wealthier residents living within the gated communities, however, had both transportation alternatives such as the Metro or luxury cars with drivers who could navigate the incessant traffic for them, which could ferry them to spacious and posh shopping malls, restaurants, and high-end businesses. The proximity of Indira Nagar (S. Srinivas 2015), a very upscale part of town, lying only two kilometers away, also provided a refuge for the middle class.

Walking outside of the gated community one heard Tamil, Kannada, and Telugu languages most commonly spoken.[9] Within the several local temples and mosques catering to the working-class orientation of these urban villages, priests or imams spoke these south Indian vernaculars to conduct prayers. Similarly, local shopkeepers spoke the local languages together with a smattering of English. Inside the gated complex, however, English was the most ubiquitous language, particularly among the schoolchildren living there. While their parents and grandparents might speak a mother tongue from another part of India, all the children spoke English among themselves and when speaking with their parents.

I am certain that some of these middle-class residents from the gated communities attended and patronized local shrines and temples. But the emphasis on yoga, meditation, and various ashram-based movements was much more clearly visible within the complex in the form of various notices pasted on the community bulletin boards. Famous contemporary or modern gurus or those from the recent past were highlighted in various postings. Among the most popular were Sri Sri Ravishankar, Isha, Satya Sai Baba, and Shirdi Sai Baba. *Darshan,*[10] meditation classes, or devotional worship of these figures was clearly popular.[11] Morning yoga classes were arranged within the complex for the residents. In the evenings, other classes were offered, which included aerobics and martial arts.

These brief observations mirror what Srinivas (2015) observed in the nearby neighborhood of Indira Nagar. The rise of the IT industry created, in short, new nodes of residency along development corridors. The cosmopolitan and transnational companies in turn also attracted a new kind of middle-class religiosity that tended to cluster around these newer enclaves. As Srinivas observes, property developers often emphasize resortlike living conditions within close proximity to spiritual centers that emphasize "inner engineering" and "the empowerment of selves, universal values, and cosmopolitan audiences living with a global milieu of travel, electronic communication, and neoliberal economics" (138). While some of these new physical terrains have corresponded to a rise in new spiritual terrains, there exist older and more established nodes of middle-class religiosity within the city as well that similarly attract a diverse but pan-Indian core of devotees. The Ramakrishna Mission is, perhaps, the most important and established among these. I discuss the appeal of this movement to the middle class in a later chapter.

Closely related to the rise of religious movements has been the successful marketing of holistic therapies to counter the urban stress associated with the accelerated and quickly shifting lifeworlds in Bangalore (as is the case elsewhere, of course). Ayurveda and yoga are the more famous systems of mind/body/spirit science to have gained in popularity. Ayurvedic and yoga treatment centers have even emerged and have been integrated within major biomedical institutions in India, such as at the National Institute for Mental Health and Neuro Sciences (NIMHANS) and Ramya Medical College, which in turn have been supported by government funding (Abraham 2012). Almost all affluent parts of the city, such as Indira Nagar and along the Ring Roads and townships not far from IT centers, have numerous Ayurvedic clinics and yoga centers for meditation and healing. These centers spiritualize the landscape as well as providing a sense of individual control and agency against the cultural and psychological stresses and dislocations caused by the rapid social, cultural, and spatial changes induced by the new urban domains of living. That is, as the social fabric is in flux, whether one is longtime inhabitant or recent arrival, seeking some meaningful cultural moorings seems to have become both the symptom and salve for the troubling of identities. Here, perhaps, we see the enduring significance of Geertz's thinking on this issue, as we recall from our introduction.

Geertz's perspective directs the focus of attention upon the symbols being utilized within nationalist discourse rather than upon the interests of specific social actors themselves. Though not blind to the elite-led nature of most nationalist and religious "rationalizations," he explicitly warned of a "Machiavellian" reading of motives (1968, 1979). Those who disseminated ideologies in response to a crisis of meaning also answer to a crisis of political legitimacy—which is of central concern to those in positions of dominance. At the same time, Geertz argues, the arbiters of nationalist ideology are themselves motivated by factors other than a purely instrumental concern with power and wealth. As Srinivas cogently observes, "While older devotions continue to have a life, it is impossible to ignore the flourishing of these alternative practices and therapies as citizens seek to make sense of, control, or direct the shifting, dangerous, painful, or uneven dimensions of their habitations and bodies" (2015, 143–144). In a later chapter, I also briefly explore the psychological, social, and cultural stresses within a clinical psychiatric context in Bangalore.

In sum, the past fifty years have produced new cultural imaginaries within the cityscape of Bangalore. The formation of linguistic states and the making of Bangalore as the capital of a Kannada language-speaking state produced an impetus towards the disentangling of complex cultural and linguistic formations and a serialized Kannadiga identity. In more recent decades, the dramatic growth in population, new residency patterns, and inward migration caused by the rise of the IT industry have led to some troubling of identity and increased stress and chaos within daily life. Spiritual and traditional therapies have come to fill this void for some. For the long-residing residents of the city, the influx of the "foreign" through the growth of the IT industry has stirred parochialism through linguistic and ethnic passions, which in turn coalesced with the political and state-driven forces of linguistic and religious nationalism.

The economic boom in Bangalore, together with a sizable foreign presence, have made it one of the most westernized and cosmopolitan of Indian cities. Yet, in spite of these developments and in addition to its already pluralistic past, the city has witnessed increased linguistic and religious tensions. I look now at the Tamil-Kannadiga tensions that erupted in Bangalore in response to a dispute over the kidnapping of a Kannada film icon by a Tamil bandit-would-be political rebel. I suggest in turn that this incident was related directly to a recurring conflict over the sharing of Cauvery River water between Karnataka and Tamil Nadu.

CHAPTER 3

Rajkumar's Abduction and a Dispute over Water

On July 30, 2000, the Kannada film hero Rajkumar was kidnapped by a notorious Tamil bandit and smuggler named Veerapan. Rajkumar was not just any film icon, he was the Kannada equivalent of Tamil Nadu's actor-turned-politician, "MGR." Rajkumar, a film icon since the 1960s, had long been a champion of Kannadiga identity and rights in Karnataka. His abduction led to small riots across the city of Bangalore as bands of Rajkumar fan club members and Kannada associations threw stones at businesses with glass facades, into universities, and other establishments associated with the elite. Public transport was halted in solidarity with the hero, and people were also forced to abandon private vehicles and walk home (Nair 2005).

Random attacks against Tamils occurred, particularly directed against the poor, mostly migrant laborers in the city. These attacks occurred again after the death of Rajkumar of natural causes a few years later. As one Tamil professional told me,

> After the death of Rajkumar, random attacks against the poor Tamils became a problem again. The middle class don't bother about these things. It is a lower-middle-class phenomenon. Cauvery (water) is an issue once a year, and leads to protests and violence. After the death, people were throwing stones at glass windows of auto dealerships and into the IISC compound (Indian Institute of Science). There were all sorts of atrocities for two days while they decided what to do with the body. On the TV, no Tamil stations were allowed for two months—they were blocked, even the satellite ones. Tamil shops and taxi drivers put Rajkumar photos up to survive. There was even a moratorium on Tamil movies for sixty days after their release in order to support Kannada films.

This individual's comment, which was echoed by several other professionals both among Tamils and Kannadigas, is significant as it locates the source of violence as emanating from the lower middle class, not the poor. Moreover, the poor, particularly the migrant laboring poor, are on the receiving end of this violence. This parallels what Hansen (2001) has described for the Shiv Sena–led violence against minorities in Mumbai.

For 108 days, Rajkumar was held hostage by Veerapan. Throughout his ordeal, rallies, *bandhs* (strikes), and prayer meetings were held throughout the city, organized by his fans and family members. When he was finally released, after successful negotiations between Tamil business and cultural leaders and Veerapan, the city erupted in a "carnival of joy" (Nair 2005, 235). Tamil-owned businesses survived the ordeal by placing photos of the film hero in their shop fronts.

One of the negotiators, a prominent Tamil businessman, explained to me that the consequences of the kidnapping were high, and thus the stakes for his release were consequential to all Tamils in Karnataka. Though Veerapan engaged in this criminal act ostensibly on behalf of the plight of Tamils in Karnataka, his actions were believed to endanger Tamil interests and to embolden hardline Kannadiga organizations that were increasingly anti-Tamil. Specifically, he called for a permanent solution to the Cauvery water dispute, compensation for all Tamil riot victims from the Cauvery-related violence of 1991, the inclusion of Tamil as an administrative language in Karnataka, the installation of the Thiruvalluvar (a Tamil ethicist/saint) statue in Bangalore, and investigations into atrocities committed by the Special Task Force in the forest against so-called smugglers, such as himself and his followers (Nair 2005, 236; Raghuran 2001). Veerapan had, in this kidnapping, become a Robin Hood–like figure for some Tamils, but many were also quick to distance themselves from him, particularly those in public positions. R. S. Maran, president of the Tamil Sangam of Bangalore, expressed frustration with the government's eagerness to negotiate with Veerapan, they having ignored the Sangam's nonviolent petitions for years.[1] As Janaki Nair argues, this was not just about a film hero; rather, the "predicament of Rajkumar was in fact the predicament of Kannada itself, held hostage to what was perceived as the more robust nationalism of the Tamils" (Nair 2005, 237; Niranjana 2000; Raghuran 2001).

In order to understand this feeling of being held hostage, we need to revisit the colonial boundaries and demographics of a city located between two major states. Bangalore was, in fact, bifurcated between the Madras Presidency and the Mysore State, both administratively and geographically.[2] The Cantonment fell under British control and was demographically dominated by Tamils (Nair 2005; Pani 2010). The Kannadiga parts of the city were largely in the old city, away from the Cantonment. But even there, multilinguistic practices were deeply embedded, as a result of an extensive Iyengar presence (Bayer 1986; Carlos, pers. comm.; S. Srinivas 2001). The drawing of linguistic states in 1956, however, and in particular the refashioning of this border city as Karnataka's capital, generated the impetus to homogeneity out of the traces of pluralism that mark and provoke the anxious politics of language and identity within this city. In short, enumeration, serialization, and statecraft created the conditions of insecurity, in Appadurai's (2006) terms, as identities became fixed out of more fluid and fractal possibilities.

As Nair argues, the very "cosmopolitanism" of Bangalore—both its historic pluralism and its modern IT economy, which brings people from all over India and the world to the metropolis—is its condition of lack, as far as the aggrieved Kannadiga community experience it. For one, demography is hard to pin down. According to a 1991 census, 35 percent of the city's residents considered Kannada their mother tongue, as compared to 25 percent for Tamil.[3] More recently, I have been told that Telugu outnumber both Kannadigas and Tamils but have no data to confirm this suspicion among some residents. Significantly, I have been told that many Telugus identify themselves as Kannadigas, thus blurring this boundary further. Thus, census data does not tell the whole story, though its apparent imprecision underscores my main point about the difficulty of making demarcations. Indeed, the attempt to create a census of language groups in Bangalore only underscores the difficulty of demarcating serial types, as many if not most Bangaloreans are multilingual and possess complex multilinguistic genealogies. Kannada-language activists, however, have often considered themselves increasingly a minority within their capital city and thus fear "losing Bangalore to outsiders." Suggestions for Kannadiga in-migration from other parts of Karnataka have been made, and pro-Kannada legislation in education, public spaces, and in administrative use have not assuaged this fear (Nair 2005). Indeed, prior to much of the pro-Kannada agitation, many Tamils did in fact describe their lives within the Cantonment areas as unaffected by Kannada language and politics. As R. S. Maran, former president of the Tamil Sangam, told me, "We thought we were living in Tamil Nadu." He was referring to the very Tamil nature of certain parts of the city and, as well, to the understanding that many older Tamils felt they had when living under the jurisdiction of the Madras Presidency prior to the creation of Karnataka.

In order to understand the raw sentiments surrounding the kidnapping of Rajkumar, it is important to look at one watershed (no pun intended) event in the relations between Tamils and Kannadigas in Bangalore, the so-called "Cauvery riots" of 1991 and their aftermath. Understanding the impact of this event upon the relations between communities in turn helps us understand the hardening of divisions between what was once a more integrated Bangalore. Linked to the hardening of linguistic sentiments was a worsening of Hindu-Muslim relations, particularly in the aftermath of the destruction of an ancient mosque in Ayodhya (Hansen 1999; van der Veer 1994). I examine these links between religious and linguistic tensions. In so doing, I also turn to ritual expressions of Tamilism, suggesting that even in a Tamil-Hindu revival, the vestiges of an old pluralism undercut the exclusivist claims by one community or another. In short, a historicity that confounds seriality is still part of a landscape of urban memory (S. Srinivas 2001).

A Dispute over Water?

The border between Karnataka and Tamil Nadu and more specifically the city of Bangalore have been largely peaceful since independence. But in the last thirty years, as mentioned already, tensions have flared between Tamils and Kannadigas. These tensions peaked in December of 1991, when a dispute over the sharing of Cauvery River water between the governments of Tamil Nadu and Karnataka escalated from being an economic issue between two "friendly" south Indian states into major riots in Bangalore and its surrounding areas. The injuries, loss of life, property damage, and loss of trust between the two communities affected life in Bangalore thereafter.[4]

It shall become clear that ethnic consciousness arose among many Tamils following recent social pressures and government policies that favor Kannadigas as a result of post-1956 statehood policies. Bangalore, a city that has a pluralistic linguistic and cultural legacy and was fairly recently subdivided between the Madras Presidency and Mysore State, has emerged as one of India's most important commercial centers during the last few decades. Simultaneously, a growing number of Kannadigas feel that the capital city is becoming increasingly "Tamilized." Though census numbers for the past forty years do not support this assertion, the making of Bangalore as the capital of the Kannada-speaking state certainly provoked this anxiety. The last forty years have witnessed a movement to make Kannada the sole administrative language of the state government, as well as more present on public spaces such as signboards, statues, and temples. During this period—and in response to the pro-Kannada movement—there has also been a revival of Tamil culture manifested in the increasing popularity of Tamil rituals such as *kavadi* bearing and fire walking during the Tamil festivals of Thaipusam, Adi Puram, Timithi, and Panguni Uttiram.[5] While ritualism—particularly when self-mortification is involved—is predominantly a working-class Tamil phenomenon, among the middle class there has also been an increasing interest in Tamil literature and the performing arts. Among Iyengars (Vaishnava Brahmins), however, there has been a gradual shift in linguistic allegiance towards greater assimilation with Kannadigas (Bayer 1986), a point I return to shortly.

The Cauvery Riots

The Cauvery River flowed quietly on the morning of December 13, 1991, oblivious to the battle over her waters that was waging between Tamil Nadu and Karnataka. This struggle had become a war of wits between the chief ministers of both states: J. Jayalalitha and S. Bangarappa, respectively. Two days earlier, the central government, under then prime minister P. V. Narasimha Rao, had instructed the Cauvery tribunal to award Tamil Nadu 205 billion cubic feet of water from Karnataka. It was widely reported in the national news media as a major victory for Jayalalitha over Bangarappa. This was a blow to his status (and perhaps to his ego as well) as a favored "son of the soil" among the farmers in Karnataka. For months, Bangarappa had promised that not "one drop" of Cauvery water would be given to Tamil Nadu. Now he faced the humiliation of the central government's decision.

On December 12, the Rajkumar Fans Association[6] staged a large procession in order to protest the central government's decision. This procession indulged in stone throwing and the chanting of anti-Tamil slogans. It was reported later by witnesses that the police did nothing to stop the marchers, who were getting out of hand. To the contrary, Bangarappa had ordered a "state *bandh*" (general strike) to protest the award. The *bandh*—aside from being unconstitutional—provided an opportunity for various "goondas" (thugs) to incite or engage in rioting against Tamils in Karnataka.

Riots were initially instigated by a rumor spread in the press and by word of mouth throughout Bangalore and Mysore that a Kannadiga woman had been molested and assaulted in the Nilgiri Hills in Tamil Nadu. Angered Kannadigas in Mysore and Bangalore attacked Tamils and their properties. Soon violence escalated against Tamils in Bangalore. The angry mobs focused their hostility against the poorest of all people in Bangalore, the migrant labor force living in squatter settlements and slums in and around the city. The established and wealthier Tamil neighborhoods in Bangalore were spared the worst, as poor farmers and construction laborers bore the brunt of the violence. The most alarming accusation came from Tamils in the riot-affected areas, who said that some policemen also engaged in violence against Tamils. According to an independent tribunal (the Indian People's Human Rights Tribunal)[7] investigating the riots, a number of incidents occurred that suggested police involvement, or at best, indifference to the victims:

> We also examined one Kanta, widow of one Arumugam. Her husband died in this incident. The police had taken her husband's body to the Victoria hospital and they themselves buried the body. They neither recorded her

statement nor registered a case in that regard. She herself was beaten and her daughter was also beaten by the police. After about a month or so, when she approached the Police Commissioner and complained to him about the incident, the Commissioner has told her that she would not get any compensation if she complains that the police had beaten her. We also examined one Vasantha. . . . She also says that on the 13th at about 7 p.m., a group of policemen opened the door of her house. Thereafter they assaulted her brother. At that time she was pregnant about five months. Due to fear and pain she screamed as a result of which she suffered an abortion. (IPHRC 1992, 8)

The Tamil working-class and migrant-laborer area of Srirampuram in Bangalore was the site of a major disturbance. Once again, reports by victims suggested police involvement:

There is a general report on Srirampuram. By and large the report indicates that the policemen had come in gangs with some goondas to every street and charged at all the people in the street with lathis. . . . The policemen had beaten a number of persons mercilessly and had even dragged persons who received injuries to the end of the streets. . . . The policemen also shouted at the Tamilians calling them "Kongaru" [derogatory term for Tamil migrants from the Kongu region adjacent to Karnataka, in western Tamil Nadu] and saying "you want Cauvery water you deserve our boot better than water." (IPHRC 1992, 9)

There were other incidents that repeated similar accusations against the police. In M.G. Nagar, a slum area, there were reports of violence perpetrated by Rajkumar fan clubs against Tamil migrants. One witness said that a mob of about fifteen hundred had attacked Tamils while shouting "Rajkumar ki Jai!" (Victory to Rajkumar!). Another reported that the mobs were carrying Rajkumar photos when they attacked (IPHRC 1992, 13–15). The invocation of Rajkumar was due in part to the actor's pro-Kannada activism; but it was also in response to the allegiance that Tamils showed to their film and political hero, MGR. It was not uncommon to see "MGR flags" and pictures prominently displayed in migrant labor slums with heavy Tamil populations. In this sense, we see the emergence of a "serial" identity in Anderson's sense (1998), which took root among Tamils through the film industry, being perhaps mirrored by that of another serial imaginary. That is, Rajkumar became the counterpart for Kannadigas, in the mirror of MGR's ubiquitous image.

After the riots, Bangarappa tried to reassure Tamils who had fled to Tamil Nadu that it was safe to return to their homes (though most were destroyed). It was estimated that over one hundred thousand Tamils had fled from Karnataka into neighboring Tamil Nadu. The estimated cost in damages exceeded one hundred million rupees. Also, over 290 people were injured and twelve were reported to have died as a result of the riots in and around Bangalore (IPHRC 1992). The Bangalore Tamil Sangam's own report (1992) had much higher estimates. According to their pamphlet, "A Mute Genocide," two hundred Tamils were purportedly killed, with hundreds more seriously injured. The pamphlet claimed that tens of thousands were displaced from Karnataka after their homes and huts were burned.[8]

The political fallout from these riots was also great. Ties with Tamil Nadu were further strained by the refugee problem created there. Jayalalitha complained that Bangarappa offered far too little in compensation to the victims, thus virtually guaranteeing that the poor refugees could not return and reclaim their lands.[9] Many Tamils, including influential members of the Bangalore Tamil Sangam, accused Bangarappa of inciting the riots by calling for the *bandh*. It was believed by many that he had used the Cauvery dispute as a pretext to deflect criticisms of corruption against his government.[10] Many Tamil farmers had resided in Karnataka for decades and thus had as much to lose as Kannadigas if water was given to Tamil Nadu. The *India Today* newspaper reported that these Tamils were "perplexed" by the turn of events that had led to the attacks (February 1992).

Bangarappa's critics suggested that he had utilized the Cauvery pretext in order to clear slums for economic and political gain. They argued that he was targeting the recent large influx of migrant workers who—it was being argued by certain Kannadiga politicians—were taking jobs away from Kannadigas (*India Today*, January 1992). Others suggested that Tamils were being driven off their land and properties as a political reward for the goondas and Kannadiga landlords who were loyal to the chief minister. In the rural outlying districts of Bangalore, it was suggested that Tamil tenant farmers, being outside of the village's moral economy and having no *panchayat* (village council) representation, were easy targets in riots aimed at clearing them from the lands they had helped make fertile (IPHRC 1992, 24). In fact, during the riots in and around Bangalore, the local police encouraged Tamils to go to Tamil Nadu for "their own safety." "The evidence shows that at Bangalore and surrounding towns people were put in the trains and they were sent to Tamil Nadu. In the district places the government itself arranged government State Transport buses to Tamil Nadu" (53). As a result of this action, tens of thousands of Tamils left Karnataka. The eagerness with which the Tamils were deported suggested government involvement to critics: "The police were keen to see that the Tamilians were sent to Tamil Nadu. . . . It was a planned and systematically executed conspiracy to loot the Tamilians and to drive them away" (31). Aside from seizing land and assets, it was suggested that Bangarappa ordered the attacks to "teach Jayalalitha a lesson" (*India Today*, January 1992).

There was also a growing sentiment among some of Bangalore's Kannadigas that the city was slowly turning into a "Tamil city." According to yet another census done in the 1980s, Bangalore's Kannadigas outnumbered Tamils by only 31 to 29 percent (Bayer 1986). There was a growing fear throughout the 1980s, however, that the unofficial numbers might now greatly favor Tamils. Many Tamils in the Cantonment area had in fact told me that Bangalore was now predominantly Tamil, though no census confirmed this. An insecurity on the part of some Kannadigas was exacerbated by certain pro-Tamil organizations that called for the full or partial inclusion of Bangalore into Tamil Nadu.

The Bangarappa government's role in the Cauvery riots was not altogether clear; however, the Indian People's Human Rights Tribunal blamed his government for inciting violence. It argued that by calling for a general strike, the state government had violated the constitution, as well as encouraging lawlessness and rioting. The report also compiled evidence that prominent members of Bangarappa's administration played key roles in the riots. Most incriminating was the evidence that certain powerful politicians had instructed the police to "go soft" on the rioters (*Deccan Herald,* November 29, 1992; the *Hindu,* November 27, 1992).

In the aftermath of the riots, Tamil social organizations, led by the Tamil Sangam of Bangalore, demanded an inquiry into the actions or inactions of the government and the police during the disturbances. For over a year, a Cauvery riots tribunal convened and heard testimony from representatives of the Tamil Sangam and other Tamil associations that had documented cases of violence. Kannada organizations also presented evidence that Kannadigas had been affected by the disturbances as well. But, whereas the Tamil cases mostly concerned violence or property damage, the Kannadiga groups seemed to justify their discontent by arguing that Tamils had become too influential in Karnataka through the help of the DMK and the AIADMK (the prominent political parties in Tamil Nadu).[11] Kannada Shakti Kendra (a pro-Kannada organization) president and professor of Kannada, Dr. M. Chidananda Murthy, argued before the tribunal that Kannada should be made the sole administrative language in Karnataka in an attempt to thwart the growing influence of the DMK and AIADMK in Bangalore. He mentioned that the most popular Tamil newspapers in Bangalore had political connections to the DMK and AIADMK and further argued that Kannada was endangered through the increasing political power of Tamils in Bangalore. He also criticized the state government for not issuing an "executive order" preventing people from conducting political and legal transactions in languages other than Kannada or English (the *Hindu*, January 16, 1992).

Aside from the physical costs of the riots, there was a loss of trust between the Tamil community and the state government. *India Today* reported that Tamils began to question their security in the state (January 31, 1991). Businesses that had been vandalized for having Tamil signboards replaced them with Kannadiga ones. "Traveling Talkie"[12] movie houses that catered to Tamil migrant labor audiences were also damaged in the disturbances. Many of these closed up for good, as the exodus of Tamils had left them without an audience.

The incident, moreover, produced a heightened consciousness of Tamil identity. Some Tamils, it was reported in the *Deccan Herald*, the leading local newspaper, wanted central government rule for Bangalore as a result of the riots. This position angered Kannadiga politicians and the deputy commissioner of police in Bangalore. Deputy Commissioner Kempaiah reported to the Cauvery Tribunal that it had come to his attention as early as 1984 that some Tamils felt discriminated against and had requested that Bangalore come under the central administration's control. He said that the Rajkumar Fans Association and other organizations had taken "strong exception" to this request. Kempaiah went on to explain that the Tamil Sangam and local DMK and AIADMK branches were the only major organizations in Bangalore that did not support the December 13 *bandh*. This, he argued, resulted in tensions between Tamils and the Kannadigas. Furthermore, Kempaiah pointed out that the Tamil Sangam in Bangalore had been an active supporter of the LTTE (Liberation Tigers of Tamil Eelam in Sri Lanka) cause prior to Rajiv Gandhi's assassination (*Deccan Herald*, November 1, 1992).

The deputy commissioner of police suggested that if the Tamil organizations had called on its members to support the *bandh*, then the cause for tension between the two communities would not have existed. Also, he argued that during the last eight years Tamil groups had "lacked loyalty to Karnataka" through their continuing allegiance to the Tamil language. Kempaiah reported that even after Rajiv's death, there were members of the Tamil Sangam who were willing to help the LTTE: "Mr. Jaganath, a member of the Tamil Sangam and employee of HAL [industrial township] in Bangalore, and Mrs. Jaganath had provided assistance to Shivarasan and Shubha, the masterminds behind the Rajiv Gandhi assassination, Mr. Kempaiah said the couple had got accommodation provided in Bangalore for the stay of same LTTE activists" (*Deccan Herald*, November 1, 1992).

Kempaiah also criticized the Tamil Sangam for unveiling a large Sri Thiruvalluvar statue in front of the organization's premises.[13] He said that many pro-Kannada organizations were against the unveiling of this statue as there were not any statues in the city honoring Kannada poets and saints.[14] During the riots, the statue of Thiruvalluvar was removed from outside of the Sangam out of fear that it would be defaced by Kannada activists. I return later to the politics surrounding the unveiling of this statue, as well as its symbolic significance.

Deputy Commissioner Kempaiah had utilized a platform—which he knew would be reported in the local papers—to make a case against the Tamils. He chronicled many of the grievances against Tamils and by extension rationalized the behavior of the Rajkumar Fans Association and other groups. Also, by invoking the Rajiv Gandhi assassination—still an open sore at this time—he was indirectly accusing Tamils of antinationalist sentiments and activities. The DMK had long agitated against "Aryan hegemony" and at one point had a secessionist manifesto. Though the party has long since toned down its strident Dravidian rhetoric, there are still organizations within Tamil Nadu that adhere to a radical and perceived antinational Tamilism. Some of these were implicated in the LTTE plot. Raising the bogey of Tamil radicalism and hinting at anti-Karnataka activities and sentiments reinforced Tamil suspicions that the police were instructed by the state government to not interfere with the rioting. Perhaps the tone taken by the commissioner exemplified the attitude of the police department. In addition, the testimony from other police officials and politicians in Bangalore suggested that the *bandh*-related disturbances were interpreted by the police in this manner. Such public anti-Tamil sentiment heightened a sense of Tamil insecurity and, subsequently, identity and solidarity.

Arguably, the violence at the heart of the law was revealed to the Tamil community through these acts and their rationalizations. That is, the arbitrary foundations of linguistic statehood were made clear by the collusion of the police and the chief minister with the violent acts, even if it only came through its rationalization. As Agamben (2005) has argued, a "state of exception" to legal rights shores up an "anomie" at the heart of the law, born of its arbitrary nature. In this case, the law's weddedness to an identity claim born of the serial imagination, in Anderson's sense, over and against the more plural and porous identities that existed prior to 1956 and, indeed, for centuries, opens a fissure in the whole of the law. While the arbitrary nature of the law provides grist for its critique or deconstruction for some, the claims made by the law also gain traction in the serial imagination of many. The primary mechanism by which this happens is through the utilizing of mass media and legal technologies. Through these mediums, feverish attempts are undertaken to retroactively make true that which is arbitrarily imposed. As Derrida (2002) argues, building on Benjamin and Schmidt, the interpretability of a legal decision or act is always retroactive in the sense that it becomes grounded in subsequent decisions or criteria. These subsequent decisions serve as the supplement to the "arche-violence" of an original (and arbitrary) decision. In the context of an ethnonationalist claim, the supplementary logic comes in the form of an archive of ethnic, linguistic, or religious difference that is often retroactively constructed in the form of rationalizations for some form of originary violence inscribed into the law. In this instance, the "case" against Tamils became the necessary retroactive archive or justification for the police and state. Reciprocally, an emergent victim's narrative takes nurturance in the perceived lack in the Other's claim, equally generative of an archive to establish its counterclaim. We witness further these competing claims in what followed. Read more instrumentally, Bangarappa and his lieutenants within the police had simply utilized the figure of the Other, the unassimilable Tamil, to shore up a political base.

The DMK and AIADMK grew in strength and stature among Bangalorean Tamils after the riots. Jayalalitha[15] took up the cause of the Tamils in Karnataka in an *India Today* interview:

A little over a lakh[16] [one hundred thousand] affected Tamil people from Karnataka have already entered Tamil Nadu. We have requested the Centre to bear the cost of their relief—it will cost us a lot of money—and appoint a sitting Supreme Court judge to receive claims for compensation from the Tamilian refugees from Karnataka and award compensation. . . . There is still fear and anxiety in the minds of the Tamil people about their safety in Karnataka. The Government of Karnataka should deploy paramilitary forces in the disturbed areas to restore the confidence of the Tamil people. (January 31, 1992)

She clearly capitalized on this event by mobilizing the AIADMK behind the Tamil cause in Bangalore. As a result, many Bangalorean Tamils began to look up to her as a protector of their interests. The Tamil newspapers in Bangalore began to print more stories about her, and posters of her appeared in Tamil-dominated sections of the city.[17] Jayalalitha went so far as to directly accuse Bangarappa of instigating the "dastardly attacks" on Tamils, and she refused to engage in further discussion on the Cauvery water dispute so long as he took part. Bangarappa, on the other hand, was perceived as manipulative and unsympathetic to the riot victims. A report in *India Today* described a relaxed Bangarappa playing badminton and doing yoga and juxtaposed this with pictures and stories of destitute Tamil victims of the riots. The almost comical extent of Bangarappa's insensitivity was chronicled in this short interview he gave in *India Today*:

> Reporter: Has your position as chief minister changed after the Cauvery-related violence?
>
> Bangarappa: It's safe. By looking at me, don't you feel so?
>
> Reporter: Several ministers have declared themselves as chief ministerial candidate. Comments?
>
> Bangarappa: I can go only laugh at them.
>
> Reporter: What went wrong with your handling of the dispute?
>
> Bangarappa: Nothing. Whatever we've done is according to the law and to protect the interests.
>
> Reporter: Why was the Karnataka bandh not peaceful as it was in Tamil Nadu?
>
> Bangarappa: Tamil Nadu wasn't peaceful. Some incidents took place as in Karnataka. Sometimes violence is okay.
>
> Reporter: Has the initiative passed to the people?
>
> Bangarappa: I don't think so. We politicians always keep the aspirations of the people in mind. We've kept in mind the larger interests of the farmers of the Cauvery delta.
>
> Reporter: Have some ministers instigated the violence?
> Bangarappa: All baseless. I deny it. (January 31, 1991)

While living in Bangalore just six months after the Cauvery disturbances and during the media coverage of the inquiry proceedings, I found that Tamil-Kannadiga tensions ran high. When I mentioned to Kannadigas that I was studying Tamil language and culture, I was often told that Bangalore was "a Kannada area," and some suggested that I "go to Madras to learn about Tamils." I was often told that the Tamils in Bangalore did not want to interact with Kannadigas. The Tamils, I heard, kept to themselves, spoke their language with each other, refused to learn Kannada, and patronized businesses in their own communities. One Kannadiga woman told me that Telugus and Malayalis (Malayalam-speaking inhabitants of the Malabar Coast of India) were more "integrated" with the Kannadigas than the Tamils were. The impression I received from Kannadigas was that the Tamils were "insular" and "kept to themselves." Another Kannadiga said that the Tamils were successful because "they worked hard" and had good business sensibilities. Kannadigas, on the other hand, she said, were "lazy and apathetic." This sentiment was echoed by others. Tamils would sometimes say that they were resented because of their "hard work" and success. There was a common sentiment among Kannadigas that because they were "so easy-going and tolerant," they were slow to react to the increased Tamil presence in the state. The Tamils were perceived by many to be industrious, wealthy, and politically influential. In subsequent years and on several return visits, I heard similar stories, though the tensions were gradually reduced, with the exception of the period during and immediately following the Rajkumar kidnapping.

Most Tamils I encountered in Bangalore spoke proudly of their cultural heritage. I was told numerous times that Tamil was the "oldest continuously used language in the world" and that Dravidian culture stems from the genius of the "Tamil civilization." These ideas were consistent with those of earlier Tamil revivalist movements (Ramaswamy 1997; Ryerson 1988). But I was rarely told by any Tamils in the city that they felt loyalty to Tamil Nadu over Karnataka. To the contrary, loyalty to Karnataka was displayed in all Tamil-speaking areas. In fact, I could not find a signboard in Tamil before any businesses—even in Tamil enclaves. On the other hand, I was told that this was due to threats to burn down or vandalize shops with signs in Tamil. One Bangalore-based DMK activist that I spoke with explained: "I used to have the signs in front of my bookstore in Tamil, but now, for the last ten years—especially after Cauvery—almost all of the Tamil signs had to be taken down. . . . It is because of the politicians." Another Tamil activist said that "Kannadigas and Mewaris [Rajasthani merchants] support one another in attempting to hurt the businesses of Tamils." The same activist suggested that the ethnic stereotypes really served the economic interests of these non-Tamil businesses. Threats against businesses having Tamil signboards sometimes made news in the local papers.

Most Tamils I met proclaimed complete loyalty to Karnataka. They celebrated Rajyosatva Day (Karnataka Statehood Day) and spoke proudly about the prosperity, cleanliness, and orderliness of Karnataka as compared to Tamil Nadu. But Tamils were aware of negative Kannadiga perceptions of them, and they resented the stereotypes that were expressed in the newspapers. Some Tamils even suggested to me that the Kannadigas were "jealous" of them because of their work ethic. One elderly Tamil woman from a middle-class background told me that she had gone into a shop in the Cantonment she had patronized for years and spoke in Tamil as she always had done. A policeman who happened to be in the store told her to speak in Kannada because she was "not in Tamil Nadu." She said that this frightened her and made her self-conscious about her Tamil identity for the first time in her life. The implication for her and others was that one could no longer take one's neighborhood for granted as a place to interact in the native tongue. Rather, there were now precautions to take, whether it be removing Tamil signboards or watching out for Kannadiga police (or Rajkumar fans) before speaking Tamil. Moreover, the notion that Tamil was alien was also novel, given the historical fluidity and porousness of linguistic boundaries in this Deccan crossroads. Bangalore was being incorporated linguistically as it had been politically, post 1956. Serialization, in its bound sense, had torn asunder the normalcy of multiple selves.

The awakening of ethnic and linguistic sentiment in Bangalore cannot be understood in terms of the Cauvery dispute in and of itself—though this provided a catalyst to mobilize chauvinistic forces. A look at the pro-Kannada movement and the subsequent awakening of Tamil consciousness in Bangalore highlights the historical antecedents to the riots. It is to the pro-Kannada movement and the subsequent response among Tamils that I now turn.

CHAPTER 4

The Kannada Movement and Tamil Revival

Karnataka was formed in 1956 after a successful struggle for the establishment of a Kannada-speaking state. The idealism that prompted the formation of the state has not completely dissipated (Vasavi 2009; Nair 2005, 2011). Though Bangalore, the capital of Karnataka, had become the dominant economic powerhouse in south India, being the center of the computer industry and the preferred location for foreign multinational companies, some felt that Kannada language, literature, and culture had been marginalized in the process. There had been, especially among the burgeoning middle class, a move towards English in most levels of government and commerce. The reasons for this, according to Kannada activists, may have been twofold. On the one hand, there was a lack of commitment to the development of Kannada by the central government, which promoted English and Hindi (Vasavi 2009); and second, the influx of recent immigrants to Bangalore from other states had marginalized the Kannada language within the capital city. That is, the cosmopolitan nature of the city made English the lingua franca among educated residents, while also attracting enclaves of Tamil laborers. The Kannada movement[1] sought to awaken the Kannadigas to the plight of the Kannada language and applied political pressure to ensure that the state government was committed to funding and legislation designed to promote the Kannada language and its literary tradition, while also making it the sole administrative language of education, business, and government (Nair 2005; Vasavi 2009).

The president of the Kannada Shakti Kendra (Center for Kannada Power), Dr. Chidananda Murthy, was one of the most outspoken proponents of the Kannada movement. He argued that Tamils were fast growing in population and influence in Bangalore; but, he maintained, they did not assimilate or attempt to learn the Kannada language. Furthermore, he felt that Tamil migrants had taken jobs away from Kannadigas. Arguing before the Cauvery inquiry, he said, "Many Tamils maintain their separate identities and do not mix with the locals. This had given rise to an apprehension in the minds of Kannadigas that Tamils may claim Bangalore city in course of time" (*Deccan Herald,* January 14, 1993). He suggested that Tamil organizations should bear the responsibility and costs for offering Kannada courses to Tamils. Saying that the state government should not have to bear the cost of educating Tamil migrants, he added that those who come to Karnataka should take it upon themselves to learn Kannada (*Deccan Herald,* January 16, 1993). The Kannada Sahitya Parishat president, Go. Channabasappa, called upon the state government to regulate the influx of immigrants and to show the political will necessary to "insure the primacy of Kannada in the State" (*Deccan Herald,* October 20, 1992).

Various pro-Kannada groups applied pressure to the state government in response to a perceived threat to their language. The growing Kannada movement helped Bangarappa get elected as chief minister, as he had campaigned on a pro-Kannada platform. In the year following the riots, in September 1992, the Kannada Development Authority (a state-sponsored organization) announced that 1993 would be "Kannada Awareness Year." The state government promised to act on the recommendations of the Kannada Development Authority. The authority asked for assistance implementing extensive Kannada education in border areas with Tamil Nadu, and they requested five thousand Kannada typewriters be made available. Also, the authority argued that although the state was supposed to have conducted all administrative affairs in Kannada since 1963, in 1992 only 5 percent of administrative work was conducted in Kannada—this in spite of the fact that 90 percent of all government employees were Kannadigas.

In addition to these pro-Kannada political pressures and demands, there were more moderate and intellectual forces within the Kannada movement as well. Perhaps the most prominent voice belonged to U. R. Ananthamurthy, the award-winning author of the Kannada and English bestseller, *Samskara: Rites for a Dead Man.* On the occasion of Rajyosatva Day (Karnataka Statehood Day), Ananthamurthy argued in the *Deccan Herald,* "The absurdity [in India is] . . . the more literate you are, the less languages you know. There are two issues which need to be addressed—mobility and selfhood. We need to be mobile within the country even while we retain our selfhood" (October 30, 1992). Ananthamurthy suggested, like many Tamil activists, that the Cauvery violence was state sponsored and "shameful." But at the same time, he requested that the state government help "reconstruct" Kannada by de-emphasizing the importance of English and Hindi (Vasavi 2009; Nair 2005).

Following this sentiment and moving it towards a general critique of the "westernization" that the opening of markets to foreign investors in India was creating, D. R. Nagaraj, a leading academic and noted Kannada literateur, argued as follows: "The movement can be used effectively as a weapon against the onslaught of the so-called universal market culture which seeks to destroy local cultures and traditions. It can be a very genuine protest against the cultural invasion of the commercial West. But unfortunately, I don't find such a larger understanding of issues in today's Kannada movement" (*Deccan Herald,* October 30, 1992). While providing a cultural and intellectual justification for the Kannada movement, both Ananthamurthy and Nagaraj were also unhappy with recent settlers who, in the words of Nagaraj, "are yet to integrate themselves with Kannada culture and Karnataka." At the same time, they cast the struggle as one between English and/or Hindi and Kannada rather than focusing their criticism on the Tamils or other recent settlers (also see Vasavi 2009). Instead they seemed to suggest that the recent ethnic strife was a symptom of neoliberal market forces and globalization.

"History, Not Water"

While there is apparently room for debate and disagreement within the Kannada movement (Nagaraj 2009), I was told that the climate had changed dramatically for Tamils in Bangalore in the 1980s and 1990s. A local Tamil academic explained how he had to show public sympathy for the Kannada movement as he was one of only five Tamil-speaking faculty at his college. Also, Kannadiga colleagues, while privately sympathetic to the Tamils, would not speak in support of the Tamil plight publicly. The aforementioned Tamil academic spoke of the passions over language that guide the "historical consciousness" of Tamils and Kannadigas, noting that such sentiments are easily manipulated by political leaders. Quoting Chidananda Murthy, the pro-Kannada activist who said of the riots, "They are about history, not about water," he described the use of "Vijayanagar motifs" (architectural designs) used as decorations throughout Bangalore during Rajyosatva Day. He added that the "Cholas and Pallavas are part of the average Tamil's consciousness." Criticism was also leveled against leaders of the Tamil movement: "Most Tamil academics are 'fundamentalists' with little or no respect for Kannada." His criticism also took a more negative turn:

There is a fundamental flaw in the Tamil mind and culture. One can look at a Tamil today and see one thousand years of thought guiding him. The emphasis on subjectivity is such that the dissenting or questioning mind is not present. Why else would people kill themselves for a man who did nothing for them?[2] It is this emphasis on the "One" and surrendering to the "One" that leads to the despotic leaders' ability to rule over others. The gurus don't want you to question them intellectually—they want absolute control and surrender on the devotee's part. Those like Vivekananda and

Radhakrishnan who interpreted Indian thought as being skeptical and democratic were influenced by English thought. They were at least 50 percent Western. Thus their message was completely misunderstood.

The "One" he speaks of is whatever ideology motivates people towards emotionalism over reason. Or more precisely, he is referring to the strong identification, almost absorption in his mind, that Indians and particularly Tamils have with their leaders, be they religious or secular.[3] Thus he was equally critical of religious, ethnic, or linguistic fanaticisms—all of which, he maintained, were tearing at the fabric of India and Bangalore. Here we witness an avowedly culturalist understanding of the political dynamics that had unfolded.

But he seemed to also imply that linguistic and religious tensions in Bangalore were ultimately underscored by economic concerns. He cited the rise in Hindu fundamentalism that corresponded, he maintained, with the increasing corruption of the state government. That is, he suggested that those most vulnerable to corruption charges (the business and political elite) were pouring money into various pro-Hindu movements. At the same time, those unhappy with the perceived corruption within Bangarappa's administration were turning towards Hindu right-wing parties and organizations as the "clean alternative." As Vasavi (2007) argues, politics is increasingly structured around "darshan," or establishing the spiritual connection between leaders and led through spectacle. I return to this point later. About the Tamil situation in Bangalore, my academic informant said,

> Tamils are accused of not mixing with the Kannadigas because they like to live in places like Ulsoor and Sivagi Nagar and patronize their fellow Tamil businesses. Lots of Tamils work in Hosur [about forty kilometers from Bangalore] in Tamil Nadu in some industry, but they live in Bangalore to reap the benefits of the climate and amenities. They are resented because they work in Tamil Nadu and pay taxes to that state. Tamils are always thought to be loyal to Tamil Nadu.

He is suggesting here that Tamil professionals or wealthy industrialists (laborers working in Hosur would live there, as Bangalore rents are far costlier) are buying up properties in Bangalore and, as others pointed out earlier, turning it into a "Tamil city." Ultimately, the pro-Kannada movements' efforts to homogenize the city's cultural identity were linked to an insecurity that a growing Tamil bourgeoisie is laying claim to the city. The impossibility of a Tamil capture or annexation of Bangalore notwithstanding, what was revealed by such sentiments, precisely, was the impossibility of Kannadiga homogeneity and linguistic hegemony given the porous historical and contemporary boundaries between large populations of Tamils, Kannadigas, and Telugus, among others.

The apparent need for enemies reveals a political technique born out of contradiction and complexity (Hansen 2001; Bailey 1998). The discourse of Tamil exclusivity and fanaticism being suggested by pro-Kannada leaders—while drawing upon certain Tamil extremist sentiments—was tied, too, to economic concerns (Vasavi 2007). Recall also the earlier comment about Kannadiga and Mewari businessmen boycotting Tamil businesses. This, of course, suggests the importance of an instrumentalist analysis of the various beneficiaries and victims of economic globalization, statecraft, urbanization, and internal migration—all of which had dramatically impacted upon Bangalore in modern times.

Beyond a strictly instrumentalist reading, however, I am suggesting that the very sense of endangerment of identity through language affiliation was created through the redrawing of state boundaries in 1956, which provided the impetus for imagining a linguistically hegemonic Kannada-speaking Bangalore. Given the economic growth of the city and region in the latter half of the twentieth century and early twenty-first, this imagined nation had been challenged by the prominence of the English language. The parochial sentiments regarding the threat of Tamil were thus symptomatic of larger structural trends. I suggest, too, that this "threat" guards a fragile and modern sense of identification by serving as a supplement to it. That is, the more fragile yet ironically rigid the identity construct, the more fluid the underlying reality. Complex and protean local identifications both pose a sense of imagined threat once serialization has taken root through statecraft and law. But I also assert that this complexity serves as its remedy. As we will see, ultimately, Tamils and Kannadigas share much that mitigates against the kind of radical othering that has affected other parts of South Asia and beyond. In this sense, the cosmopolitan past that Nandy (2002) celebrates for Cochin as its condition of hospitality is also found to be true for this Deccan metropolis, the strains described here notwithstanding.

Rajyosatva Day

The annual Rajyosatva Day (Karnataka "re-unification," or Statehood Day) celebrations on November 1 have grown in size and potential volatility in Bangalore. The day commemorates the redrawing of states in 1956, which resulted in the creation of Tamil Nadu and Karnataka out of Mysore State and Madras Presidency.[4] I heard that the celebrations had often turned into anti-Tamil parades. For example, I was told about an altercation between the Rajkumar Fans Association and a line of moviegoers waiting to see an MGR film. This, according to certain Tamils in the city, had turned into a minor riot.

This day also features a Rajkumar film festival. Rajkumar made dozens of films in which he played heroes and kings from the Vijayanagar or Hoysala periods. His films romanticized the greatness of the Kannadiga-dominated empires and have served as a potent symbol of Karnataka identity. The "reunification" day recalls past glories and makes explicit the primordial link between the old empire and the modern state of Karnataka (see Nair 2005). That is, the creation of the state in 1956 was imagined as the "reunification" of Vijayanagara in cultural-nationalist terms. As Tamil cinemas are often "stoned" on this day, I was warned to avoid being near one. This was especially true, I was told, if a Kannadiga film had a scene in which Vijayanagara soldiers are defeated in a battle by Tamils.[5]

The focus of attention for many Kannadigas in Bangalore on Rajyosatva Day was a temporary fairground that was erected near the Central Market and Kempegowda Circle, in the heart of the city. Spectacular wooden arches and pillars were propped up and decorated with paint and thousands of lights. The festive atmosphere was the principal site for speeches and special events. Famous Kannadigas such as Rajkumar,[6] Chidananda Murthy, and Bangarappa often gave anti-Tamil speeches in the public square. A professor of Tamil and Kannada literature in Bangalore informed me that in addition to anti-Tamil speeches, the decorations—that is, the arches, pillars, and banners—were charged with meaning to Kannadigas and Tamils. The arches utilized motifs from the Vijayanagar era—a golden age of Kannadiga political and cultural hegemony over most of south India.[7] Minor incidents, I was told, often broke out when processions from this site passed through Tamil-speaking areas. The Tamils, for their part, would sometimes carry a Chola-style (architectural) arch in reaction.[8]

For the most part, however, Tamils made it a point to celebrate Rajyosatva Day. Decorations were highly visible in Tamil sections of town. Cardboard Vijayanagar arches acted as facades in front of many Tamil-owned shops. In the neighborhood where I lived, in the heart of the former Cantonment, was a vigorous display of loyalty to Karnataka. Along the business district of the neighborhood were decorative lights, streamers, and music. A Tamil-Muslim merchant indicated to me that Tamils were mostly responsible for the colorful display, and in the same breath he asked me, "Do you know of our language problems?" He then suggested that the ostentatious display of loyalty was born out of fear of vandalism by gangs of young Kannadigas. After singling out the Rajkumar fans as particularly "against us," he spoke of the "sweetness of MGR's face" in comparison with Rajkumar's apparent harshness of character. As we spoke in his shop, auto rickshaws buzzed by us with the Karnataka state flag prominently displayed. In fact, for the entire month of November, all transport vehicles (buses, taxis, rickshaws, and lorries) displayed, at the minimum, the Karnataka flag.

Perhaps most striking about the "performance" of ethnicity that this celebration exhibited was the trend to seek historical antecedents to make sense of existing sentiments. The imagining and archiving of past glories in golden ages strategically naturalizes difference. That is to say, revivalisms of various kinds often require "inventions of tradition" (Hobsbawm 1983) to mobilize sentiments around the historical consciousness of a particular group. In short, contemporary battles are imagined—such as the competition for jobs, privileges, and water—as contested origin myths. These are boundary-making devices for defining the moral community (Bailey 1960).

Bailey's pioneering instrumentalist work (1960) demonstrated that individual subjects located within traditional value systems were capable of appropriating local (real or imagined) as well as rational-legal structures and discourses in the service of political and economic ends. Through what Bailey called "bridge actions," certain individuals were able to utilize the emerging structures and ideologies of the nation-state in order to challenge their marginal status within the traditional moral economy of the village (also see Cohn 1955; Srinivas 1966). Within the local systems of tribe and caste were strategic appropriations and inversions of both Hindu ideologies and the traditional basis for power. In analyzing specific social actors' engagement with traditions in a widening social field being created by the state, Bailey also anticipated a later concern in anthropology about the internal tensions within dominant discourses (e.g., Dirks 1994; Herzfeld 1997; Daniel 1996; Irschick 1994). For our purposes, we can see how the imagined differences between empires and linguistic groups helped solidify political sentiment and override more fluid boundaries in the service of a more exclusive identity. In this case, it was not marginal and rural "bridge actors" appropriating moralizing discourses to further caste or tribal rights but rather the political deployment of strategic essentialism, built upon invented traditions and as championed by political leaders. This was a bridge unto an imagined past; but, at the same time, a vision of the past that carried instrumental value to specific actors and groups.

Evocative symbols seem to generate (though they are assumed to represent) primordial ethnic attachments. For some, however, when battles came to concern the ancient empires—or even regional film stars—rather than issues of economic or social substance, there was little hope for productive dialogue. Indeed, many Tamils and Kannadigas viewed the whole exercise surrounding the festival as propaganda for the chief minister.[9] A powerful factor in the imagining of the primordial seems to be the mass media—and especially the impact of film images.

The emergence of separate Tamil and Kannadiga film industries has played a significant role in the creation of linguistic nationalism. The DMK had first utilized the Tamil film industry to popularize the non-Brahmin movement (Ramaswamy 1997; Dickey 1993). Similarly, Kannada films, albeit a smaller industry, played a significant role in romanticizing a glorious Kannadiga empire.[10]

As Anderson's (1998) notion that the "serial" imagination takes hold through mass mediation and the homogenous time and space it creates, we can conclude that a necessary but not necessarily sufficient condition for the imagining of communities arose through popular new media forms such as novels, films, and newspapers (Anderson 1991). But invention is the mother of necessity. In this case, the violence of naming serial types (or "bound serialism," in Anderson's terms) opens up a breach or an impossibility in what it purports to separate—in this case, distinct ethnic and linguistic groupings. This performative act requires its supplement, in Derrida's (2002) terms, or secondary and sustaining forms of violence, in Benjamin's language (1978), in order to foreclose or suture the impossibility of the breach through the naming of difference. But as this supplement is temporary and inherently deconstructible, the haunting engine of supplementation, an "archive fever" (Derrida 1995) is never exhausted (Deshpande 2000).

The intellectual critics, however, either lament the inattention to literature and fine arts that film fanaticism contributes to (recall the pro-Kannada views of U. R. Ananthamurthy) or condemn the "fetishizing" of culture and ethnicity altogether at the expense of Nehruvian socialistic ideals; the more ardent progressives worry about the eradication of poverty and the widening gap between the bourgeoisie and the working class (Vasavi 2007).

In sum, the Kannada movement produced a climate that contributed to the election of Bangarappa, which in turn led to his handling of the Cauvery dispute in an apparently reckless manner. Even before Bangarappa was chief minister, the project of awakening Kannadiga cultural identity had been fueled by the rapid economic growth in the city and the subsequent arrival of more immigrants to an already multilinguistic city. Underlying the linguistic and cultural pride of Kannadiga nationalism, however, was a pragmatic concern as well: without pro-Kannada legislation, what would be the economic fate of the capital city, and who would protect the economic privileges of the Kannadiga bourgeoisie? "Bumiputraism" was one solution to this problem.[11] Arguably, and reading the situation in instrumental terms, the bourgeoisie legitimized their economic agendas through politically charged populist campaigns aimed at the lower middle and working class. These campaigns in turn required invented traditions, and transmission of these images seemed to rely upon the mass media. But such an instrumentalist perspective does not at the same time explain the phenomenology of identity attachments and the force that these carry within the imagination. Moreover, the cultural antecedents that are invoked by modern forms of mediation, such as the use of processions, iconography, and spiritual imagery, must also be examined seriously. So-called invented traditions can only be invented from a wellspring of symbolically resonant possibilities (van der Veer 1995; Kapferer 1988). In Bangalore's case, these cultural materials are imbued deeply within an imagined landscape that makes the contestation over said landscape meaningful (Srinivas 2001). One way the imagined landscape becomes material is through museums that simplify history into a coherent nationalist or ethnic narrative (Anderson 1991).

In the summer of 2015, for example, I had an opportunity to visit the fairly recently created Kempegowda Museum in the heart of downtown Bangalore. This museum, set in the distinguished colonial-era Mayo Hall, along MG Road, purported to tell the story of Bangalore's putative founder in visual form through drawings and photographs of the Yelahanka chieftainship, which ruled the region around Bangalore in the fifteenth and sixteenth centuries and of which Kempegowda was said to be a local leader. At the heart of the exhibit was a large photograph of Kempegowda's likeness in statue form taken from an old temple. The Yelahanka chieftainship in turn was described as having political ties and loyalties to the great Vijayanegara Empire. Thus, the golden age of Kanndiga hegemony over the south of the subcontinent was extended, by vassalage, to the local Yelahanka chieftainship, made palpable by the illustrious figure of Kempegowda. While there was nothing particularly misleading about this vague description, coupled with the lovely images of maps, temples, and forts built by the Yelahanka that were on display in the museum, a different and more nuanced version, perhaps, of history was decidedly absent.

Many scholars have suggested that Kempegowda's grandfather hailed from the Kanchipuram region of Tamil Nadu in the fourteenth century, coming from a farming community that later were identified as the Thigalas, an important community of farmers in the Bangalore region that claims both Tamil and Kannadiga descent and important patronage from rulers during the sixteenth to eighteenth centuries (Srinivas 2001; *Deccan Herald,* October 8, 2013). To this day, the Thigala Karaga Jatre, an important Hindu festival honoring the goddess Draupadi, is one of the most important ritual celebrations in the city (Srinivas 2001). By not discussing the Thigala linkage or showing the purported migration from today's Tamil Nadu to Yelahanka, a claim of contiguity and sovereignty, not to mention homogeneity, is made for Vijayanegara and Yelahanka within the

Kannadiga imaginary. The alternative narrative, however, would have marked if not celebrated the close Tamil and Kannadiga ties that had been forged over the centuries and as epitomized by the complex genealogy of Kempegowda.

While the Kempegowda Museum may seem an innocuous if historically thin monocultural representation of Bangalore's past, it presents a visually arresting narrative and buttresses an idea of Kannadiga difference and regional sovereignty. Such cultural-nationalist projects, of course, also produce strategic and tactical resistances (de Certeau 1984; Deshpande 2000). Thus, long before the museum came into being, there was a heightening of Tamil cultural identity in response to other claims within the Kannada movement and, as we will see, a sharpening of religious identifications in response to the rise of Hindu nationalism as well.

Tamilism

Ever since Annie Besant[12] made the "mistake" of equating Brahmin and "Aryan" in south India, I was told by a Tamil academic colleague, the Dravidian movement, and more specifically, "the Tamil movement was born" (see also Irschick 1969). The anti-Brahmin movement gathered much momentum in the early part of this century in response to the Indian nationalism that Annie Besant and Mahatma Gandhi espoused. The Dravidian movement, however, had begun more than a century earlier as various individuals, ranging from colonial officials, scholars, linguists, and religious reformers, began to reconstruct a Tamil golden age.[13] This golden age, it was presumed, was an age of economic prosperity and relative social equality (Irschick 1994; Ramaswamy 1997; Ryerson 1988). Dravidian civilization provided an alternative model for Tamil cultural identity at a time when the Indian nationalists were constructing a national identity based upon Sanskritic or Brahminical symbolism:

> The Backward Classes Movement [Dravidian] from its earliest days developed a mythology of its own. Contemporary speculations identifying the Brahmins with Aryans, and Tamil with the original Dravidian language, were eagerly seized on by the leaders of the non-Brahmin castes to manufacture an elaborate theory of Brahmin Machiavellianism throughout the centuries. The Brahmin invader had brought the evil institution of caste into India, and had used his great prestige and power to strengthen his hold on the society by making laws in his own favor, and worse, by shackling people's minds with the ideas of *varna*. . . . Pristine Dravidian society, which created the glorious literature of Tamil, was caste-free till the

Brahmin came, established his hegemony over everybody, and suppressed Dravidian culture. (Srinivas 1966, 104)

The most vociferous critic of Brahminism was E. V. Ramaswamy Naicker.[14] He founded the Dravidian Kazhagam and staged dramatic burnings of the *Ramayana* and public beatings of Rama images—which he maintained symbolized the Aryan conquest of the Dravidian south: "According to it Rama was not a Tamilian. . . . He was a Northerner. Ravana, who was killed by him, was the king of Lanka—that is southern Tamil Nadu. . . . The men of Tamil Nadu are derided as monkeys and monsters. . . . In the Ramayana war not a single Northerner or Aryan lost his life. . . . All those who lost their lives were only Tamils who were called Rakshashas" (Ramaswamy, qtd. in Ryerson 1988, 94–95).

The emergence of a contemporary Tamil literary tradition, aided by print technology, also played a key role in the imagining of a Tamil identity.[15] The Tamil film industry also played a large role in the DMK's rise to political prominence in Tamil Nadu (Ryerson 1988). As Anderson (1991) has argued, print technologies (and by extension, popular films) allow for the creation of an "imagined community" or the "unbound serial" forms of identification I have discussed earlier. It should not go unnoticed, however, that those propagating such imagery were not themselves the "downtrodden" but were from elite non-Brahmin backgrounds (Irschick 1969).

The struggle for Dravidian as opposed to "Aryan" or Brahminic culture has at various times pitted Tamil Nadu (and earlier the Madras Presidency) against the central government—particularly on the issue of a national language. Also, within Tamil Nadu itself, the dominance of Brahmins (though they are a minority) in higher-level jobs and education was successfully reversed through legislation by the Justice Party, the DK, and the DMK throughout this century (Irschick 1969; Ryerson 1988). M. N. Srinivas (1966, 102) illustrated the extent of their former dominance:

While Brahmin dominance in certain areas is general to peninsular India, it is particularly striking in Tamilnad. Like other Brahmins . . . Tamil Brahmins have a tradition of scholarship, but what distinguished the latter was the striking lead they had obtained over everyone else, including non-Tamil Brahmins, in Madras Presidency, with regard to English education. . . . In 1918 the Brahmins in the Presidency numbered 1.5 million out of 42 millions, but 70 percent of arts graduates, 74 percent of law graduates, 71 percent of engineering graduates, and 74 percent of graduates in teaching were Brahmins. Out of 390 higher appointments in the Education Department 310 were held by Brahmins, in the Judicial Department, 116 out of 171.

Srinivas and Irschick also note, however, that while there were many wealthy non-Brahmins—particularly in business and agriculture—the emerging Brahmin elites benefiting under colonialism were also the key players in the Indian nationalist movement. The leaders of the non-Brahmin movement were not from the "low and oppressed castes but from the leaders of the powerful, rural dominant castes" who were worried about the Brahminization of local politics (Srinivas 1966, 103; Irschick 1969).

Though the Dravidian movement seemed to be a reaction to north Indian hegemony and Brahmin dominance in the south, the movement again became ideologically salient among Tamils in Bangalore in response to the Kannada movement. I was told by a Tamil academic in Bangalore that the movement is strong in areas where Tamil is not "pure." He explained that while the goal is to purify the language from Sanskritic influences, it is popular in areas where Tamils are politically weak. Bangalore, Pondicherry (a former French colony in Tamil Nadu), and even Malaysia, he said, were the places where the "pure Tamil" movement was particularly strong.[16] It also has political and social meaning. One could argue that there is an element of diasporic longing born out of unique social and political pressures facing Tamils living in multicultural environments outside of their "imagined" homelands. The non-Brahmin element of the movement is also revealed by the lack of Brahmin support for it in Bangalore, particularly among the Vaishnava-Brahmin Iyengars.

The Iyengar Shift

The desire to rid Tamil of foreign elements calls attention to a Tamil-Kannada interface that Ramanuja[17] and the Alvars (Vaishnava saints) produced across south India during the twelfth and thirteenth centuries, a point I return to later. Indeed, Tamil Brahmin influence can be seen in the large Iyer and Iyengar communities across south India. In addition to finding Tamil-speaking Brahmins in southern Karnataka, they exist in substantial numbers in Andhra Pradesh and Kerala. Two brief examples might help to illustrate this.

We may recall the opening vignette, when I was in a small village outside of the city of Kuppam one evening. Kuppam lay close to the border of Tamil Nadu, Andhra Pradesh, and Karnataka but is now firmly located within Andhra Pradesh. The priests and Brahmins in the village all spoke Tamil as their mother tongue. This was especially true of the older generations. The children of the village, however, primarily spoke Telugu, as this was the language of instruction in school (and, of course, the state language of Andhra Pradesh). Within a generation, it seemed, there had been an attenuation of Tamil. But among Brahmins the use of Tamil was more resilient, as it was a language of devotion within the large and ancient Vishnu temple in the village. On another occasion, while traveling with some colleagues in Kerala, close to Cochin, we encountered an entire Tamil-speaking *agraharam,* or Brahmin community. Here we were told that many such Tamil Brahmin communities existed in Kerala. In the past, many rulers in Travancore and Cochin had invited priests from Tamil-speaking areas. Indeed, as Nandy (2002) shows, many seminal Tamil sacred texts were composed in and around Cochin in ancient times. This plural and multilingual past for much of south India was probably the norm, I have been suggesting. That is, a kind of linguistic cosmopolitanism existed that has only been disrupted by the formation of linguistic states in the 1950s (Pollock 2006).

The popular Vaishnavism that emerged led to a close development between Tamil and Kannada for some period. Ramanuja once converted a Hoysala Jain king at Belur after healing him of some sickness.[18] The king and his followers adopted Tamil and Vaishnavism in gratitude. To this day, some Iyengars in Karnataka say that they are Kannadigas but learned Tamil as their mother tongue as a result of this incident (Bayer 1986). The Iyengars, though often speaking Tamil in the home, speak as much Kannada as Tamil (Lal 1986) and live integrated within Kannadiga communities. As most of them can speak Kannada, they do not meet opposition and hostility in the same way that the non-Kannada–speaking Bangaloreans do. They were a well-entrenched part of Bangalore prior to the Cantonment[19] and speak a heavily Sanskritized dialect of Tamil, which also converges linguistically with Kannada. Part of this linguistic convergence can be attributed to the long-term linguistic interactions with Kannada speakers. Especially among the wealthy and middle-class Iyengars, there is a tendency to identify more strongly with Kannada and the Kannadiga community than with Tamils (Lal 1986).

In addition, the revival of the "Pure Tamil" movement in Bangalore, with its strident anti-Sanskrit (and thus anti-Brahmin) stance, further alienated the Brahmin Tamils from the non-Brahmins. The Vaishnava tradition, in particular, was deemed "Aryan" or "alien" by the leaders of the Tamil movement, as compared to the belief that Saivism is an indigenous Tamil tradition.[20] Thus Iyengars were derided as caste-minded by the Tamil movement.[21] Indeed, I heard many non-Brahmins, including Tamil Muslims, speak disparagingly of the Iyengar community. Some said they were "racists" who often refused to mix with other castes. I was also told that the Iyengars were prominent in neo-Hindu organizations, including the increasingly popular Vishwa Hindu Parishad (VHP) and their sister organization, the Rashtriya Swamisevak Sangh (RSS)—both leaders of the Hindu right wing or Sangh Parivar (Saffron brigade).

Lal suggests that the politics of the pro-Kannada movement, with its strident anti-Tamil rhetoric, affected Iyengar linguistic identity when he states that "socio-political factors are the main contributing factors for the linguistic convergence and shift. . . . That is, the convergence is towards the direction of the dominant language of the area (Kannada)" (1986, 15). In other words, the shifting of linguistic—and, one could argue, cultural—identity was directly related to the redrawing of state boundaries. That is, after Bangalore fell solely within Karnataka's borders, Tamils who had benefited under British patronage were now at a political disadvantage. Their identification with Kannada and the politically dominant community was thus strategic; and this allowed the Iyengars to distance themselves from the "subversive" and "antinational" elements within the non-Brahmin Tamil community, not to mention the many Tamil migrant laborers who have been drawn to Bangalore for economic reasons. As Bayer (1986) also points out, Iyengars, though having a dual Tamil-Kannadiga identity, increasingly avoided living in Tamil enclaves and showed a shift in allegiance towards Kannada-language use. In contrast, non-Brahmin Tamils still identified strongly with the Tamil language—particularly in the Cantonment areas. Bayer also found that the wealthy Iyengars, many of whom were civil servants under the British, also exhibited a trend towards English education and language use in the home.

Here I might note a parallel with Malaysia (Willford 2006, 2014), where the English-educated elite Tamils were recruited for prestigious administrative posts, and in postcolonial times they found other ways to distance themselves from the stereotypes attached to working-class Tamils. But in contrast, the Iyengars found common linguistic and religious grounds in addition to political privileges through their assimilation with Kannadigas, whereas the Malaysian Tamil elite were not afforded any avenue for attaining Bumiputra status. This similar postcolonial predicament—in which ethnicity is redefined (or reinscribed) by the changing of political control—also calls attention to the enduring impact of the state as arbiter of rights and privileges. This granting of rights has an impact on how one chooses to identify oneself, if viewed pragmatically or instrumentally.

The fluidity of the Iyengar identity illustrates that ethnic boundaries are more complex in stratified capitalist economies than Barth's (1969) classic transactional model of boundary maintenance suggests; and the same would hold true for culturalist or "primordialist" arguments. Barth, in my opinion, rightly argues that cultural or racial differences do not constitute ethnic differences. Rather, he emphasizes that "ascription" is the "critical feature of ethnic groups." He suggests that the "dichotomization between members and outsiders allows us to specify the continuity, and investigate the changing cultural form and content" within an ethnic group (14). That is, the "boundary" between the group and the "other" is the critical feature of definition. Though the boundary is flexible and open to manipulation, Barth suggests it is identifiable particularly when "the complexity is based upon the existence of important, complementary cultural differences; and these differences must be generally standardized within an ethnic group" (19). A larger implication was raised by Barth: To what degree does the demarcation of ethnic boundaries act as a constraint upon social actors? If one considers the production of ethnic stereotypes within a political field, the question of power becomes immediately salient. Stereotypes of identity are ascribed by more powerful groups upon less powerful others within a competitive political field. Abner Cohen (1996), for example, noted how ethnic demarcations created by colonial governments were part of a "divide and rule" policy—and a policy that had residual ethnic implications within the politics of the newly independent state.

I am arguing, however, that boundaries are more fluid than this. The Iyengars, recognizing state policies and their own economic interests, have enacted a strategy of assimilation. But assimilation coupled with exclusions and/or selective amnesia is bound to generate some discomfort about the foreign presence within. While this can fuel the demarcations between imagined others and selves, it also troubles identities within individual subjects and communities (Hansen 2001; Willford 2006).

The class of a group and their relationship to the state also figures large in the creation of moral communities. Groups make use of the cultural and political categories—the two cannot be separated—in order to pursue status-based and economic interests (Bailey 1960; Brass 1990). The critical part of defining the moral community is in the casting of the struggle—that is, in defining the group by what it is not—in which the "enemies," deviants, and minorities are clearly identified (Bailey 1998). Though hardly a novel observation, ideological constructs—religious or cultural—often mask bourgeois or elite interests. But against purely economistic or instrumental reading, I also suggest that the powers of serial identification present new resources for the imagination, although these are generative of specters (Anderson 1998). As Iyengars perceive themselves as subjects of a Kannadiga-defined state, as buttressed by law, they also draw upon their own Kannada-ness—the porousness of their own linguistically fluid pasts—to rationalize what is Kannadiga about them. At the same time, the phantom of suppressed Tamil identities produces a displacement upon the external figure of the foreign "Tamil." This figure serves as the necessary supplement to an imagined Kannadiga identity, more homogenous than history and genealogy, if not memory, suggest.

One Tamil college student described to me a growing reluctance to speak Tamil in public as the pro-Kannada sentiments were growing in the city. A law was passed, he claimed, that now prohibited the use of Tamil signboards. In addition, a statue of Kempegowda was installed in the city with a Kannada-only inscription. There was also talk by Kannada "extremists" of removing the Tamil inscriptions from other statues in the city. There are a number of statues that were installed during the British period. These, particularly those in the Cantonment (especially in Cubbon Park), have inscriptions in four languages, owing to the perception at the time of Bangalore being a multilingual city, covering the four sides of the square base. The languages used were Kannada, Tamil, Urdu, and English.

Paradoxically, though in accordance with Bayer's (1986) finding, English-medium schools were expanding in size in spite of the political posturing of pro-Kannada activists. Having an English education, the aforementioned student explained, was the best way to benefit from Bangalore's increasing economic importance—especially as it attracted many foreign companies under the increasing liberalization of India's economy. The Tamil student also explained to me that the university quota system in Karnataka was designed to protect the interests of Kannadigas. Universities had an 80 percent reservation for Kannadigas; but more significant was the way they determined if one was a Kannadiga. One was considered a Kannadiga after having lived twelve years in Karnataka. That is, ethnicity was ascribed, along with the political benefits that came with it, based upon length of residency. That, and the fact that the entrance examinations were in Kannada, favored an increasing percentage of "Kannadiga" students.

Several other college-aged students voiced concerns about the trajectory of Tamil-Kannadiga relations in the post-Cauvery riot atmosphere of Bangalore.[22] One student stated, "Bangalore is not the place for Tamils to live in. Tamils are treated very badly in Bangalore. Whatever may be the problem, Tamils are affected the most. Many Tamils lost everything to return to their native [place] empty handed due to the Cauvery problem." Another stated that because Bangalore is a cosmopolitan city, Tamils should live there and that although there were problems before, the Cauvery water dispute caused increased problems for Tamils.

In a slightly different vein, a student stated, "Others respect Tamils, but some consider Tamils [to be] low. They are like 50 percent ignorant people gazing at sweets in the shop. Bangalore is a city where Tamils can make a living. But people there create problems for Tamils." In this statement, I believe the student meant that many of the working-class migrants from Tamil Nadu come to Bangalore dreaming of wealth but have no idea what challenges lie ahead. Even

Queen Victoria Statue, Cubbon Park. At the base, the inscription appears in four languages: English, Kannada, Tamil, and Urdu, demonstrating the multilingual status of the city under colonial rule.

more alarmist, one student said, "Tamils are afraid even to mention that they are Tamilians. They [Kannadigas] hate the Tamils to that extent." The most ubiquitous theme I heard among the Tamil college students concerned the "low" status that Tamils suffered in Bangalore, mostly as a result of the migrant laborer presence in the city. As one said, "Some think that Tamils are a low people." But others were fearful for Tamil safety: "Bangalore is not a safe place for Tamils. During the Cauvery dispute, Tamils and Kannadigas fought each other." The following combined a sense of Tamil stigma with a fear of persecution: "Others rate Tamils low. Tamils are uneducated. Tamils remain farmers without educating themselves. Others do not like Tamils. In Tamil Nadu, we live with all our rights. In Bangalore—Tamils live as slaves. Bangalore language and customs are different. Though it is a city, Tamils should not live as slaves." Similarly, another student said, "Bangalore Tamils are different from Tamil Nadu Tamils. Tamils live like slaves. We are afraid to speak our mother tongue. Bangalore is not safe for Tamils. There is no place for Tamil. Everything should be in Kannada." It appeared that Tamils considered themselves "slaves" for fearing to assert their Tamil language and identity.

Finally, one student, while underscoring a kind of shared cultural intimacy between Tamils and Kannadigas in Bangalore, stated strongly their victimization:

> Bangalore Tamils are different from other Tamils in food and habits. Tamils in Bangalore eat ragi [millet] balls[23] or gruel. Their Tamil is influenced by Kannada, as if they translate Kannada into Tamil. Bangalore used to be a safe place for Tamils. Now the Cauvery problem turns out to be a language issue. Tamils are tortured. Tamils were driven away from Bangalore. Tamils were even afraid to speak Tamil. Tamil women who wore turmeric chords or Tamil *thalis* were not spared.[24] Tamils have to live in fear in Bangalore. All their belongings were destroyed. Karnataka government supported this act, as it did not give any protection to Tamils. Even other places, Tamils are tortured. For instance, the Ayodhya issue.[25] In Mumbai, within three days, more than three hundred Tamils were killed.

Here the student directly points to a cultural interface between Tamils and Kannadigas—so much so that the Tamil language passes through Kannada and presumably vice versa with each utterance. While perhaps hyperbolic, it marks an important truth about the closeness of these languages and the intimate contact zone that Bangalore has been over the centuries. Thus, the acts of aggression by the activists and government that egged them on are poignantly felt as a betrayal between kin.

While the benefits of assimilating with Kannadigas seemed obvious, there were many Tamils, mostly non-Brahmins residing in the former Cantonment, who identified strongly with the DMK or AIADMK, maintained the mother tongue at home, and transacted business in Tamil.[26] In these Tamil enclaves there was an increasing awareness of the declining political capital their language carried in Karnataka. In response to this was a revival of interest in Tamil literature and religion—the latter oftentimes manifested in dramatic public rituals, journalism, and other forms of activism. Turning briefly to a meeting of academics, journalists, businessmen, and activists, we witness some of the resentment that pro-Kannadiga politics and policies engendered.

The Meeting in Cubbon Park

It was a brisk day in December 2003 when I met with a group of Tamil activists and leaders in Bangalore's verdant and popular Cubbon Park, at the heart of the city. Present was a prominent business leader, the publisher of a Tamil newspaper, a professor from Bangalore University, and a poet and activist.

We chose to sit in a circle on the grass, away from other listeners. The intent was to speak freely, unconstrained by political realities and sentiments in the city. After explaining my interests in language and identity in Bangalore, as well as my research on Tamil identity in Malaysia, one of the men began by talking about the Tamil cause. He spoke of the "Brahamanism" that had been resisted by Tamils for centuries. This had erupted in twentieth-century politics and had been worsened with the rise of Hindu nationalism. With the Liberation Tigers of Tamil Eelam (LTTE) proclaiming itself a Tamil and not a Hindu struggle, there was great sympathy among non-Brahmin Tamils within Tamil Nadu and Karnataka. But this had incurred the wrath of non-Tamils, who tended to more strongly support the Hindutva (Hindu nationalist) cause and considered Tamils increasingly anti-Brahmin and antinational. There were nods of assent to this brief summation of the Tamil predicament. But while Karnataka, particularly Bangalore, was increasingly anti-Tamil owing to chauvinist sentiments, it was a "lack of courage" among Tamils that was their concern. Recently, it was explained, a Tamil writer who expressed sympathy for the LTTE had been arrested in Bangalore. While a few spoke out, the majority were silent, fearing reprisals from Kannadigas. The problem, I was told, was that Tamils in the city lacked "guidance." There were no leaders who would speak out on behalf of the aggrieved Tamil population. Like the aforementioned college students, this shackling form of fear, though not necessarily "slavery," was indicative of a loss of nerve.[27]

But, although Tamils were intimidated by anti-Tamil rhetoric in the city—especially in the wake of the Cauvery violence and continuing debates about both Cauvery water and language use in Karnataka—there would be a time when "Tamils will fight back." Looking around to be sure that nobody was listening to our conversation, one of the men then said, "How long can Tamils take it?" The same man claimed that Tamils outnumbered Kannadigas in Bangalore at that time, though this was never admitted by the government or media. Moreover, in 1956, at the time linguistic states were drawn, "Tamils controlled Bangalore." If Tamils were bold and brave, it was said, they would not be "cowed by threats." When I mentioned hearing that Tamil signboards on businesses were no longer visible, fearing vandalism from Kannadiga thugs and "Rajkumar" fans, one man said that the fault lay with the Tamils, who allowed themselves to be intimidated. If they were brave and proud of their language, their unity in numbers would protect them, it was said.

In addition to their fear, there were divisions within the Tamil-speaking communities in Bangalore. The "rich ones don't care" about the sufferings of the poor laboring Tamils who bore the brunt of anti-Tamil violence. Moreover, the poor Tamils were often "recruited for votes." That is, "their innocence was exploited" by crafty politicians who cared little for them and would turn on them in a moment's notice if it could offer them political gain. A "divide and rule" political strategy among Karnataka's leaders had thus weakened Tamil unity. The Bharatiya Janata Party (BJP), described sarcastically by one of these men as the "Brahmin Janata Party," practiced "casteism against Tamils." While the BJP was weak in Tamil Nadu, it was growing strong in Karnataka among Kannadigas, it was said. Moreover, Tamil Brahmins, particularly the Iyengars in Bangalore, were sympathetic towards the BJP, more so than they were to their fellow Tamil speakers, it was claimed. This division, facilitated by case and religious politics, weakened the Tamils of Bangalore, despite their large numbers.

But there were some differences of opinion voiced by the group as we talked. For one thing, the business leader said, to the displeasure of the others, that Tamils "must learn to blend in." His assimilationist tone contradicted the more confrontational notion that Tamils must assert themselves against pressure groups. Moreover, the LTTE, he asserted, was not a good solution or model for the Tamils of India. Their methods and extremism, he suggested, alienated Tamils from other groups. Finally, the government of Karnataka, at that time headed by Krishna Moilly, was generally "good" and nothing like the anti-Tamil chauvinist tendencies of the Bangarappa government before (which he blamed for the anti-Tamil violence that erupted during the Cauvery water dispute of 1991). In one critical area, he agreed strongly with the others. He suggested that Tamil film culture contributed to the degradation of Tamil values. Moreover, the hero worship and violence in Tamil movies was intellectually stultifying.

The publisher of the Tamil newspaper agreed with this sentiment wholeheartedly. Tamils, he claimed, needed a complete break from the moral degeneration exhibited in Tamil movies. And the hero worship of film icons had an enervating effect on a true political awakening, he claimed. While the masses enjoyed the escapism of song, dance, and heroic fight scenes, this depoliticized their plight, ultimately offering them a false sense of justice when real political struggles were at hand. On the other hand, the publisher believed Tamils needed to be more, not less, assertive when dealing with policies that discriminated against them. The Tamils of Karnataka, he maintained, were an important and historically rooted community, having every right to their continued cultural and linguistic presence. Indeed, Tamil "suffering" in the state began, he lamented, with Kamraj, then the chief minister of Tamil Nadu, "agreeing to give Bangalore to Karnataka" with the drawing of linguistic states in 1956.

As outlined earlier, both Tamils and Kannadigas can find historical grounds to lay claim to the city. The ancient kingdoms were vast, somewhat decentralized, and to some degree linguistically plural. Nevertheless, the "pure Tamil" movement divests itself of its Kannada influences and of the cultural fusion that grew in the Deccan. The Tamil movement looks back further to the Sangam age (approximately 500 BC–AD 500), an era of Tamil history that is imagined to precede Sanskritic influences upon Tamil (Hart 1975). Non-Brahmin Tamils told me that Kannada had more Sanskritic influences than did Tamil. I observed much pride among Cantonment-living Tamils—even among Christians and Muslims[28]— when discussing the classical Tamil civilization as imagined by non-Brahmins. In fact, one of the common complaints about the DMK and similar pro-Tamil groups concerned their alleged complicity with Muslims and Christians in denigrating Brahminical Hinduism. Indeed, supporting the pure Tamil cause pitted one against the rising tide of Hindu fundamentalism, as exemplified by the VHP and RSS. Before addressing this conjoining of language and religious imaginaries, however, let me conclude by raising once again the issue of class in determining the form of protest taken by non-Brahmin Tamils.

There has been a revival of religious ritualism among Tamils within Bangalore.[29] While Tamils no longer have enclaves where they are free to put signboards up in their native tongue without fear of harassment, they can express their Tamil identity through ritual performances. In Ulsoor, a predominantly Tamil area, a Murugan temple is the site for a very dramatic display of *kavadi* during

Thaipusam, Panguni Uttiram, and other Saivite festivals. *Kavadi,* fire walking, *karagam* dancing, and other Tamil religious practices are said to be on the rise in Bangalore. Though the details of this revival are briefly addressed again later, it has been suggested to me by some Tamils that this is an expression of ethnic identity and solidarity in the only way possible. I was told by one Tamil man that the *kavadi* ritual, in particular, allowed a "psychological freedom to chant and sing aloud in Tamil," and that this will "not be tolerated by Kannadigas during non-festival days." By this he suggested that open expressions of Tamilness are confined to the spectacle of the religious ritual, where, one could argue, its potential political significance is defused. I will describe in more detail such a festival later.

Those who participate in the *kavadi* rituals are generally from working-class backgrounds, with little or no interest in the intellectual or political debates surrounding the pure Tamil movement. I was told that one reason for the growing popularity of these folk traditions stemmed from an increasing demand for migrant labor in the construction industry. A high percentage of these migrants are poor Tamils from the border region. The increasing numbers reflect a growing population of poor Tamils from rural areas; and at the same time, their poverty and political insecurity resulting from anti-Tamil rhetoric and riots lead them to seek divine intervention through vow taking and ritualism. In spite of the exodus of many of these Tamil laborers as a result of the Cauvery riots, there has not been a decline in ritual participants.

Drawing an ethnic distinction between Tamils and Kannadigas is more ambiguous—and, as I have suggested, requires greater historical imagination—than is the case, for example, in Malaysia (Willford 2006), where Malays, Chinese, and Indians not only speak differently but also look, eat, and pray somewhat differently. Making this demarcation of difference thus also requires the use of stereotypes as a necessary supplement. The revival of Tamil folk traditions that are considered unorthodox to Brahminical Hinduism serves to identify the "backward" Tamil laborer as an "alien" in modern Bangalore. This, however, is complicated by working-class Kannadiga participation in the same rituals and the substratum of *bhakti* religiosity that defines them. But the Tamils advocating the pure Tamil movement—particularly those who have openly expressed hostility to Brahminical Hinduism, the state of Karnataka, and the Indian nation—are easily labeled as "subversive" and "deviant." Moreover, when radical members of the local Tamil movement call for the partition of Bangalore, the idea that Tamils are not loyal to Karnataka is reinforced. Though few Tamils have openly expressed this desire, the local papers have aired the views of pro-Kannada politicians and organizations suggesting that this is a very real threat to the future of Karnataka. Thus, any glorification of Tamil culture, language, or political leaders (in India or Sri Lanka) is increasingly portrayed as subversive to the interests of Karnataka and India. The Bangalore Tamil Sangam's rumored complicity in the Rajiv Gandhi assassination[30] also allowed local politicians to deepen the line of division between the Kannadigas and Tamils, and those Tamils who were publicly sympathetic to the LTTE were also accused of disloyalty.

At this juncture, we can now see with some confidence that Tamils and Kannadigas have an intertwined and complex history in Bangalore (Srinivas 2001). Thus, assertions of a "pure" Tamil or Kannadiga identity must be understood as simplified figures of difference, forged out of a dissonant dialectic, which in turn was constituted by the legal creation of linguistic states in 1956. While a ground of commonality will be demonstrated in the realm of practice, the threat of the "alien" or "other" was conjured by the impossible disentangling of complex histories of cultural and linguistic sharing.

To understand why Tamils[31]—and Muslims, as we will soon see—were increasingly becoming the "Other," one must consider Bangalore's position with regard to national economic interests. As an economic center for the IT sector, Bangalore has a strong postindustrial bourgeoisie who seek close political patronage from the state government and who in turn must cooperate with New Delhi. Unlike the openly antagonistic stance taken by the DMK in Tamil Nadu to the central government at various times in its history, Karnataka has strong ties and shared interests with New Delhi. As mentioned, both the Congress I (Bangarappa's party and the ruling party of India for most of her independence) and BJP parties have strong followings in Bangalore. In Malaysia, for instance, the utility of Islamic modernism and Bumiputraism in state policies and rhetoric helped legitimate bourgeois interests under the guise of ethnic politics. In India, a resurgent Hinduism has similarly gained momentum, particularly among the middle class (Vasavi 2007; Vanaik 1990; McKean 1996; Hansen 1999). The extent to which this resurgent Hinduism gained center stage in Indian politics became painfully clear in 1993 when the Ayodhya temple-mosque dispute erupted into India's worst religious riots since independence. It is to resurgent Hinduism in Bangalore that I now turn.

CHAPTER 5

"What? Legitimacy? Just Use Vivekananda in the Name of the Movement"

A new and colorful Swami Vivekananda statue stood above the Bangalore suburb known as Banashankari 3rd Stage. This somewhat affluent area was still relatively green in 1992, with only a few "huts" dotting the fields between the large houses. At night, the new memorial of the Swami radiated a brilliant pink off its crowning dome. By day, its pastel-colored dome and pillars could be seen for some distance. Approaching the statue, one found that the Swami had been freshly garlanded, surrounded by cobras—as if Shiva himself was gazing majestically at the middle-class housing below. Before the Swami a large flagpole flew the saffron flag. Underneath a banner read, "Welcome Swami Chinmayanandaji." A few days later, Chinmayananda, the VHP founder and ideologue, inaugurated the shrine with great fanfare. A number of prominent politicians, including the chief minister, attended the ribbon-cutting ceremony. Later, a Tamil friend told me that the memorial was the brainchild and project of an "unscrupulous money man" who happened to have a lot of "political influence."

With this entry point, I now turn to the political uses of Hindu nationalism in urban space. I return to the question of "statue politics" later. But my main aim in this chapter is to map out the factors that contributed to the symbolic struggle over Vivekananda and his legacy and whether there is any convergence between struggles in the religious and linguistic spheres, respectively. In light of the extended length of this chapter, I have divided it into three sections. The first explores the politics surrounding the centenary of Swami Vivekananda's famous address at the Parliament of Religions in Chicago. Second, I examine the spiritual allure of the Ramakrishna Mission, the organization Vivekananda founded. Finally, the conclusion to this chapter assesses the theoretical terrain that helps explain the forces that exacerbate differences and conflict, drawing from instrumentalist, culturalist, and psychoanalytic perspectives.

The Vivekananda Centenary

India entered 1993 in the midst of political and social upheaval. As the Babri Masjid-Rama temple issue dominated the news throughout 1992 and the destruction of the mosque in Ayodhya on December 6, 1992, was followed by terrible rioting throughout India, the centenary of Swami Vivekananda's historic appearance at the 1893 Parliament of Religions in Chicago approached. One hundred years earlier, Vivekananda's fiery rhetoric mixed Hindu revivalism and "progressive" social ideals in a manner that inspired the Indian nationalist movement in Bengal.

Vivekananda was the principal disciple of Ramakrishna Paramhansa, one of the most revered and influential Hindu saints of the nineteenth century. After his master's passing in 1888, Vivekananda organized the other disciples of Ramakrishna into a monastic order and social service organization called the Ramakrishna Mission and Math (a monastic order). This organization was instrumental in fostering a revival and reform of Hinduism in modern India. After wandering on foot across India, Vivekananda, while sitting on a rock at land's end at Cape Comarin, in the little fishing town of Kanyakumari, received the inspiration to travel to the West in order to bring the message of Vedanta. There, in turn, he hoped to raise funds to ameliorate India's poverty.

After raising sufficient funds for the journey, Vivekananda sailed to America in order to address the Parliament of Religions in Chicago. From the Indian point of view, this event had been organized by Christian groups aiming to demonstrate Christianity's "superiority" over other religions. Vivekananda, it was reported, gave a stunning speech that galvanized his audience. Reports back in India suggested that the swami had demonstrated "Hinduism's greatness" and that he had "conquered the West" as an exponent and personification of India's "spirituality." This event, and the media coverage of it, did much to awaken Hindu pride in India. The swami went on to lecture and raise money in Europe and the United States, and in India he engaged in social work and lectured throughout the subcontinent until his early death in 1902.

Perhaps no other modern Hindu figure, except for Mahatma Gandhi, is hallowed throughout India more than is Vivekananda.[1] His striking image, no less than his writings, has made him popular across a broad spectrum of Indian society. Because of the range of his writings, he has also become a figure easily appropriated by different political and religious groups who often attempt to position him into their ideological camp. His ubiquitous image—the virile, turbaned monk gazing out with large, intense eyes—can be seen throughout India on statues, posters, and prints. Iconographically, he is projected as both a mendicant and masculine hero. Like Gandhi, his image evokes saintliness; but unlike that saintly politician, Vivekananda is seen as a masculine, heroic figure with a robust face and body. This combination of traits makes him a popular figure for mass reproduction.[2]

Given his broad appeal in India today, it was not surprising that numerous *melas* (festivals) were organized throughout the country and throughout the Indian diaspora to mark the centenary.[3] In an attempt to "fight communalism," the central government declared 1993 to be "Vivekananda Year"—a year to propagate the teachings of the swami. A government counsel, under the leadership of human resource minister Arjun Singh, was formed in order to organize a series of celebrations, exhibitions, broadcasts, and publications. The VHP, RSS, and their affiliates were also sponsoring their own festivals and publishing their own materials to mark the occasion. On the one hand, the Hindu revivalist forces drew strength from the writings of Vivekananda and utilized his image for the "Hindutva" (Hindu nationalist) cause. On the other hand, there were those who saw Vivekananda as the apotheosis of "secular humanism" and Gandhian pluralism. I will not, however, interpret the swami within this debate. Instead I look at the critical role that media technologies played in the harnessing of cultural symbols by different parties. While it is true that varied media forms allow us to view cultural developments as a reflection of critical issues and concerns, we must also consider the role that these technologies play in the dissemination of political ideas.

As social identities are in flux, so are the culture and political networks with which they dialogically interact. The use of processions, statues, public events, and the media coverage of these is, in the end, contested and made meaningful locally, even spatially (Vasavi 2007; Deshpande 2000). But it is still important to see how the use of media technologies enables the construction of a public sphere that demarcates the "true" cultural identity from the "Other." This public sphere utilizes an iconographic tradition in an attempt to craft a relatively homogenous cultural identity (Freitag 1989; van der Veer 1994). The images created by the Vivekananda procession throughout India, as well as his address at the Parliament of Religions, provided idioms that potentially united disparate (and diasporic) groups against imagined others (van der Veer 1994). Following Anderson (1991, 1998), we might say that the serialization of identity in India requires these standardized images as a necessary condition. This standardization prefigures the imagined community, allowing people from disparate groups and territories to imagine themselves as parts of a whole.

VIVEKANANDA BHARATA PARIKRAMA

The Vivekananda Kendra, an organization based in Kanyakumari (a district in Tamil Nadu), was an affiliated organization of the RSS.[4] The Kendra, under the leadership of Dr. Lakshmi Kumari, recreated Vivekananda's 1892 journey throughout India on foot—a trip that culminated in the town of Kanyakumari, at the southernmost tip of the subcontinent, where the monk was inspired to travel to the West with a neo-Hindu interpretation of Vedanta. The Vivekananda Bharata Parikrama (India Pilgrimage) was recreated by a dedicated group of devotees. They chose the precise routes taken by Vivekananda a century earlier. Accompanied by a large van that acted as a mobile museum, bookstore, and gift shop, tapes, T-shirts, videos, and pamphlets were sold along the procession. "Vivekananda is my Hero" bumper stickers and T-shirts were sold at the procession when I witnessed it in Bangalore. Thousands of devotees and curious onlookers observed the colorful spectacle. The streets in Bangalore where the procession passed were decorated with saffron banners, flags, and posters of the swami. Many locals joined the procession for a short time, thus creating an illusion that the march was comprised of thousands of people. In the center was a truck decorated as a "minitemple" (resembling the famous Vivekananda rock memorial in Kanyakumari) carrying a garlanded statue. *Bhajans* (devotional songs) were heard from speakers on the truck. The truck-temple stopped within the Ramakrishna Mission Ashram at about five in the evening. Devotees prayed, circumambulated the truck, and received the *darshan* (visual blessing) of the swami icon. Long lines of people approached the statue, touched the base, and performed a *namaskaram* (reverential folding of hands in front of the chest or above the head).

At six in the evening, a cultural program and speeches in Kannada and English were given by the leaders of the Vivekananda Kendra, Ramakrishna Mission, and other local religious and political figures. About three thousand well-dressed and mainly middle-class devotees assembled within a large open-air auditorium within the ashram. One of the resident swamis then led the congregation in the singing of *bhajans*—during which *arati* (the waving of the flame before the deity) was then performed to Ramakrishna, Vivekananda, and Sarada Devi (Ramakrishna's wife, who is also worshipped). After this, a series of ecumenical prayers were offered, followed by a vocal duet. Then a short drama was performed in which a Muslim, Hindu, and Christian all turned away a miserable beggar only to be redeemed after witnessing Vivekananda helping the same man. After seeing his compassion, they too were able to approach the beggar and offer comfort.

Following a few speeches by various organizations, including the RSS and a government official from the Congress I Party, the woman spearheading the march—Dr. Kumari, who was also the energy and organization behind the Vivekananda Kendra—spoke with a fiery passion that, I imagined, evoked the forceful personality of the charismatic swami. Dr. Kumari, who wore an unadorned white sari (a sign of renunciation or widowhood), spoke of India's great "moral crisis." Speaking in English, she recounted many exhilarating moments experienced while trekking across the country. Her speech then turned serious as she decried the "moral decay" that India had "fallen to." She described the social service work of the Vivekananda Kendra in Kanyakumari but called upon everyone present to make "Swamiji the guide of our lives." Asking devotees to emulate him, she claimed that India could soon "reawaken." But she warned that India could see "even worse days if it does not now dedicate itself to the ideals of Swamiji." Resources were not the problem with India's poverty; rather, the problem lay in her "loss of spiritual values." In particular, she chastised those seeking "Western luxuries" at the expense of "spiritual responsibilities," adding that "people are trapped by that idiot box, the *asura* [demon] of the household, the TV." This, she maintained, was why "people no longer have the heart to help their fellow man." Finally, she exhorted the audience to "look to a higher ideal in leadership" than that personified by those presently occupying the Indian political stage. Then she boldly (given that a government leader was present) compared Vivekananda to some of the current political leaders, suggesting that the disparity between them proved her previous point. Lastly, Dr. Kumari ended by telling the mostly middle-class audience that "singing a few *bhajans* once a week" would not help to save the country in crises. On the whole, in spite of her misgivings about the present political leadership, her message was one of social activism aimed at "uplift" for the poor. Devotion to Mother India, she preached, could best be realized by ameliorating poverty among her children—a message preached by Vivekananda one hundred years earlier.

The entourage stopped in major towns and held rallies in which prominent leaders spoke. Towards the end of the journey, as the procession approached Kanyakumari, Congress I Party leaders spoke at the celebrations. Media coverage of these events in the newspapers, All India Radio, and Doordarshan[5] was considerable. President Dr. Shankar Dayal Sharma addressed the Parikrama on October 28 in Kochi, Kerala. The *Deccan Herald* carried the headline, "Sharma says communal thinking is ruinous."[6] Sharma was quoted as saying,

> Communalism is alien to our traditions and heritage and it will only spell ruin wherever it exists. . . . It benefits none, not even those who seek to propagate it for selfish reasons. . . . Just as Vivekananda's Parikrama helped weave the threads of our cultural unity into a harmonizing pattern and became an important link in the reawakening of national consciousness so also at Chicago he gave a new perspective of religion and introduced India to the West, indeed to Indians themselves. (October 29, 1992)

The *Hindu,*[7] on the same day, quoted President Sharma as saying,

> "Some years later Mahatma Gandhi taught us the same lesson, namely that we should remain fearless. . . . Let us, therefore, resolve anew to act upon Swami Vivekananda's inspiring message and endeavor to become strong of heart, strong of mind and have the strength never to submit to injustice and wrongdoing." Recalling that Vivekananda had been a source of inspiration for those who led the country to independence, the President said that the Swamiji "had set in motion a process of national rejuvenation and regeneration directed at ridding society of archaic and obscurantist practices." (October 29, 1992)

Clearly the tone and content of his words suggested an anticommunal and iconoclastic interpretation of his writings. He positioned the nationalist Hindu philosopher ideologically closer to Mahatma Gandhi (and by extension, Nehru) than to Subhas Chandra Bose, Aurobindo,[8] or the supreme Hindutva ideologues, Sarvakar and Golwalker.[9] From the same speech, the Ramakrishna Mission journal, *Vedanta Kesari,* quoted Sharma:

> Secularism and socialism are not the only fields in which Swami Vivekananda helped to build the climate that obtains in modern India. His understanding of Vedanta and of different religions made him an inveterate opponent of the terrible practice of untouchability which he strongly denounced. . . . Gandhiji wrote about him in 1941: 'Surely Swami Vivekananda's writings need no introduction from anybody. They make their own irresistible appeal.' (December 1992)

Once again Sharma positioned Vivekananda within the Nehruvian Congress I framework. Nowhere in the speech did he demonstrate how the swami made a direct case for secularism in India. Instead emphasis was placed on the religious tolerance and "anti-caste" viewpoints of the swami. Also significant was the lack of recognition given to the Vivekananda Kendra's procession in the press.[10] Sharma's speech was reported in all the major papers, and I heard excerpts of it on All India Radio and the Doordarshan television network.

After the tragic events at Ayodhya and rioting in its aftermath, the Parikrama reached Kanyakumari on December 28. There, before the Vivekananda Rock memorial (which was managed by the Vivekananda Kendra), a panel of political and religious leaders including then prime minister P. V. Narasimha Rao, union human resources development minister Arjun Singh, chief ministers Jayalalitha

(Tamil Nadu) and Karunakaran (Kerala), Dr. Karan Singh, a philosopher, and Swami Lokeswarananda, vice-president of the Ramakrishna Mission, spoke about Vivekananda to a large assembled crowd. This was then broadcast throughout India on Doordarshan that evening. Prime Minister Rao spoke: "The renouncer stands above everybody else . . . in our society. . . . The great leaders have given more moral fibre than mere book knowledge to the society. He [Vivekananda] anticipated the seminal transformation brought by Mahatma Gandhi. We know from Mahatma Gandhi's writings how profoundly he was influenced by Ramakrishna Paramhansa and his disciple, Swami Vivekananda." Rao went on to speak of the "deep moral crisis" that the country was facing. He said that "Hindu society" could achieve a "social revolution through spiritual revolution." But he tempered this by saying that "material civilization" could not be neglected in this process. Rather, Vivekananda "could see both sides" and balance them. Again we see an attempt to draw upon the Gandhian legacy and its historic links with the Congress Party. But rather than characterizing the swami as an ideologue of secularism, Rao appealed to the Hindu majority by speaking of the "renouncer" and his/her role in defining the morality of "Hindu society." In doing so, the prime minister seemed to equate Indian and Hindu society—the explicit position taken by the BJP-VHP-RSS combine. On the following day, the front-page headline of the *Hindu* read, "Nation needs the help of spiritual leaders." The first paragraph under the top headline began with the following: "Prime Minister, Mr. P. V. Narasimha Rao today said the country needed the guidance of spiritual leaders as they could handle crisis better." But the Kanyakumari address by Rao and others did not escape criticism. In a letter entitled "Whose Vivekananda" printed in the *Hindu* on January 13, the author pointed out that the Vivekananda Kendra's long-planned celebrations were overshadowed by the "official apparatus which sprung into action when the PM's visit was announced." He offered this criticism:

> This highly politicised jambooree was very much restricted to mainly the Congress I and a few AIADMK "sponsored crowds." The public and the youth who should really be his torch-bearers were significantly absent.
>
> Yet another distortion is the PM's repeated calls to the spiritual leaders, as if the Ayodhya episode and the role played by the Saffron Brigade had not already done enough damage. Must not our national leadership realise the folly of playing this religious card again and again?

Indeed, the prime minister appeared to some to be pandering to Hindus with his embracing of Vivekananda and "spiritual leaders." Some critics recalled that it was

Rajiv Gandhi himself who had started the Ayodhya crisis when he had allowed the disputed structure (the Babri mosque) to be used for Hindu prayers. It was clear to many Bangaloreans I spoke with—including members of the Ramakrishna Mission—that the government was trying to capitalize on the Vivekananda procession by appearing as the "true" and "tolerant" upholders of Hindu values. It was not so much that Hinduism and politics did not mix as it was that the Hindu "fundamentalist" opponents of the government (BJP-VHP-RSS) were violating the "tolerant" spirit of the religion.[11]

Others approved of the prime minister's words, such as the author of an editorial that appeared in the *Hindu* under the title, "The new relevance of Vivekananda":

> There is little doubt that an effective way of overcoming the serious crisis which the propagators of the basically fascist Hindutva of the RSS and VHP type have brought upon the country is to launch a sustained and concerted campaign to reach Swami Vivekananda's message to the masses, particularly the majority community. And there could be no better occasion for doing it than the centenary of the Swamiji's cross country pilgrimage and Chicago address. The Prime Minister . . . has done well to seek the guidance of religious leaders on how to remove what he calls the "moral disquiet" that has overtaken the people following the murky Ayodhya episode. (December 30, 1992)

Arjun Singh, then union human resource development minister and the one responsible for organizing the celebrations across India, also spoke, but ironically in Hindi, a language not understood by most of the attending audience members;[12] however, Singh knew that the broadcast on All India Radio and Doordarshan would reach millions of listeners throughout the country. This in itself showed the power of media technologies transforming events and making their distributive trajectory wider. But on January 11, Singh did give a national address in English on Doordarshan following a documentary film about the life of Vivekananda. Before his speech, however, mention was made of Dr. Kumari's Bharat Parikrama and the social work of the Vivekananda Kendra. Naturally, no mention was made at this point that this organization was related to the then-banned RSS.[13] In his address, Singh attacked those "sectarian" or "communal" forces that had brought the country to a "dangerous" juncture. He described Vivekananda as the "most luminous" figure to "guide us through the darkness against communal forces." Singh quoted Vivekananda to illustrate the swami's views on religious fanaticism.

He referred to a time in Vivekananda's life when he had become "outraged at the destruction of temples" in north India by past Muslim dynasties. Vivekananda reportedly heard the goddess say to him, "Is it you who protect me, or do I protect you?" This "humbled" the monk and made him realize that "God need not be defended by humans." The timing of the address in its post-Ayodhya context made it clear that Singh was attacking the BJP-RSS-VHP combine through this anecdote.

More significant, perhaps, than the rhetorical strategies employed by Congress I leaders at the climax of the Bharata Parikrama and inauguration of the Vivekananda Year was the media appropriation of this event. The images and words broadcast across the nation firmly placed the swami in the Congress I camp. This media campaign was also used to characterize the BJP opposition as having produced a "moral crisis" by fomenting communal enmity. In other words, the Rao government's strategy was to claim "mainstream" Hinduism, while casting the BJP and its allies as "fundamentalists." In turn, the BJP was also accused of inciting an Islamic fundamentalist response. Nehruvian secularism was nowhere to be heard or seen as the Congress I Party waved its own saffron banners. As Vasavi later argued (2007), politics was enacted through public "*darshan*"—a conjoining of the visual spectacle and spiritual. I return to this theme in a later chapter.

Media coverage of the Bharata Parikrama was conspicuously light after the Ayodhya episode—especially considering it was at the climax of its arduous journey. Dr. Kumari, who had given rousing speeches about Vivekananda, was completely overshadowed by the Congress I leaders.

The BJP-VHP-RSS voice, without control of the legitimate press,[14] was seen mainly in small and dubious newspapers. An example was seen in the "officially banned" RSS newspaper, the *Organiser*. BJP president L. K. Advani exhorted a crowd of devotees gathered in Calcutta for the 125th birth anniversary of Sister Nivedita[15] to serve the nation as a form of devotion: "Advaniji then urged the Central government to celebrate the centenary of Swami Vivekananda's address at the Parliament of Religions. . . . Shri Advani also stressed the fact that Vivekananda considered devotion to God and devotion to Nation as synonymous. Shri Advani reminded the people of Swamiji's message that dharma was the soul of India, and if we ignored dharma, the nation's roots would dry up" (December 13, 1992). It was interesting that Advani urged the government to honor the centenary when it was known that it had formed a special committee headed by the home minister in order to carry out the celebration of "Vivekananda Year." Clearly, Advani's message was one of ultranationalism, cast in Hindu terms.

In the December 6 issue of the *Organiser*—the day the Masjid fell—a headline read, "The Triumphant Hindu." In the article, K. Suryanarayan Rao offered tribute to Vivekananda. Like Advani, he did not emphasize religious harmony and pluralism; rather, the emphasis was on total devotion to Hinduism and India:

> Swamiji was very forthright in his admonition of Christian missionaries. In one of his speeches, he warned: "You Christians who are so fond of sending out missionaries to save the soul of the heathen, why do you not try to save their bodies from starvation? . . . From Colombo down South to Almora in the Himalayas, Vivekananda emphasized the unification of all Hindus. Organisation, discipline, character are the need of the hour. . . . This was the Swami. He was for the total defense of the Hindu, not only with intellectual arguments but with physical prowess as well. . . . I appeal to one and all to study Vivekananda's life and works in detail. This alone will make us understand the greatness of our Motherland, the value of *sanatana dharma* and its Hindu heritage and make us proud of being born Hindus.

This typified the *Organiser,* and by extension, the RSS utilization of Vivekananda. Nationalism was equated with religious duty (dharma) coupled with a defensive attitude towards Western or Islamic "attacks" on Hinduism.[16]

Shifting briefly to the United States we witness similar "ownership" debates played out in the Indian-American media. The focal point of these debates was the VHP–sponsored "Global Vision 2000" conference.

Global Vision 2000

Global Vision 2000, sponsored by the VHP of America,[17] was intended to be a celebration of Vivekananda's address at Chicago and a way to teach "Hindu values" to second- and third-generation Indian-American children. The conference had been planned two years earlier. and money had been raised through various fundraisers held by the "Overseas Friends of the BJP." *India Today,* on November 15, 1992, reported that the BJP-VHP-RSS raised $32,000 at a single dinner in southern California for the purpose of the conference. According to this article, the VHP of America had hoped it would be able to collect close to $1 million through fundraising activities. The article claimed that many affluent Indian-Americans were eager to help the BJP back home. It also claimed that there were more than twenty thousand members supporting the "Overseas Friends of the BJP."

Global Vision 2000 was advertised in the Indian-American newspapers. A large one-page advertisement in *Hinduism Today* appeared:

> We cordially invite you to join us in a spectacular three-day celebration of Swami Vivekananda's historic delivery of the Advaitic vision at the

Parliament of Religions. . . . This event formally launches World Vision 2000,[18] a series of creative programs initiated by the Vishwa Hindu Parishad to provide forums to explore a greater Vision of Wholeness for our future on Mother Earth. Many eminent Hindu and world leaders (the Dalai Lama is invited and President Clinton is invited to inaugurate the festival) will address the mammoth gathering of over 15,000 with inspiring messages.

As the event neared, it also attracted a fair amount of criticism in the main Indian-American papers. *India West, India Abroad,* and *India Today* (Western edition) all ran highly critical stories about the conference and the VHP's motives behind it. Many questioned why the VHP of America—with its links to the banned VHP and RSS in India—would sponsor a conference purporting to promote religious tolerance. Novelist and journalist (and later Congress I politician) Shashi Tharoor spoke out in a letter to the *Washington Post*: "Its organizers have no claim to the all-embracing tolerance and wisdom of the late sage. They are the Vishwa Hindu Parishad, whose vision extends most famously so far to the destruction of the Babri mosque at Ayodhya in northern India in December, an act that unleashed violence and rioting on a scale not seen in India since independence." He added that the "strident chauvinism" of American Hindus is "one more installment in a long saga of zeal abroad for radicalism at home." *India West* reported that many activist groups and individuals had come together to protest the conference. The Coalition for Communal Harmony, comprised of "secular minded Hindus," argued that "the VHP never believed in the essence of Vivekananda's teaching—religious tolerance—yet it has the audacity to organize something in his name to promote its own agenda in America."

The criticisms of the conference, both within India and in the United States, had an impact. President Clinton, it was reported in *India West,* along with the Dalai Lama, did not want to be associated with the organization sponsoring the conference after the negative publicity gained some traction.[19]

While the conference attracted criticism from VHP detractors in the United States and in India, some participants were surprised by the controversy. They claimed that the VHP of America was independent of the organization in India and thus had no connection to the political events in the last couple of years. But *India Today* suggested otherwise:

That the VHP means business is clear from the list of speakers: leaders of the Bharatiya Janata Party (BJP) Atal Behari Vajpayee and Murli Manohar Joshi would be addressing the audience. "The VHP has an even bigger task. It not only has to continue the religious education of Americans, but also has to anchor the second and third generation firmly in Hindu tradition and culture," says Gaurang Vaishnav, programme chairperson. "The Vivekananda centenary celebrations would certainly give the VHP a new status across North America." (July 31, 1993)

A front-page headline in *India West* on August 13 read, "Leaders Call for 'Resurrecting a New Hindu India.'" The article claimed that the conference had "deviated" from its initial objectives and had clear "political overtones." It reported further that the conference "spoke of fostering 'Hindu consciousness' and a 'distinct Hindu identity,' particularly in India, for evolving what they termed a 'new social, economic and political order.'" VHP president Ashok Singhal was quoted as saying, "December 6, 1992, would be written in golden letters in the history of India and on the canvas of people's awakening."

After the conference, the North American version of *India Today* carried a cover story entitled, "Gift-Wrapping Hindutva: Colour, crowds and controversy mark the VHP's show of strength, as Vivekananda becomes just a facade." The report claimed that the conference turned out to be one of the most controversial "overseas Indian jamborees" in recent times. While some critics of the BJP considered the event a disaster because President Clinton and the Dalai Lama did not show up, some enthusiasm was generated by the more than ten thousand delegates that attended throughout the three-day fest. The report claimed that Vivekananda was nearly excluded from the conference, except for a "token tribute" in the form of an art exhibition on his life and work. *India Today*'s coverage ended with a rather strongly voiced criticism of the conference: "There is no denying it was a show of Hindutva strength. The VHP campaign to legitimise and consolidate its presence in the international arena after being banned in its own country had yielded dividends. 'America will realise with this programme that Hindutva has asserted itself and now there is no force that can stop it,' maintained [Ashok] Singhal [VHP president]. Vivekananda had served his purpose: a gift-wrapping for the Hindutva Package."

What conclusions can we draw from the "Vivekananda Year," and how it was reported in India and the United States? It was obvious that Global Vision 2000 was affected by arguments in India. In fact, many Global Vision organizers felt that their "spiritual" conference had been politicized by the critics of the BJP-VHP-RSS. At the same time, we saw that the VHP leaders had themselves asserted pro-Hindutva statements and positions at the conference.

Clearly, both sides of the debate utilized Vivekananda for political gain through the media. Moreover, very little discussion was actually focused on the writings of the swami. As Tharoor argued, the immigrant experience may have in fact contributed to a zeal for religious symbolism, as this can be a vehicle for the expression of patriotism in the midst of feeling displaced. The impact of the media widens the distributive trajectory of symbolic icons from the "imagined homeland"; and as Appadurai (1991, 193) suggests, this may take on a "fantastic and one-sided" quality that provides "fuel for ethnic conflict." Anderson (1998) labeled this "fantastic" quality of diasporic sentiment "long distance nationalism." In Anderson's formulation, it is the experience of cultural and psychological displacement within an adopted homeland that gives rise to "one-sided" yearnings for certitude and symbolic mooring. The consolidated figure of the Hindu holy personage within the iconography of Vivekananda provided this certitude, one could argue. While here we see an example from a transnational and diasporic flow, similar principles might accrue when we look at a global city in flux.

As witnessed in this study, Bangalore's identities appear most troubled when in rapid change and flux—a factor not removed from globalization. Moreover, the serial imaginary is aided by "mediascapes" (Appadurai 1996) and the temporary unity or symbolic homogeneity provided by key symbols. Nevertheless, we must be careful when we assign too much agency to these technologies. We must consider that competing nationalistic (or transnational) religious discourses represent the interests of parties that have the material resources to strategize through the media and, hence, the enduring utility of instrumentalist perspectives. That is, the appropriation of Vivekananda represents a political struggle between competing political parties—in this case, the Congress I and BJP. Cast as a struggle between "secularism" or "pluralism" and Hindutva, or Hindu nationalism, it was clear that both parties claimed ideological congruency with the Hindu nationalist leader. More broadly, we can see that focal icons of identity are contested from within, destabilizing any single narrative, whatever such yearnings for certitude and morality represent. Moreover, and following the more phenomenological logic of Appadurai and Anderson, we note that instrumentalism, while important, is analytically insufficient to explain the zeal and passion such symbolic constructs provide, not to mention their resonance, culturally and psychologically.

While a full examination of Hindu nationalism is well beyond the scope of this book[20] (Hansen 1999, 2001; Menon 2010; Jaffrelot 1998), I am suggesting that there has been a gradual accommodating of the religious sentiments of middle-class Hindus in India since independence—but especially within the last thirty years. Moreover, Hindu revivalism in modern India was and is spearheaded by a growing number of middle-class–based neo-Hindu organizations crusading to make the sometimes amoral (some would say immoral) world of capitalism and industrialization have a moral or dharmic face. The coinciding and overlap between Hindutva and other regionally based identity constructs based on language and ethnicity, furthermore, cannot be underestimated (see Hansen 2001; Appadurai 2006; Vasavi 2007). As has been pointed out, the Tamils in Bangalore have been stereotyped as simultaneously antinational (and in Hindutva discourse, anti-Hindu) and a threat to Kannadiga identity.

Nationalist ideologies seek to legitimate and naturalize a social order that naturally is more economically favorable to some than it is to others—an instrumental baseline, so to speak. This does not discount the visceral and phenomenological compulsions of identity politics. But it is not controversial to suggest that putting a moral face upon politics allows for the continued domination of certain groups by more powerful others; and as I have suggested, creating a counterdiscourse requires capital and access to material production and media technologies. However, it is not necessarily the case that followers of Hindutva or regional chauvinisms are elites. Rather, the evidence in Bangalore suggests that a lower middle class is attracted to xenophobic discourses out of insecurities associated with a more elite class (Nair 2005). That is, scapegoating of minorities might be best seen as a symptom of other challenges blocking a more progressive political agenda (Vasavi 2007), a point I return to later.

While it could be argued that Hindu nationalism justifies economic structures that favor the burgeoning Indian middle class, an interest in religion among the middle class and professionals cannot be understood solely in hegemonic terms. Instead, the search for a new Hindu identity—particularly one that is "scientific" and "modern"—is indeed a spiritual calling and a quest for meaning (Geertz 1973). Looking briefly at the Ramakrishna Mission, the organization founded by Vivekananda, we can better understand how the urban Indian middle class is drawn to a combination of both Hindu nationalism and otherworldly mysticism in such movements. In doing so, the devotee can fulfill the twin goals of dharma (duty to the religion and nation) and *moksha* (spiritual liberation). The other two classical goals in Hindu life—*artha* (worldly success) and *kama* (pleasure)—have, arguably, already been largely fulfilled by the professional middle class.

The Ramakrishna Mission

The Ramakrishna Mission (RKM) has enjoyed the patronage of the Indian government since independence. Even the agnostic Nehru[21] committed government support to RKM hospitals, schools, and disaster relief efforts. In a Hindu-majority nation, the nonpolitical RKM has attracted a large following of devotees due to its combining of intellectualism, mysticism, and social commitment. It has also benefited from the canonization of Ramakrishna as a saint and Vivekananda as a national hero. The movement also attracts prestige due to its international following, which began as soon as Vivekananda first traveled to the West in 1893. Today there are over one hundred principal RKM centers throughout India. Most are on land donated by wealthy patrons. It is one of the largest religious institutions in the nation and has extended to branches throughout the Indian diaspora, especially in the United States.

Though the RKM was founded with an explicit mission to serve the poor, most lay members come from elite or middle-class backgrounds. The RKM appeals to educated Hindus who seek a "rational" and less ritualistic variety of religious experience. Also, the poor and working class lack the means to donate money and time to the RKM's charitable causes. This was the case in Bangalore, where I attended cultural functions and rituals and interviewed monks and devotees at two RKM ashrams in 1992–1993.[22]

One of the RKM ashrams in Bangalore was a large complex located near the center of the city on Bull Temple Road. I was told that this part of town was a "Brahmin (Iyengar)-dominated area." The ashram had a large auditorium; but it also had a large and ornate temple,[23] a bookstore, library, residence hall for swamis, and a large botanical garden. Every day, the ashram attracted hundreds of devotees for prayers and worship in the early morning and again at sunset. Classes on Hindu philosophy were held twice a week, once in Kannada and once in English. These classes were also well attended. A number of special programs were also held in the ashram. The birthdays of Ramakrishna, Vivekananda, and Sarada Devi, in addition to major Hindu holidays, were marked by special *pujas,* lectures, and cultural programs. These events would often draw well over a thousand devotees. Many RKM centers also have a publications department. A number of journals, magazines, and pamphlets are produced by different branch centers. Also, English and vernacular translations of ancient religious texts are published. RKM publications receive government subsidies, allowing prices to be kept low and thus widening their distribution throughout India.[24]

The RKM's principal appeal for devotees comes from its highly trained monks and nuns. These individuals were and are venerated by devotees. Acting as traditional gurus, they instruct individual devotees on spiritual and personal matters. Their many years of training and personal asceticism, particularly among males, accord them great respect and devotion from disciples. There is usually more than one resident swami at any ashram. RKM swamis meet with disciples during regularly scheduled times. Many times it was suggested to me that as social, personal, and spiritual problems were increasing in large cities—particularly among the English-educated middle class—individuals sought the comfort and advice of gurus. Even swamis told me that they often felt overwhelmed by the many problems faced by devotees. One even complained that he had little time to pursue meditation, as he was busy meeting devotees much of the time. Gurus seemed and seem to fill an important psychological role as anomie and alienation increased with the stresses of modern urban life. As Kakar (1982, 1988) has often argued, the guru is the Indian version of the psychotherapist (Narayan 1989). And it follows that the increased alienation produced by urban stress factors is also productive of other forms of psychic stress. But intensified religiosity or other forms of excessive attachment to an identity are not the only symptoms of modern life in Bangalore. Mental health disturbances are also said to be on the rise, a point I examine in chapter 8. At the same time, gurus also recast troubling individual experiences in ways that are culturally meaningful. That is, they mitigate against a "crisis of meaning" by providing coherent models "of" and "for" a cultural and social reality (Geertz 1968, 1973). Gurus also act as loving and idealized parental figures (Kakar 1982; Narayan 1989). I will comment again upon devotee aspirations shortly.

A key element in Vivekananda's teaching—and hence of the RKM—is his call for social activism. Vivekananda spoke of an almost chivalric need to protect "Mother India" by serving the poor and suffering. The VHP and RSS, in turn, were inspired by this message, adding to it a martial sense of duty. The "Mother" had to be protected from all attacks and diseases (McKean 1996; van der Veer 1994; Madan 1997). On the one hand, social reform and charitable work must be carried out in order to make the nation strong. On the other hand, minorities, particularly Muslims, had to be prevented from damaging the nation. Ashis Nandy (2002) has gone so far as to argue that Hindutva's intolerance to the threat of internal diversity can be linked to the project of secularism in India, itself a universal project hostile to a religious presence in public life. Thus the universal impulses of secular humanism have produced a religious variant, following a similar logic that does not tolerate difference—and one that goes against the more protean pasts of religious pluralism and accommodation in India (Kaviraj 1992; Deshpande 2000). In any event, deifying and gendering the nation inspired a sort of patriotic devotion. While I am glossing over the Hindutva ideology, the call to social action (particularly to the middle class) continues in RKM rhetoric. This is seen in the following example.

On December 2, just before the Ayodhya riots, the RKM held its own Vivekananda celebrations in Bangalore. Once again, the large ashram was filled with thousands of devotees. This time, after the *puja* and *bhajans,* the vice president of the RKM, Swami Ranganathananda, was present to deliver a talk entitled, "Vivekananda 100 Years after Chicago." The elderly and much-venerated swami held the audience's attention with a fiery yet patriotic speech. He began his talk by comparing Vivekananda to Buddha and Shankara (the systematizer of Vedanta), saying that they continue to "work long after death" through their followers. Then he described his meetings with Nehru in the 1950s, claiming that the latter credited Vivekananda for "bridging the past and present." This was followed by Mahatma Gandhi's appraisal of the swami. He then began a long critique of present conditions in the nation, which I recorded in my notes:

He [Vivekananda] created history. Gandhi also created history. You must create a new India free from evils of past. You must have his [Vivekananda's] love for India. . . . What is wrong with India today: evil, corruption, everything. . . . Downwards since independence—we may have more buildings, but as a people we are going down. People love themselves—not the country. In the temples, we ask: "God give me this, give me that." We are stunted in growth. . . . Middle classes are self-centered [with] no love for country. How can India grow as a nation? [Former president] S. Radhakrishnan said, "Vivekananda will show us how to use our freedom." But we just ask for our own—a good cushy job, success . . . no concern for others. Just my belly and my self. Is this what freedom means? Poverty should have been eliminated after freedom. Slaves are not free. Vivekananda asked why there should be so much poverty in our country. [Here] charity ends with temple alms. . . . Western people solved it better. In Holland, the streets are clean and tidy—even dogs are well fed. They loved their country. In Norway there are no status distinctions. . . .

He came for us but we don't care for him. Love the nation. Be good citizens. Status is high being a citizen, not an employer. The power in that speech [in Chicago] . . . Swamiji went through many difficulties to make that speech. . . . Every student should memorize that speech in Chicago. He was undoubtedly the greatest figure at the Parliament of Religions. . . .

I have been around the world fifteen times, and in other places there is such respect for Indian philosophy—Vedanta. But here, 20 percent kidnapped all the wealth after freedom. You care only for yourself. No other country has this "what can I do for you"[25] attitude. We realize this is a "sick" India. The whole world pities this "sick" India. Every student must have this instilled in him. . . . We must put heart into society. . . . Buddha was gentle; Sankara was extraordinary; but Vivekananda was concerned about common people. . . .

Its [his message] impact on government will take some time. As a democracy, it will take some time. The Centenary should be a time to remember his words and spread these ideas.

The swami then went on to describe how Indira Gandhi had earlier announced that Vivekananda's birthday would be celebrated as a "youth day." He also mentioned that Arjun Singh, P. V. Narasimha Rao, and other prominent members of her government had formed a committee to "better understand Vivekananda." Out of their efforts (in the early 1980s), a pamphlet entitled *Rebuild India* was produced and distributed by the government. Additionally, sixty passages by Vivekananda were selected and aired on television between programs. Clearly, the Congress I, both under Indira and Rajiv Gandhi and now under P. V. Narasimha Rao, had cooperated with the RKM on promoting Vivekananda's brand of reformed Hinduism. The vice president of the order seemed sympathetic to Congress and Congress I,[26] tracing the influence of Vivekananda upon Mahatma Gandhi and Nehru; and he made it a point to show how the then-ruling party had involved the RKM in its planning of various Vivekananda-related projects. No mention was made of Hindutva.

On the other hand, we see that patriotism—and shame for a lack of it—among the middle class is a key thematic. India is personified as "sick"—a mother neglected by self-interested "kidnappers." Vivekananda has given his life for the redemption of the nation, yet he is ignored by a "greedy" and materialistic middle class. Indians, particularly those who are wealthy, should feel guilty for letting Vivekananda and Gandhi down. One way to expiate this national sin is to now commit oneself to propagating the ideals of Vivekananda through service to the nation. But it is not too late, as he ended his talk by saying, "More living people will appear in the next ten years" as a result of an increased awareness of Vivekananda resulting from the centenary. They will be hit, he predicted, by "thought bombs" uttered by the swami one hundred years earlier.

While the previous RKM leader emphasized the moral and patriotic duty of serving the nation by serving the poor, the following swami voices concern over past and present governments in India, suggesting that "secularism" threatened the future of Hinduism and the nation. My interview with him began matter-of-factly, as he detailed the rules of ordination and the training involved in becoming a swami in the Ramakrishna Order. Though critical of the Congress-led government, as we will soon see, he acknowledged that financial support was given to the RKM by the government:

It is the responsibility of each branch center to find its own resources, and funding is mostly from public subscriptions (membership) and donations. Occasionally, we also get grants from the government provided the work falls under the category of the grant, say for instance, in the running of an educational institution—say a school or college—the Education Department can give us grants provided we follow their norms and standards. Similarly, suppose we are running a dispensary or hospital, the Health Department can give us a regular expenditure every year—or a lump-sum grant. . . . As far as possible, we try to depend on the public money. That is, our collections from the public as subscriptions and donations.

When I asked what his views were on the rise of "Hindu fundamentalism," however, he reacted strongly. He said that the so-called Hindu fundamentalism was a mistaken notion. "Fundamentalism is impossible to a Hindu. . . . Hinduism is and has always been tolerant. Zoroastrians and Christians had found a home among Hindus without persecution." The more aggressive sounding tone taken in recent times by the VHP and RSS was "a reaction to the pampering of minorities by worthless politicians." He complained about the "uneducated and narrow mullahs" who made many demands for Muslims that violated the constitution.[27] Government leaders had "no guts" when they caved in to these demands in order to secure votes from minorities. Of course, he was singling out the Congress I Party, which traditionally relied upon Muslim votes. He praised the BJP, claiming that it was the "best party" and "very sensible." Also, he maintained that the BJP-VHP-RSS "were not anti-Muslim but simply wanted what any majority in any country should enjoy—equal rights." Because Hindus were "naturally peaceful," he claimed, they had "allowed themselves to be bullied for a long time." The swami also said that "partition was a tragic mistake," adding that India should have been "a Hindu state." Once again, he blamed the politicians who caved in to the demand for a separate Pakistan.

On the whole, this swami, like the earlier one who was more generous in his comments about the government, was convinced that the call to service (dharma) that Vivekananda had loudly proclaimed was essentially patriotic. Both saw India as synonymous with Hinduism and argued that citizens and government should strengthen the nation through service. But, whereas the former viewed Mahatma Gandhi, Nehru, and to a certain extent the modern Congress I Party as fostering a reawakening of Vivekananda's message, the latter blamed the party for everything from partition to the marginalization of Hindus in their own country. Moreover, rather than limiting his critique to "materialism" and "greed," he also suggested that non-Hindus are antagonistic to Hindus and hence subversive to the nation. Whereas the first swami blamed societal problems associated with modernization and capitalism for India's internal ills, the second claimed that Hindus were under siege—even by their own government. Similarly, an anonymous "Hindu monk" wrote the following:

> Though Islam means spreading peace and Muslim is one who lives in peace with Allah and His creation it is an ironical fact that "there has not been a religion which has shed so much blood and been so cruel to other men" [quoted from *The Complete Works of Swami Vivekananda,* vol. 3, p. 350]. The story of Islam in Bharat [India] has been one continuous story of invasions and wars, arson and plunder, rape and wanton destruction. Though almost all Muslims here are converts from Hinduism and hence the same blood of the ancient Rishis is flowing through them, their hostility towards Hinduism does not seem to have abated in the least. . . . Until enlightened Muslims . . . take over the leadership of their society, the Hindu society cannot afford to shut its eyes to the dangers from this quarter. (Anonymous 1972, 63–64)

The author is said to be an RKM monk in Bangalore—perhaps the same one interviewed here. But his views are clearly too hostile sounding to represent that organization, although they are not totally uncommon within the RKM, as Golwalker—the RSS ideologue—was originally an ordained RKM monk (Anderson and Damle 1987).

But it could be argued that the vice president, being a public figure speaking to thousands of devotees, might have chosen his words carefully. Yet, it is clear that he saw a direct lineage from Vivekananda via Gandhi and the Nehru dynasty to the present government—all had worked to propagate his teachings. This much is clear when he outlined recent efforts by the government to promote his brand of reformed Hinduism.

As in the Vivekananda Bharata Parikrama discussed earlier, it appeared that both the government and opposition were ostensibly promoting neo-Hinduism. One RKM monk even joked to me of an inevitable "Vivekananda Party" being formed by some self-serving politicians. This suggested a trend in which the dominant political parties in India increasingly invoke Hindu religious leaders and symbolism in order to appear moral and legitimate to voters. Not surprisingly, even within the "nonpolitical" RKM, there was difference in opinion over what the role of the government has been or should be. On another occasion, while conversing with an elderly and much-respected swami in the second and smaller of Bangalore's two RKM ashrams, I asked him if those who use "Swamiji in their political struggles or politicize his message cause problems for the RKM?" The monk smiled and said, "We have no copyright on Swamiji. They have their programs and we have ours, there is no conflict."

"THE SILKWORM IS BUSY MAKING NOT HIS HOUSE, BUT HIS TOMB"

I have suggested that the RKM—and by extension, other ashram-based neo-Hindu movements[28]—call upon Hindus to engage in social service as a patriotic and spiritual endeavor. Indeed, the RKM has a sterling reputation for its many social projects. There are hundreds of free clinics, orphanages, schools, and housing and sanitation-system projects in rural villages and slum areas and flood/cyclone relief centers. The swamis and nuns in the order are expected to participate in these projects. In addition, lay devotees, particularly those with professional training (doctors, teachers, engineers, etc.) are urged to donate their services to these projects. I had the privilege of witnessing their work in rural Bengal, Karnataka, and Tamil Nadu. But equally strong attraction to the RKM is prompted by an inner search for meaning and enlightenment. This is a more individualistic pursuit, which, perhaps ironically, deconstructs notions of patriotism and community.[29] The otherworldly attraction of RKM swamis to their devotees undoubtedly arises from their many years of meditation, study, and social work. Most of them radiate a peace of mind that is only seen in people who have long cultivated detachment from "worldly pursuits." A cultivated disposition, no doubt—they themselves will tell you this—but to the devotee their peaceful countenance suggests awareness of a higher reality. It is believed that insights will be gained or miraculous powers revealed in the presence of a "holy man." The monks themselves—most hailing from middle-class, English-educated backgrounds—are seeking a deeper meaning to their existence than the one promised by modernity's creature comforts.

To a degree, monastic life is about iconoclasm—questioning traditions and ideologies aimed at motivating the individual desire for worldly success. One swami I interviewed suggested that all assumptions must be questioned. When I asked for his estimation of the RKM's role in modern India, he answered as follows:

> I don't know if I can make any generalization about the so-called Ramakrishna movement and the role it plays. Generalizations can never be made about anything. I hate it when Indians ask about Americans just because I lived there [he served at the Vedanta Society in Hollywood]. I meet some people in one particular place—one cannot make generalizations about this to the whole country. I also hate the artificial division between East and West that so many make. Get the fundamentals from Vivekananda's writings, then patiently observe the extent to which his teachings are realized among some of the followers, but do not make hasty

generalizations—either positive or negative about the RKM. Be scientific and liberal; and always be truthful about your methodology and agenda. The guarding of a doctrine or ideal can only lead to blood, thus we must never cling to our truths or theories.

This rather Socratic-sounding swami seemed to suggest that the only "truth" was found in realizing that other people's "truths" were indeed contingent upon assumptions—all of which were in turn built upon other assumptions or generalizations. Proving his point, we see that he is right about the RKM in one important sense: the ideology of its followers cannot be generalized. Yet that is precisely what I am trying to do here, albeit in a highly truncated form and contrary to this iconoclastic monk's wishes.

For six months in 1992–1993 I attended both Bangalore ashrams, also making trips to Madras (Chennai) and Mysore RKM centers. As I was living in the Tamil-oriented Cantonment area, I chose to visit the closer Vivekananda Ashrama (RKM) in Ulsoor more regularly. This ashram, though smaller, had six resident swamis. Five of them were semiretired due to old age. They would meet with devotees and give classes on scripture and philosophy, but they spent much of their time in meditation. One very young swami ran the daily affairs of the ashram and also participated in a charitable project in a nearby village. I spent many hours in this ashram speaking with monks and devotees, observing rituals, devotional singing, and classes. Perhaps it was the unhurried atmosphere and the fact that these swamis were no longer active in any public projects (except the younger one) that made the ashram more conducive to reflection and meditation than the larger and more socially active ashram. Here, devotees came to the sagacious monks in pursuit of wisdom and the techniques for inward-directed spiritual inquiry.

Swamis sometimes utilized metaphors and analogies to get the point across that life is transient; and they urged devotees to direct their energies towards finding "that which is imperishable." Here are a few characteristic quotes from what I recorded in the ashram:

> The perishable is all around us, that there is an imperishable is very good news.
> Death means birth—man is born to die and dies to be born, without end. Yes, if there is a focus on the Lord, and self-control, one casts off the body as a worn-out garment. . . . It is possible for everyone. Discrimination helps one walk away.

> A hero is he who seeks nothing in this world of change. . . .
> The Lord is easily reached by one who is absorbed on Him. . . .
> The name of God must be like water to fish—Do you think it is

difficult? Remembering God's name must be like breathing. This
is the easiest way, so don't ask for anything easier than this. . . .
This body or life, is it so nice? It is misery and suffering. It is the
abode of suffering. Everything is changing, moving towards death
and decay. Is life happy? No exception, sickness—mental or physical comes to everybody . . . old age, and then Death. . . . He comes
and goes, therefore He is real. Therefore we must know that there
is a person who lives in us and comes and goes. . . .
Would you like the bird to stay in the cage? Here the bird is in a
mood of sorrow. Wings are given by God, but we cannot use
them. . . . The Lord has not restricted man from choosing the
cage. Buddha and Shankara broke the cage; but if you pray for a
better cage, then you will get a better cage. "Ask and thou shalt
have it." But we must act in accordance of our asking. We are
afraid because our wings have lost their freedom. Daring heroes
will succeed. . . .
Unmanifested, the imperishable, without which the other side
would not be possible. It is the silence over which speech is overlaid. Activity begins in time. . . . Silence, where did it begin. One
cannot say where silence began—only the speech overlaid on
it. The imperishable is like that—it cannot be perceived . . . the
Supreme being is that over which everything comes and goes.
Silence is One, without beginning or ending. . . .
The silkworm is busy making not his house, but his tomb. Let us
work out our destinies. . . .
One should constantly repeat the name of the Lord. The Lord is
pure, so in all states of body and mind you can repeat the name of
God—even in the latrine.

From these excerpts, we might conclude that there is nothing novel about the
RKM's message: human life is only made meaningful by realizing a hidden yet
underlying reality behind the world of appearances and change. Without realizing
this, we suffer feelings of loss over changes, identify falsely with our bodies and
limited perceptions, and live in constant fear of the unknown. Even in meditation,
fear of losing our "false self" (ego) overwhelms us like "a gravitational force": "a
time comes in deep meditation when we become frightened because all is going
and we cannot feel our self." Here the "self" refers to the individual ego. This fear
must be overcome: "Let go of the piece of wood in the river and climb to safety
aboard the boat." Most ordinary people, however, are unable to grasp the "imperishable" through mental disciplines alone, thus the *bhakti* path is prescribed. That

is, the devotee is instructed to "repeat the Lord's name." Gradually, by repeating the name of God, "all other thoughts go away."

The aforementioned younger swami was himself so consumed by his ashram-related activities that he yearned for the freedom to pursue his own spiritual awakening. He complained that too much social service—to the exclusion of meditation—was a problem that needed to be corrected. He spoke of an earlier experience sitting before a "Great Swami" in Brindaban:[30]

> I went for a few days just to sit with him. I never asked any questions, but in those few days in his presence I learned much. I have met many great saints and you can sense their aura around you. Once I sat before a great learned and saintly monk of our order. Another talkative monk began asking all sorts of questions to the Swamiji. Finally, the Swamiji said, "Can't you learn in silence?"
>
> I desire to go to a place where I can meditate for six months. There I will exist by God's grace alone—never knowing where the next meal might come. Perhaps I will go to Madhya Pradesh because in the Himalayas there are so many trekkers and tourists. This can disturb your mind. I have put in my request for leave to the order. I hope they grant it.
>
> For sixteen years I have worked in the order without introspection. I must charge my spiritual batteries in order to do the work in the right spirit—that is, looking upon and serving others as they are divine

Vivekananda Ashrama of the Ramakrishna Mission, Ulsoor, Bangalore.

Statue of Swami Vivekananda within the Vivekananda Ashrama.

beings—work as worship. There is a spiritual gap between the younger and older monks right now. The first three generations of the order were spiritually advanced. The younger monks, like myself, are beginning to recognize that there is a greater need for meditation, study, and prayer— and not merely work.

In sum, devotees and monks are also drawn to ashrams in search of the spiritual. The call for social activism as devotion to "Mother India" is certainly Vivekananda's lasting legacy; and the RKM has become the primary vehicle to pursue these aims. The monastic tradition, of course, is ancient within Hinduism, Buddhism, and Jainism. In any important Hindu temple in India, one still sees wandering ascetics (*sadhus*) who are not affiliated with any organization. Seeking *moksha* (spiritual liberation) is nothing new. Indeed, it is the final aim of life according to the *Dharma Shastras,* a canonical Hindu text. The Upanishads and Buddhism had already formulated the philosophical premises behind the idea of individual enlightenment as release from the cycle of rebirth (*samsara*) long before. But those drawn to the RKM were attracted to more than yet another otherworldly hermitage (though this was also appealing); they were also attracted by the call to service and social reform, as well as the synthetic "rationalistic" and ecumenical philosophy, which not only influenced the Hindu-Indian nationalist movement but also gave it a modernist framework. Hinduism is "scientific" and "rational"—the RKM suggests—in fact, it is said to be more so than any other religion. Vivekananda was sophisticated enough to craft a Hindu view of modernity that could saddle science and tradition within an assimilative Vedantic discourse, as van der Veer cogently observed:

> It was the genius of Vivekananda to systematize a disparate set of Hindu traditions and make the result intellectually available for a partly westernized bourgeois audience and defensible against Western (Christian) criticism, and incorporate it into an essentializing notion of "Hindu spirituality." This spirituality was borne by the Indian (Hindu) nation and it was superior to "Western materialism," brought to India by an aggressive and arrogant "British nation." . . . Vivekananda saw his project very much in terms of a revitalization of the Hindu nation. National self-determination, social reform, and spiritual awakening were all linked in his perception. He founded the Ramakrishna Mission to enable monks to become politically active in ways it had not before. (1994, 87)

Most of the active members of the Bangalore RKM centers were English-educated professionals from the middle class. Brahmins were well represented. The ecumenical message posited a Vedantic underpinning to all religious philosophy and practice, thus absorbing minorities within its "tolerant" and rationalistic vision. In doing so, it assumed a position of superiority over the "sectarian" forms practiced by others. In this sense, the RKM paved the way for both the BJP-VHP-RSS combine and Gandhian pluralism. Both defended Hinduism against the West, and both cast Indian nationalism in religious terms.

The prestige associated with the RKM could be seen in its clientele. Doctors, lawyers, professors, and engineers were frequently members. On the other hand, it was rarer to see working-class devotees in their urban centers. Once while I was visiting with one swami, the chief of police in Bangalore visited the ashram together with the minister of telephones. I was told that both were regular visitors, as were many other "prominent figures." As noted, Nehru, Indira and Rajiv Gandhi, and P. V. Narasimha Rao had close relationships with the RKM (RKM 1989; Gambhirananda 1983).

The combination of patriotism, ecumenism, and spirituality can be observed in the following devotee. Mr. Basappa was a retired flight engineer who had lived in the United States during his training. He had a comfortable house in a prosperous section of Bangalore, three servants, and a driver for his car. In his house was a shrine-meditation room with pictures of Ramakrishna, Vivekananda, Sarada Devi, Swami Sivananda (recall the Divine Life Society and TFA), and Sai Baba. Though a direct disciple of Sivananda—who had initiated him years earlier—he said that "as long as they speak of God, I will listen." Mr. Basappa visited an RKM ashram at least twice every day for the morning and evening worship, in addition to classes and special celebrations. He often donated kerosene and sugar to the ashram. When I first met him, he told me that it was "divine will" that I had come to meet him within the ashram. The fact that I "had traveled so far to a country without proper food, lodging, and water" made me "more Indian" than him, he mused. "Religious life comes easy to us in India," but those from the West must "sacrifice a lot" in order to come to India. He meant this as a compliment.

Basappa spoke of the "greatness of our country," claiming that "miracles were quite common in India." India possessed a "miraculous peacefulness," he maintained, in spite of her many religious and linguistic communities. This he attributed to the "tolerance of Hinduism." He spoke to me of the "scientific" nature of spiritual life, claiming that one need not have faith; rather, Vivekananda and Ramakrishna taught that spiritual realization came from discipline and practice. One of his fascinations concerned the "basic differences" between East and West:

> In the East, people are only concerned with the higher mind. Therefore, time as money mentality will never help India to achieve material prosperity. Rather, India only cultivates a way of thinking which goes against the realities of this world. India does not have the capacity to elevate herself materially. In the West, on the other hand, people only cultivate the lower mind. Thus much material wealth has been obtained, but there is little or no spiritual development for the people as a whole. . . . Both minds are needed in order to have a vigorous and prosperous mind and body. Thus India is destined to search a higher path and be materially poor.

This construction of East and West, though stated simply here, was Vivekananda's. Informed by a Hegelian sense of national spirit, India's "destiny" is to be world teacher. Or, again, in Hegel's sense, spirit emerges first in the bondsmen and not the master, who remains blinded by his expropriative material power. Though rationalizing India's poverty, it is also an assertion of spiritual superiority. The world, after all, is "the abode of sorrow"; and with the "true" aim of life being spiritual realization, India seems to have best solved the puzzle. This message—particularly among the English-educated middle classes, who during colonialism and after experienced some ambivalence of their cultural identity (Chatterjee 1986; Anderson 1991)—resonates deeply, as it allows for the simultaneous critique of "backward" social practices while also valorizing a "Mother India" more spiritually advanced than any other human civilization. Pride and shame were tightly bound within Vivekananda's rhetoric. Devotees drawn to the RKM were able to reconcile these emotions by devoting themselves to the ideals of service and reform.

Basappa described religious tensions as being symptomatic of a "religious kindergarten" where names and dogmas were observed. In a "higher state," there are no differences that can produce conflict. This "higher" plane is, of course, the religious philosophy of the RKM—a neo-Hindu interpretation of Vedanta. In spite of this philosophical positioning, the lure of the "miraculous" was still there. He told me that while "swamis are not gods—only elevated humans," one of the swamis in the ashram could read his "thoughts and feelings." The philosophical and rationalistic arguments aside, gurus are there to show devotees evidence of the "higher" reality through the thaumaturgical powers that they harness.

"The Apocalypse Has Come"

The BJP-VHP-RSS agitation to establish a Rama temple at the exact spot where a mosque existed in Ayodhya gained momentum in the late 1980s and early 1990s partly as a result of two factors. First was the huge success of the *Ramayana* television serial. The show, which ran for over a year (1986–1988) on national television, made Rama a more popular deity across India, allowing the BJP to gain political support agitating for the temple (Lutgendorf 1997). Even Rajiv Gandhi and the Congress I initially supported the BJP on the issue of the Rama temple, both during his administration and particularly after losing elections in 1989, when a series of scandals had rocked his administration (van der Veer 1994). Among the Hindu middle class, the BJP's consistent Hindutva ideology was seen by many as honest and principled. Certainly, the dramatic rise of the BJP to the political center stage (except in Tamil Nadu) indicated that Hindu nationalism was growing (Hansen 1999). Second, the perception that Congress I—the only other party with mass support—was highly corrupt also strengthened the BJP's appeal. Before speculating further about the root causes of Hindu nationalism and to their linkages to regional identity politics, I return to Bangalore and describe how the Ayodhya crisis was experienced by some of its Tamil-speaking residents.

Bangalore, like the rest of India, was tense in the days leading up to the demolition of the mosque in Ayodhya. Daily news reports of the standoff between the central government and the followers of the BJP-VHP-RSS—particularly as hundreds of militant Hindus arrived in Ayodhya—created a perception that something volatile was about to happen.[31] Muslims were especially alarmed by the growing realization that the government would not stand in the way of the marching Hindus. Their worst fears were confirmed when the mosque was completely destroyed by the Hindu agitants on December 6, 1992, while the police and army looked on helplessly.[32] The first reports of the incident were guarded. On All India Radio, a nervous Bangalore heard that "some acts of vandalism" had been committed by the Hindus. But by that evening, a weary-looking Prime Minister P. V. Narasimha Rao appeared on national television to announce that the BJP had "betrayed the constitution." It was then clear that the Babri Masjid had been razed to the ground.

The leaders of the BJP-VHP-RSS were arrested for their part in the destruction. But by this time, riots had erupted between Hindus and Muslims in many parts of India. Thousands were killed in the ensuing violence. Bangalore was not spared. Though violence was less severe in Bangalore, at least thirty were killed in clashes.[33] The central government called for a "Bharat Bundh" (all-India strike) to protest the demolition of the mosque.

All shops in Bangalore were closed the following day. There was an eerie silence in my Cantonment neighborhood. One of my neighbors, an elderly Tamil woman, proclaimed that "once a mosque is destroyed there will be endless violence, because these people [Muslims] are lunatics." She and two other neighbors who had gathered together agreed that "this is only the beginning." One Tamil Brahmin spoke of the "deep hatred between Hindus and Muslims." He said that as small children, Hindus and Muslims will play together. "But if the [Hindu] parents find out that their child is playing with a Muslim, they will disallow further contact," he claimed. A few days later, the same man had a Kannadiga Brahmin houseguest over. The Kannadiga man said, "Muslims must leave . . . go to Pakistan, or behave. They can go to America and try to act in this way." The man also added, "Muslims are a cursed people because they do not respect their women." The Tamil Brahmin then said, "Hindus and Muslims have inborn hatred for each other. Hindus and Muslims are opposites in every way. If a baby is born in a Hindu house there is joy; but if a baby is born in a Muslim's house there is sadness. Death brings sorrow to a Hindu and joy to a Muslim. Hindus write from left to right, but Muslims write from right to left." While I cannot say whether such extreme stereotypes of the other were typical or simply exacerbated by the communal riots on a national stage, it was clear that the Hindutva movement had acted as a catalyst behind anti-Muslim sentiments, particularly among upper-caste Hindus. At the same time, as we will see, at the level of grassroots, working-class neighborhood interactions, Hindus and Muslims retained friendships and intimacies, though these too faced some challenges in light of the Ayodhya incident.

As violence escalated in the following days, a curfew was imposed at night. People were allowed to shop during daylight hours but were expected to stay off the streets otherwise. Police walked the streets armed with semiautomatic rifles to make sure that the curfew was observed. There were also fears that looting might occur in riot-torn sections of town. During the noncurfew hours, I visited with shopkeepers and residents of the neighborhood. On one occasion, I was standing in front of a vegetable shop speaking to its Tamil-Muslim proprietor when a policeman approached us. The policeman questioned the shopkeeper in Kannada about me (he did not know English or Tamil, nor I Kannada). After a few tense moments, he left us alone. The Muslim then told me to sit down within the vegetable stand, out of sight of passersby, to continue our conversation. He told me that the policeman had asked whether I was a reporter. Public gatherings (three or more people) were banned. At night, one could hear the firing of tear gas canisters. I was told that police fired these in the nearby Tamil-Muslim neighborhood if anyone took to the streets. One friend, a Tamil-Hindu male, told me that he was questioned by the police for "walking on Miller's Road" (a nearby road) at sunset. He told me to "not even think of leaving Vasanthanagar [my neighborhood]. It is the only peaceful place in Bangalore."[34] Rioting occurred in nearby Sivaji Nagar, Commercial Street, Rajaji Nagar, and Tannery Road. These areas are also within the former Cantonment side of town and had a heavy concentration of Tamil-speaking Muslims. Chamarajpet and City Market, in the densely populated center of old Bangalore, were also affected by rioting. These areas also had a large Muslim presence.

It was true that Vasanthanagar was more peaceful than many parts of Bangalore. No incidents were reported within the neighborhood. Part of this stemmed from the high Tamil population, as they were less attracted to the BJP's Hindu nationalism, despite the strong sentiments expressed by my Brahmin neighbor and his friend. Also, the neighborhood was very old and Hindus and Muslims were well integrated for decades within it. In fact, on the evening of the demolition, an already planned festival for the Hindu deity Ayyapan had been scheduled.[35]

As evening approached on December 6, most were already aware of the demolition of the mosque. Though not announced by Indian radio or television, many had heard the news on the shortwave radio broadcasts of the BBC and Voice of America. In the center of Vasanthanagar was a main road with small businesses, two temples, and a mosque. The mosque and one of the temples were only fifty feet apart. A long-planned procession of the Ayyapan image commenced (the curfew was not yet in effect) from the nearby Sri Ayyappa temple. Led by fifty children carrying candles, the image of Ayyapan was seated regally upon a much-decorated elephant. The golden, garlanded icon sat upon a palanquin and was illuminated by lights. A priest preceded the elephant with a camphor flame, while musicians followed from behind. Before each home and business, the procession stopped and received an offering of fruit or sometimes cash. The priest performed *arati* before Ayyapan and offered the flame for the devotees to touch. Many people offered bananas to the elephant, which it would then eat. As the procession approached the mosque, I wondered if the events earlier that day would provoke tension. But to my relief, there was none. The procession did in fact stop before the mosque. There the priest performed the *arati* before the mosque. Rather than being provocative, the ritual was deemed respectful. From inside the mosque, a man appeared with a tray of fruits and milk and gave them to the priest. A Tamil-Hindu friend at that point said to me, "They say that Hindus and Muslims are enemies, but look, here is a *puja* before the *masjid*." Indeed, many Muslims gathered on the street to enjoy the festivities—a far cry from the "fanatics" or "antinational" subversives they were sometimes made out to be by partisan Hindus.

This simple act illustrated the shared spiritual repertoire between Hindu and Muslim as part of the neighborhood fabric in Bangalore and elsewhere. Though not as elaborate as the shared ritual and historical space seen in the works, for instance, of Mayaram (2003), Gottschalk (2000), and Flueckiger (2006), a fabric of Hindu-Muslim interaction persisted, even at one of the darkest hours in recent Indian history.

Nevertheless, many expressed pessimism to me about the future of India as a result of the riots. One Tamil poet and DMK activist talked to me of a turbulent period to come:

The "Apocalypse" is the only way to return the nation to nonviolence. The Apocalypse has come—it will end in holocaust. . . . There is an unspoken rule that one should not burst crackers [firecrackers] in front of a mosque; but the RSS cadres stop and burst crackers and bang the drum before the mosques. Some fanatical Muslim is bound to throw stones and start a riot. The hatred between Hindus and Muslims is growing. . . . A civil war will hit India and there will be another partition.

The same man had returned recently from Madras (Chennai), where he reported on the lack of violence there between Hindus and Muslims. It was in fact reported that only Tamil Nadu had not experienced any communal clashes as a result of the Ayodhya crisis. This Tamil activist suggested that the BJP was very weak in Tamil Nadu because of its pro-Hindi and "pro-Aryan" philosophy— something that the Tamils had already feared from the Congress Party. The DMK, he maintained, had widespread support among Muslims and Christians in Tamil Nadu. This was an accurate assessment (Ryerson 1988; Ramaswamy 1997); however, the AIADMK, headed by the Brahmin Jayalalitha, was far more sympathetic to the Hindu nationalist cause.[36] Jayalalitha had angered many allied to the non-Brahmin Dravidian movement by her patronage of Brahminical institutions within Tamil Nadu. Still, at the time of the Ayodhya crisis, she and her government were allied to the ruling Congress I.

The DMK activist said that a number of allied pro-Tamil organizations and parties had met in Tamil Nadu recently for a conference called "Tamils' Right to Live." At this conference—which he claimed was attended by more than twenty thousand Tamils—the "threat to Tamil culture and identity" from the BJP's "fascist Aryan" philosophy was discussed. A number of activists and politicians[37] were arrested at the conference, he claimed, after they voiced their support for Prabhakaran, the leader of the LTTE in Sri Lanka. Of course, by doing so, the radical Tamils only confirmed the suspicion of their alleged antinational sentiments. Perhaps, significantly, the notion that Tamils were antinational and anti-Brahminical had repercussions in Bangalore and, more broadly, Karnataka. Accusations against Tamils were different, more charged with contempt than those directed at other minorities. Moreover, there was evidence that the Kannadiga chauvinist groups that decried the Tamil presence in Karnataka had alliances with the BJP and RSS (Nair 2005; Vasavi 2007). Thus, the rise of Hindutva and language xenophobia were related phenomena, as was the case in Mumbai (Hansen 2001). We could say that xenophobia and fear of the minority other were in fact symptoms of a broader malaise relating to class polarization within urban India (Appadurai 2006, 2013; Vasavi 2007). The serial imaginary answered to this malaise, producing solidarities based upon stereotypical forms of othering, aided by an iconography of difference.

WAHEED

Though I had many Tamil friends in Bangalore, one that stood out was a working-class Tamil Muslim man.[38] He and his family impressed me with their kindness and generosity, in spite of having very limited financial means. Waheed, a twenty-five-year-old merchant, suffered the stigma of being both a Tamil and a Muslim at a time when both were increasingly held in suspicion in Bangalore. His best friend was his Hindu neighbor, four years older than he. The three of us spent many afternoons together drinking tea and discussing the politics of Bangalore and the United States. His family was not wealthy, and what little money they had went for his older sister's dowry and his younger sister's education. The latter had shown academic talent and was attending a nearby private Catholic college. Waheed spent his days in his small shop attending to the family business. In his free time, he read magazines and books in five languages (Tamil, Hindu, Urdu, Kannada, and Telugu). He also liked to practice his English with me, which was almost as weak as my Tamil was at that time. His concerns about the escalating linguistic and religious tension are worth noting:

> The BJP wants Muslims to go [to] Pakistan. Why should I go? This is my country. . . . The tearing down of the mosque will lead to civil war between Hindus and Muslims. In the Hindu parts of town—such as Malleswaram[39]—the BJP has harassed Muslim homes and people. It might be our fate. . . .
>
> The BJP is doctoring school textbooks in Uttar Pradesh,[40] leading to the removal of Akbar and even Mahatma Gandhi. Children are being brainwashed. There are one thousand mosques which have been marked by the BJP for destruction. . . .
>
> You know of our language problems? Kannadigas, especially the Brahmins, are against Tamils and Muslims. . . . Last year I could tell angry Kannadigas that I was a Muslim when they questioned me in Rajajinagar. Now I have no excuse. Even Tamils in places like Malleswaram and Frazer Town (middle-class areas), especially Brahmins, support the BJP more now. It is hard to be both a Tamil and a Muslim. . . .
>
> The police are massacring Muslims in Sivaji Nagar. They are searching their homes and firing upon Muslims if they gather for a meeting. I saw this with my own eyes. There is a rumor that a group of pro-BJP miscreants are going to attack Friday *namaz* (prayers), so the police have been called to protect the *masjids*. But the police may disperse the Muslims, especially if the imam [religious teacher] in Sivaji Nagar tries to address the crowd. Stay off the streets during prayer hours on Friday.

There was despair in his words. I also saw much worry on his face as he interpreted the recent political changes in Bangalore. His fears may have been slightly exaggerated when he suggested that "one thousand" mosques were targets of the Hindu nationalists. It is also possible that rumors of police "massacres" reflected a growing fear and insecurity generated by the crisis more than it did a genocidal anti-Muslim policy. Still, the perception among many Muslims to whom I spoke echoed these fears. Hindutva activists, from a Muslim standpoint, would accept nothing less than the violent suppression of Muslims. One senses a foreboding of approaching "Aryan" mobs; and when they catch him this time, he "will have no excuse." But this fate arises from a conjoining of Tamil and Muslim otherness to the imagined unitary identity of the Kannada-Hindu nation. Only the Brahmins among Tamils harbored sympathies towards the Hindu nationalists, a narrative that non-Brahmin Tamils had long leveled against Brahmins in Tamil Nadu (Ramaswamy 1997; Irschick 1969). Recall such sentiments expressed in the Cubbon Park meeting discussed in chapter 4. Waheed even suggested that this calamitous othering by the majority was their "fate." But he also defended his religious convictions and imagined a glorious Indian Islamic past and future in challenge to what he perceived to be Hindu misperceptions of Muslims:

The BJP makes Muslims sound intolerant. In Islam there is much religious tolerance. A few fundamentalists are there, but the majority want to live in peace with neighboring Hindus. . . . I am for people first, and religion secondly. I hope India remains secular. . . .

We are born in India. What to do? Someday—maybe in forty years—the country will be ruled by Muslims again. It is said that India was ruled eight hundred years by Muslims. They will someday rule again. I hope and dream that this comes. But all the religions will be tolerated and no group will be singled out. The country will remain secular—as Islam says it should be—and we will live in harmony. . . .

The police are RSS trained and fire mainly upon Muslims. They are taught to view Muslims as the enemy. The police do most of the bad.

There are actually 200 million Muslims in India—more than Indonesia—but the government will not admit that because they fear Muslim fundamentalist groups in the Middle East and the impact these could have on India's Muslims. This is just the beginning of the problems. But it is my dream that we live in peace and harmony.

Muslims wanted peace and, if given the chance to rule India, would be able to maintain a "secular" and tolerant society better than the "bad" RSS-influenced Hindus were able to do. Moreover, the Muslim community was stronger than most people realized, both in terms of population size and through political linkages with the Middle East. This suggested that any suppression of Muslims in India by Hindutva forces was "just the beginning of the problems." Finally, Waheed spoke of a growing north/south, Hindu/Muslim divide in the nation; and echoing or mirroring Hindutva ideology—but from a Muslim perspective—he suggested that Hindu fundamentalists wished to erase history and turn the clock back to medieval times, while Muslims, on the other hand, lived in a modern and "scientific" way when following their sacred traditions correctly:

> The Tamil movement to secede results from a lack of power distribution to the Tamil Nadu. If the BJP wins power, India will consist of only four states: Uttar Pradesh, Haryana, Madhya Pradesh, and Rajasthan.[41] The rest will break off. . . .
>
> The RSS and BJP want to make Sanskrit the national language.[42] They want to return India to the sixteenth century. *India Today* shows that the Muslim-Hindu and north-south relations are becoming worse. They [BJP] want Urdu to be thought of as an "alien language" even though there is a seven hundred-year-old tradition. Hindi is only four hundred years old, yet they push it on the south. . . .
>
> In India now, the BJP is telling that you are fundamentalist if you try to follow your religion as in the Book. They say you should go to Pakistan. In our Quran—it is more than a Holy Book—it tells how to live our lives. They [BJP] say if we follow the Quran we are going back to the sixteenth century, and not going towards the twenty-first century. Actually, in our scriptures there is science—all these things are there already. If we follow the instructions for the modern age that the Quran is giving, then we will prosper. Our problem is that the Muslims, unlike the Sikhs, have stopped practicing the Quran. That is why we suffer. People turn to Satan in lotteries, alcohol, gambling, and drugs. . . . People think of Islam as jihad [holy war]; but the jihad is against devils [the aforementioned vices].
>
> It is wrong to say that Muslims are loyal to Arabia first. First, we are loyal to India—then to Arabia. So many Muslims fought and sacrificed in the freedom struggle. But their names are never on statues in our highschools. . . . Even the Gandhi film made Muslims look bad—especially Jinnah.[43] Jinnah was not for partition. He was forced to take that position because of the hard-line RSS people.

Like the RKM swami who blamed Muslims for the defensive posture taken by the BJP, Waheed's spirited defense of tradition made a claim of "secularism" and humanism ("for people first"); yet, both were equally alienating to the other—particularly as the Other was caricatured as "medieval" and fanatical. A defensive posture was assumed in both cases; but it was equally true that both had been influenced by modernist (and liberationist) religious discourses that emerged in the anticolonialist struggles a century earlier. But "progressive" and "scientific" Islam or Hinduism still seemed to require an antagonist: a medieval, fanatical Other that was hell-bent upon its destruction (Hansen 1999; Ghassem-Fachandi

2012). The discourse of freedom and universal right is also one of conflict, as it excludes all that is deemed a threat to its ideals (Nandy 2002). Thus, as Nandy argues, so-called fundamentalisms were spawned by universal secular ideologies that found religious difference threatening (also see Madan 1997; Chatterjee 1993; Deshpande 2000). Pluralisms could in fact be eroded, Nandy argued, by universal logics, be they secular or nonsecular. In India's case, the secular state had engendered contorted religious responses that sought to eliminate threats to the universal community as imagined. Put in the language of Benedict Anderson, the serialization of types created outliers, minorities, and scheduled communities. This in turn created hitherto unthreatening pluralities into "mediaeval" and antinational others from whom the state had to protect, contain, and inoculate itself. Moreover, consistent with the argument I am forwarding in this study, the seemingly solid cage of religious (or ethnic) discourse and the antagonism it engenders masked a growing disparity between classes and the state's role in managing and/or masking this inequality.

As I left Bangalore a couple of months after the rioting, Waheed still expressed worry about the future:

> I think it is time for you to leave. The civil war has begun. My Uncle's cousin in Bombay was stabbed in three places. His shop was first looted, then he went to the police station. Because he was a Muslim, they did nothing. As he left the station he was attacked by an angry Hindu mob. He was just an innocent man. . . . The RSS is also planning attacks against Muslims in Bangalore . . . the situation will get worse. But nothing will affect my friendship with Kumar (his Hindu friend), we have been like brothers since we were boys.

As he and Kumar saw me off at the train station, I thought of his words and hoped that their friendship would endure.

Conclusion: A Modulated Instrumentalism

Since 1993, India changed leaders many times, but the nation did not disintegrate into the civil war that some feared after the Ayodhya episode. A degree of pragmatic restraint was adopted by most politicians. Some in Bangalore predicted that this would happen—even if the BJP were to come into power. One Telugu Muslim man had told me that "the BJP is using religion to get votes, but once they capture power they have to get the support of minorities as well." Sure enough, when the BJP finally did form a central government, they chose a well-liked "moderate" as prime minister in Atal Behari Vajpayee. In doing so, they bypassed the leader of the party, Lal Krishnan Advani, who was seen as a more strident Hindu nationalist. Under BJP rule, India remained committed to economic reforms begun under Congress I leaders; and most importantly, there were fewer processions, agitations, or demonstrations that could provoke communal riots on the scale of those witnessed in 1992.[44] Consolidating a coalition government required a more pragmatic and diplomatic approach than did agitating for a Rama temple.[45] In that sense, the "rhetoric of struggle" can employ moral absolutes without compromise; but once in a position of power, a degree of pragmatism and compromise must be utilized to maintain power (Bailey 1998).[46]

This study has thus far addressed two problems in Bangalore: linguistic and religious nationalism. First I described how Tamil-Kannadiga tensions had increased over time. I followed this with a discussion of how the dominant political parties positioned themselves as the defenders of the dharma, or "true" Hinduism, prior to and after the dramatic Ayodhya-related events unfolded. We have now identified some of the key factors that made Bangalore more volatile in the 1990s and 2000s. The second half of this book focuses upon the persisting civilities that mitigate against the effects caused by what I have called the serialization of identities, following Anderson. But at this point, some analysis of the rise of Hindu nationalism and its links to Kannadiga identity vis-à-vis the Tamil community is warranted.

Recent scholarship on Hindu nationalism (e.g., Vanaik 1990; Hansen 1999, 2001; Menon 2010; Ghassem-Fachandi 2012) has underscored the ways in which the perceived "Hindu nation" is said to be under "attack" by minority separatists—Muslims, Christians, and "Western materialism." During the Nehru era, opponents of his socialist and secularist policies from the Hindu right would speak of a threat posed by communist "materialism" to India's spiritual values. McKean (1996), for example, has demonstrated the links between the Hindu nationalist forces and a free-market philosophy in the conservative and pro-Hindu Swatantra Party.[47]

Though the Swatantra Party was formed in 1959, it shows that the "present nexus of capitalism, Hindu nationalism, and appropriated Gandhianism had been articulated well before the 1970s" (McKean 1996, 35). Having the support of many prominent industrialists and bankers, the party's procapitalist ideology and close ties to communal Hindu organizations, such as the Hindu Mahasabha (an important precursor to the VHP), seemed similar to the positions articulated later by the Congress I and BJP from the 1980s onwards. While Swatantra's (and later, the Jana Sangh's) openly procapitalist ideology drew support from conservative Hindu groups, particularly aristocrats, businessmen, and wealthy landlords but was clearly out of fashion in the 1950s and 1960s (the heyday of Nehruvian socialism), it did play a part in the "Hinduizing" of Indian politics. Moreover, it cast a "moral" urgency upon capitalist relations through the idea of "trusteeship": "The language of spirituality was used to promote its ideology of responsible individualism and trusteeship. Rajagopalachari combined the language of liberalism with its emphasis on the individual's political and economic freedom with that of brahmanic orthodoxy whereby spiritual values would regulate capitalist social relations" (McKean 1996, 37). Rajagopalachari was earlier a Congress leader and chief minister from Madras Presidency before founding this pro-Hindu and pro-capitalist party. His stance on Hindi as the national language and Brahminical Hinduism (he was a Brahmin) as the national religion earned for him the wrath of Tamil non-Brahmin movement leaders. Sometimes violent and always spirited opposition to "Rajaji" helped the Tamil movement gain momentum. So in a sense, Hindu and Tamil nationalism fed off one another—though not always symmetrically (Ramaswamy 1997).

One can also recall that the Indian nationalist movement—originally led by elite politicians and lawyers—grew into a mass-based struggle after the successful interjection of religious symbolism introduced by Gandhi (Chatterjee 1986). In this chapter, we have seen how the prime minister called upon "spiritual leaders" to save the nation during the Ayodhya crisis—a clear departure from Nehruvian socialism. Moreover, the Congress I Party has often pursued the Hindu vote in recent times by promoting their own brand of "moderate" Hindu nationalism. Vanaik notes this trend: "The Congress, after the end of the era of one-party dominance, had to mount a constant search for the winning electoral arithmetic. It turned first to the core minorities. With the rise of the intermediate castes and the growing volatility in the voting behaviour of Dalits ['untouchables'] and Muslims, the Congress party's pitch to Hindu nationalism became more pronounced" (Vanaik 1990, 145). From this and other examples (e.g., Brass 1990; van der Veer 1994; Embree 1990), we can see that electoral gains figured prominently in the growing Congress government and opposition support for various shades of Hindu nationalism.

Vanaik's (1990) critical study of India's political economy complements recent ethnographic accounts of Hindu nationalism (e.g., McKean 1996; Fox 1990; Menon 2010; Hansen 1999). Vanaik demonstrates that a shift in economic policies begun under Indira Gandhi and greatly accelerated in the middle and late 1980s under Rajiv Gandhi's liberalization programs corresponded with a dramatic rise in Hindu nationalism. This occurred in the rhetoric and activities of the BJP, which inherited much political and religious ideology from the Swatantra and Jana Sangh Parties and was matched by a similar Hindu posturing within the

Congress I Party. The assassination of Indira Gandhi also created a Hindu backlash against religious minorities and separatist demands. Later, the killing of Rajiv Gandhi by Tamil extremists linked to the LTTE also created sympathy for Hindu nationalism and produced anger directed at "subversive minorities," particularly Tamils. Vanaik suggests that the more radical version of Hindu nationalism being propagated chiefly by the RSS-VHP-BJP was led by dominant classes who had benefited under increased privatization and liberalization of the economy. Vanaik analyzed two dominant classes—the rich farmers and landlords (also see Gupta 1998) and the industrial bourgeoisie—and their involvement in Hindu nationalist politics. These groups have reached out politically to the "backward" or "intermediate" castes through Hindu nationalism.[48] In particular, as the "intermediate" castes have increasingly joined the ranks of India's expanding middle class (see Hansen 1999), now estimated to be 150 million people strong (or 20 percent of India's population), they have been drawn to Hindu nationalism.

As we will see, Vasavi (2007) in more recent times has drawn attention to this trend in Karnataka, calling it "political darshan" at the expense of progressive political work. I have suggested something along these lines in this and preceding chapters. Tamilism is indeed one such reaction to Hindu nationalism and its purported links to regional chauvinism in Bangalore. Similarly, Islamic radicalism seems to be on the rise in reaction to Hindu aggressiveness (and as we saw, some Hindus would say the reverse has happened). Certainly, Waheed was more concerned about the status of Islam in contemporary India than he was about the potential arrival of supermarkets or fast foods that could threaten his livelihood. There is, perhaps, no tool as powerful as religion in imagining the moral community. The serialization or homogenization and purification of religion seems remarkably potent as a means to unify disparate groups. But the serial imaginary requires external "threats" or enemies in order to shore up or supplement (Derrida 1976) its own ideological inconsistencies and overreach.

Picking up on Vanaik's theme that religion serves particular class interests, McKean (1996) has analyzed the relationship between neo-Hindu religious organizations and the thriving Indian middle class. She found that involvement within organizations and parties sympathetic to Hindu nationalism provided opportunities for upward "cultural mobility": "Involvement in religious organizations is reported as being increasingly respectable and an important means to attain respectability. The terms respectable and respectability camouflage complex political and economic processes whereby persons and social groups invest money and time in religious organizations as a means to expand local, regional, national, and transnational power bases" (32).

In addition to carefully chronicling the political aspirations and affiliations of several middle-class neo-Hindu ashram-based movements in her ethnography, McKean also collected quantitative data on the expansion of Hindu religious organizations in the 1980s. For example, she found that in Delhi alone there had been an increase from 560 to 2,000 religious buildings between 1980 and 1987. Over the same period, Uttar Pradesh has had an increase in religious buildings from 4,000 to 6,700 (1996, 32). Though buildings do not tell the whole story, she suggests (following Vanaik and Fox) that the decline in Nehruvian socialism as the dominant political ideology was signaled by the Congress I's gradual endorsement of liberalization and privatization policies. With state socialism no longer a popular legitimating ideology for the bourgeois classes, the homogenizing and moralistic discourses within Hindu nationalism filled a void. Not only had neo-Hindu activism become part of the Congress' clarion call, it also became entrenched within communities, filling social, spiritual, and cultural needs for a community insecure about their continued economic well-being. Therefore, patronizing Hinduism provided oneself respectability, not to mention loyalty, from Hindu constituencies.

Returning to the idea of "trusteeship," Vanaik suggests that religious institutions have grown more powerful from "their effective and organized insertion into the everyday life of urban neighborhoods . . . to provide recreational, cultural and genuine welfare services, that is, to meet some of the secular needs of its constituencies. . . . Such a strategy . . . should be emulated by the left" (1990, 161; also see Hansen 2001; Menon 2010). We might recall that the RKM became one of the most influential and well-regarded religious institutions precisely due to its schools, hospitals, and relief services.[49] Though "nonpolitical," the RKM has enjoyed both government and private patronage. I have suggested that service to the RKM and its many charities is a way to serve "Mother India." That is, the well to do are inspired by Vivekananda's teachings to "love and serve the poor"—it is their religious and patriotic duty. We saw how this appeal was directed to the middle class in Bangalore. But this behavior can also be a tool to gain respectability. Commitment to a religious institution carries with it status enhancement. It is, in a sense, "Sanskritization" done large.[50]

I am not arguing, however, that this is necessarily or always the primary motivation for religious involvement. We also saw that institutions such as the RKM fill an intellectual and spiritual void felt by many westernized elites. The liberalization of the economy in India unleashed "transnational capitalism" on an unprecedented scale in both urban and rural areas, though these were perhaps experienced differently. Economic and social discontent coupled with cultural alienation might account for the appeal of Hindu nationalism in reaction to the onslaught of westernization. Nevertheless, one must also concede that organizations like the RKM, or the more militant VHP and RSS, required substantial capital and benefactors for them to, in Vanaik's words, have influence upon the "local machinery" (i.e., education, welfare, police, and politics) in the community.[51] It is reasonable, therefore, to investigate the ways that religion was and is used as a "tool" to forward the interests of powerful groups (Brass 1990; Bailey 1991).[52]

To obtain appropriate support from the masses, emergent public spheres were utilized. In the case of Hindu nationalism, the use of television, movies, posters, cassettes, and, more recently, CDs, DVDs, and the Internet have all been used to spread RSS-VHP-BJP ideology. Of course, the same also holds true for the Kannada and anti-Brahmin Tamil movements. With the aid of these technologies, older public spheres took on a new relevance and homogeneity (Babb and Wadley 1995; Appadurai 1996; Anderson 1998).

Processions (*yatras*) have long been a part of Hinduism. Originally used to legitimate divine kingship, processions are a display of power and authority. They are also a part of pilgrimages and thus are intended to produce intense emotions of *bhakti,* or devotion (Fuller 1992; van der Veer 1994; Vasavi 2007; Deshpande 2000). The RSS-VHP-BJP utilized the idiom of the *yatra* and inculcated it with political meaning in order to reach out to the masses. The Rama temple agitation was popularized through a VHP–sponsored procession following the huge success of the *Ramayana* television serial. In one memorable photo, Lal Krishnan Advani, the leader of the BJP, led the Ayodhya procession with bow and arrow in hand, thus symbolizing and embodying Lord Rama (van der Veer 1994).

Analyzing the many important VHP–led processions in recent years is certainly not possible here (see van der Veer 1994; McKean 1996; Hansen 1999; Menon 2010); however, I do suggest that they, whatever their religious inspiration, are effective as a means towards obtaining the Hindu vote. Helping to sponsor such an event accords one respect. But patronage and planning also require a great deal of financial strength. Indeed, McKean has argued that the VHP–led processions have been enabled by wealthy patrons eager to appear as both patriotic and spiritually concerned. Vanaik has described Hindu nationalism as the "Hindu community in-the-making" (1990, 151) since the state of India was formed. I am suggesting that rather than asking simply how Hindu nationalism is a "cultural" response to modernity or westernization or the bureaucratization of serial types, we should also ask, "Whose community is being imagined through its work?"

Sarvarkar, the founder of the Hindu Mahasabha and ideologue of Hindutva, once said, "Nothing can weld peoples into a nation and nations into a state as the presence of a common foe." For Hindu nationalists that foe seems to be Muslims.

But when we consider the following Sarvakar statement, we see the essential tension between Hindu nationalism and Tamilism: "By an admirable process of assimilation, elimination and consolidation, political, racial and cultural, they welded all other non-Aryan peoples whom they came in contact with or conflict with through this process of their expansion in this land from the Indus to the Eastern sea and from Himalayas to the Southern sea into a National unity" (quoted in McKean 1996, 80).

Hindu nationalism explicitly endorsed a vision of the nation based upon "Aryan" conquest and absorption. It is little wonder that non-Brahmin Tamils who did not consider themselves "Aryans" took exception to this framing of nationalism. While Hindu nationalists—particularly of the Hindutva variety advocated by Sarvarkar, the RSS-VHP-BJP, and others—spoke of the Hindu nation as being under siege from separatists, Muslims, Christians, and communists, the leaders of the Tamil movement continued to decry the Hindi-speaking Aryan as the "rapacious" conqueror of a more "civilized" Dravidian population. Part of the Hindutva historiography, however, was to argue against the Dravidian-Aryan division and the invasion hypothesis altogether. From a Hindutva perspective, the Sanskrit language and the Vedas are the authochthonous traditions, not an import by alien "Aryans" arriving from Central Asia. Hindutva activists argue that Sanskrit is the root language of all South Asian languages and that the Dravidian movement was inspired by foreign colonial ideologies in order to divide and rule the subcontinent (see Irschick 1969). As a result, Tamil nationalism vis-à-vis the Dravidian movement has always been regarded by Hindu nationalists with suspicion of being anti-Hindu and, thus, antinational (Ramaswamy 1997).

Thus we can see a link between Hindu nationalism and Tamilism, as one seems to have been a reaction to the other at the ideological level (Irschick 1969). This might be the "culturalist" way of looking at the problem, but not without the risk of "mystifying" the social relations (following Marx) that produce such ideologies. When we look closer at the leadership of both the Hindu nationalist organizations and the Tamil movement, we see that bourgeois interests were at the heart of both (Irschick 1969). Taking this instrumentalist position, however, does not necessarily diminish the meaning that purportedly "primordial" symbols evoke, whatever their actual provenance. Thus I am not suggesting a retreat from the semiotic—just a consideration of power and instrumental reason (as a Weberian ideal type) as a first but certainly not final step.

It might be worth recalling the difference between Madras (Chennai) and Bangalore in order to understand the religious and linguistic tensions in the latter. I have pointed out that Bangalore enjoyed greater prosperity, a larger middle class, and was strategically more important, economically speaking, than was

Chennai in the 1980s, 1990s, and into the 2000s (Nair 2011). As such, the city has had, arguably, closer political ties with the central government than has Madras/ Chennai. Congress also had strong support in Karnataka, whereas in Tamil Nadu, the anti-Hindi position of the DMK and other parties peripheralized the Congress. Moreover, Bangalore had a stronger BJP presence than was seen in Chennai (Price 2013). In order to maintain foreign and Indian high-tech investment in Bangalore, the city required a reliable electricity supply, relatively clean water, good roads, and excellent telecommunication lines. This in turn required that Karnataka have reasonably cordial relations with the central government (Nair 2005). Therefore, arguably, the increasing Hinduization of national politics was also reflected in Bangalore more so than in Madras/Chennai. Moreover, mirroring the Hindu nationalist rhetoric, the pro-Kannada movement echoed concerns about Tamils not wanting to "assimilate" and learn Kannada. It was said that Tamils were "subversive" to the interests of the state of Karnataka. But beneath the rhetoric, we saw glimpses of the economic reality underlying such xenophobia (e.g., migrant labor status, Iyengar and Mudaliar wealth, globalization and the IT sector, etc.). Lastly, Kannadiga nationalism was imagined to be the revivification of Vijayanagara (Nair 2011), the greatest of Hindu kingdoms that thwarted the "onslaught" of Islamic aggression during Mughal times. Thus, as mentioned earlier, Vijayanagara was and is an important symbol of both Hindu and Kannadiga nationalism.

In contrast, Tamil nationalism—or Tamilism, as I have called it here—was defined, sometimes explicitly in hostile terms, against Brahminical Hinduism (Ramaswamy 1997). The anti-Aryan, anti-Brahmin sentiment was, arguably, far less salient among Kannadigas;[53] and consequently, Hindu nationalism has had a greater appeal in Bangalore than in Chennai. Before concluding with some necessary objections to the instrumentalist position I have outlined here, let me briefly sum up a couple important points raised regarding the instrumentalization of ethnicity.

I have suggested that ethnic preferencing in Karnataka has served as an effective legitimizing mechanism for economic policies that, in their essence, are increasingly liberal and free market. Working-class and poor Tamils in Bangalore have surely suffered as a result of ethnic discourses and scapegoating. The Cauvery and Rajkumar disturbances described earlier demonstrated this. Conversely, those Tamils with more open political and economic channels have made use of them by assimilating or repositioning themselves ethnically (Malkki 1995). That is, the Iyengars recognized the benefits of being "Kannadigas."[54] It is sometimes possible, ironically, to become a *bumiputra*, or son of the soil. But this of course is a function of political interest mediated by differentials in power. Ethnicity is sometimes a matter of choice. But this flexibility is an impossibility to the Tamil poor in Karnataka, as is the case with other scapegoated minorities (Appadurai 2006; Ong 1999). On the other hand, Iyengars and other non-Kannadiga groups in Karnataka can become, at least in legal terms, Kannadigas through prolonged residency. Perhaps that is why the mainly professional Tamil groups met far less hostility than their fellow laboring Tamils. Immigration laws and procedures seem to always favor "desirable"—that is, well-educated and highly skilled (not to mention taxpaying)—individuals. On the other hand, migrant laborers have, as is sadly often the case, so much to gain and very little to lose in immigrating, seem to attract negative stereotypes, are mistrusted, and serve as the scapegoats within internal political machinations.

But we should always caution against economically deterministic models to explain religious and ethnic phenomena. After all, what makes us human is our inherent sociality necessitated by a symbolic mode of understanding. All humans derive meaning and purpose within groups and the solidarities they establish through symbolic rapport. I wish to consider briefly alternative readings of Hindu nationalism and other "primordial" formulations and excesses of identity in order to clarify the continued utility, yet intractable limits, of instrumental analysis.

Sudhir Kakar (1996) has warned of the inadequacies of an "instrumentalist" reading of religious nationalism in his ethnography of Hindu and Muslim communalism in Hyderabad, India. Quoting from an earlier study of his, he suggests that "modernization" has produced anomie within certain sectors of the population—something he had predicted twenty years earlier with "prescience":

> In short, we can expect an increasing destruction of the nascent, Western-style individualism as more and more individuals seek to merge into collectivities that promise a shelter for the hurt, the conflicted and the ship wrecked. . . . As in other parts of the non-Western world, revivalism or fundamentalism in India . . . is an attempt to reformulate the project of modernity. Like its counterparts elsewhere, the leadership of Hindutva, for instance, has never been traditional but decidedly modern, consisting of individuals who turned their backs on their own Western education. (143–144)

Kakar invokes Weber's argument that the rationalization of social life had produced greater control over nature in addition to social and economic relations, thus giving individuals more stake in charting their destiny. But the "disenchantment" of social life that rationality and modernization usher in also produces a "depression" and pessimism that "are the foundation on which the edifices of the new Hindu and Muslim as well as other cultural identities in India are being constructed" (144). Modernization produces alienation and anomie as it delivers "blows to self-esteem," as there is an "increase in the complexity and incidence of bureaucratic structures, with their attendant dehumanization" (146).

In addition to the psychic "wounds" produced by modernization—at least in Kakar's Tayloristic model of it—is a crisis of meaning produced as cultural identity faces the onslaught of global culture:

> Global migrations, tourism, and communications confront people in a society with a foreignness of others which is unprecedented in their experience. All over the world our encounters with strangers are on a larger scale, over longer periods of time, with the strangers possessing a higher degree of strangeness than has ever been the case before. . . . In bringing together people in closer proximity, the processes of globalization paradoxically increase the self-consciousness which separates and differentiates. (Kakar 1996, 147)

This position echoes the global "culture of cultures" scenario forwarded by Sahlins (1993). The economic forces of modernity (i.e., "migrations, tourism, and communications") produce cultural consequences manifested in assertions of "difference" (i.e., "self-consciousness which separates"). This, like Appadurai's (1996) conception of "Culturalism," seems to imply an inseparable if not isomorphic relation between individuals and their culture. Why else would the local assertion of difference assume particular patterns or "continuity" with traditions? Agency is located, at least in part, at the systemic, structural, or cultural logic level, rather than in individual entrepreneurs acting instrumentally. We may also recall Kapferer's notion of cultural ontology here.

Kakar, being a cultural psychologist and psychoanalyst, is interested in the relationship between individual and society. Self-definitions are at the core of his concern. But we have asked who is in position to articulate and produce new referents for cultural identity? We certainly cannot assume that religious ideologies emerge from the psychic wounds of the masses or that urban modernity has somewhat uniform effects upon the population. On the other hand, as Kakar acknowledges, the discontent and insecurity can be manipulated by individuals and groups for certain political ends.

The factory assembly line—particularly in developing countries routinely exploited for cheap labor—is certainly one of the most "dehumanizing" of occupations. Management for efficiency (Taylorism) requires rigid and hierarchical bureaucratic structures. It is in these factories where one would expect to find the highest incidences of alienation under rational-legal domination. But Kakar concurs with Vanaik and McKean that the emergent bourgeoisie have spearheaded the RSS, VHP, and other Hindu nationalist groups, directing their message towards the lower middle classes. Moreover, we have just seen that the cultural "self-consciousness" of those face-to-face with the "migrations, tourism, and communications" is producing "differentiation"—that is, ethnic and religious fundamentalisms. This "self-consciousness" is stronger among middle-class and westernized elites, as it is they who have greater contact with outside ideas via tourism, literature, and communications technology. But whereas elites tend to develop, through their jet-setting and cosmopolitan tastes, flexible identities, we see among the middle class—and particularly the lower middle class who fear downward mobility—a conjoining of xenophobic tendencies to fantasies of homogenous identification. Scapegoats who can serve as displacements for anxious individuals can serve to shore up fissures within ideological projects (Hansen 2001). Cultural or ethnic nationalism, as we have witnessed, is fraught with such fissures owing to the technologies that allow for more serialized forms of identification. That is, the silencing of more complicated, nonserial, and nonmonocultural pasts continues to exert a haunting presence upon those who violently suppress pluralities. Thus, first and foremost, we must also investigate the ways in which global modernity's effects are distributed differently according to class and status positions. From this vantage, we can begin to understand which groups are more likely to engage in excessive acts of cultural rationalization, needing, as it were, continuous and supplementary proof of their claims to autochthonous or privileged status.

We still live in a world in which ideological "Truths" are inseparable from locations of power, despite the emergence of WikiLeaks, Twitter, and the Internet. There has undoubtedly been some erosion of certain privileged controls of information (Appadurai 1996), but no one would seriously argue that the means of material production have no influence upon the means of mental production, to paraphrase Marx. Perhaps no one has collapsed notions of "ideology" and the "material" more forcefully than Foucault in his conception of discourse. Discourse is not purely ideological nor material, but it is the complicated relationship between them that forms "Truths" (or "Truth Regimes"):

"Truth" is to be understood as a system of ordered procedures for the production, regulation, distribution, circulation and operation of statements.

"Truth" is linked in a circular relation with systems of power which produce and sustain it, and to effects of power which it induces and which extend it. A "regime" of truth. (Foucault 1980, 133)

The implications of accepting this aphoristic-sounding position—which, in my estimation, is not wholly removed from Marx's dialectical position—is clear in one regard: no ideology or cultural identity is separable from relations of power, of which class is an important determinant in capitalist economies. This was the gist of Asad's (1993) important critique of Geertz. Furthermore, there is no purely "economic man" operating by "calculative rationality." This is as chimerical as the emancipation of truth from power, as Foucault argues. We are agents of meaning (Weber) or subjects of discourse (Foucault). Either way, our apprehension of the world arises out of social and cultural contexts, within which power is unevenly distributed, institutionalized, and naturalized as "Truth." This more qualified instrumentalist perspective shows its continued relevance in this study. Moreover, critiquing "cultural identity" does not subsume the cultural, ethnic, or religious under an economic "reality"; rather, it aims to make visible the "power of Truth." That is, the structure of reality is a cultural phenomenon, but the self is forged within a "behavioral environment" (Hallowell 1955)—one in which disposition, self, and the social as well as material environments are inextricably linked. My unease with Foucault's notion of truth regime, however, is that it collapses the antagonisms, fractures, indeed, instabilities within any discourse.[55] Rather than a seamless confluence of power coalescing from all directions, the compelled nature of identity assertions seems often to be excessive and feverish, frantically seeking to silence their own specters of uncertainty (Appadurai 2006; Derrida 1995).

As this modulated instrumentalism is best illustrated through critique, let me now return to Kakar. Recall that Kakar suggests that global modernity's forces had left psychic "wounds" and a crisis of cultural meaning resulting, he suggests, in greater attraction to "absolute" ideological systems or "fundamentalisms." Hindu nationalism, he suggests, assumes a "healing function" by integrating individuals within the "cultural group."[56] Kakar naturally sees this group identity need as serving a "healing function" and also as a root cause for ethnic "othering" and potential violence. The in-group defines itself against what it is not, as Barth famously argued (1969). Thus the more one invests psychically in the group identity, the more likely one will take up arms to protect its honor, solidarity, and safety.

Kakar had documented numerous cases of atrocities demonstrating the potential violent impulses within seemingly normal and moral people. Yes, under the right conditions, violence is unleashed. But I think, too, that this also mutes the obverse. Passions are put to use—usually at the hands of "instigators." Pragmatic restraint is the norm, not the exception. Most of the time we practice what Bailey (1996) calls "the civility of indifference" towards those not in our moral universe. Blatant racism and ethnocentrism (especially when violent) protect some "truth"—and as Foucault says, "to effects of power which induce and which extend it." Derrida (1976) argues that "supplements" can be dangerous precisely because they shore up an unstable and deeply divided truth. Foucault downplayed this instability within his "regimes of truth." Thus many Lacanians and deconstructionists have tried to restore the unseen and unsaid to any assertion of truth (see Morris 2000; Copjec 1994; Zizek 1989). Moreover, and returning to Kakar, the "instigatees" *are* our special concern. They are the ones called upon to do the dirty work of the "instigators"—whether that be, in my case study, showing loyalty to the Tamil, Kannadiga, or Hindutva cause. It is incumbent upon us to critique those structured meanings that are taken for granted as "truth" to true believers. Demarcations of ethnicity and religion, particularly in their serial and homogenized form, determine the structure of "truth" in the modern, postcolonial world. Weber's observation, thus, seems particularly apt: "All history shows how easily political action can give rise to the belief in blood relationship, unless gross differences of anthropological type impede it. . . . The concept of the 'ethnic' group . . . dissolves if we define our terms exactly" (1996, 39–40). Where I would disagree with Weber, however, is in the notion that rational and precise anthropological work can "dissolve" the assertions of blood and belief. Instead we often witness that the sheer impossibility or absurdity of an ethnic definition serves, ironically, as the fuel of its own excess or zealousness. That is, the logic of the supplement takes hold and retroactively constructs the otherwise absurd as true. It is, for example, the absurdity of a Kannadiga hegemony in Bangalore—or conversely, its Tamil counterpart—that drives excessive rationalizations to the contrary.

Kakar is right to point out the significance of global modernity and the bureaucratic structures within capitalism with relation to self-conscious articulations of religious identity. There is indeed a connection between the phenomenon of global neoliberal capitalism and the rapid spread of religious fundamentalisms across the globe. The need to "rationalize" traditions (following Weber) seems to occur often. Geertz (1968, 1973) rightly notes that such behavior is not always Machiavellian. I too follow Weber's general principle that we all rationalize our actions with cultural meaning. That does not mean, however, that we should ignore the material and cultural consequences of such behavior upon the nonelites.

T. N. Madan has suggested that modernity and secularism, though operating hand-in-hand in the West, were extremely alienating in India because they ignored the "immense importance of religion in the lives" of Indians (1997, 276; also see Nandy 2002). He suggests that increasing religious fundamentalism in India resulted from the marginalization of religion from political life under Congress Party rule. He also suggests that Muslims never accepted—and were thus exempted from—the rules of the secular constitution. This in turn has provoked a perverse reaction from Hindus. The remedy for Madan is for the Indian state to recognize the importance of religion in Indian life and for it to promote a "pluralistic" and tolerant (i.e., Gandhian) Hindu nationalism to counter the "dangerous portent" of fundamentalism.

In Madan's case, Machiavellianism can be deterred by recognizing the alienating and hegemonic effects of Western secularism and modernity and by promoting a tolerant, pluralistic religion of the people. The assumption, of course, is that "traditional" religion was more tolerant than the new fundamentalisms, which are "reactionary" (as Madan and Kakar suggest) against modernity or derive from modernist measurements of types (e.g., bound seriality) and legalistic construction. Though sympathetic with Madan on a theoretical level, van der Veer[57] points out that "Madan's suggestion ignores the extent to which Hindu religious traditions have, from the start, been creatively used for the construction of a truly Indian nation-state. Therefore, he cannot avoid the question of which traditions should be protected and used for the construction of a truly Indian state" (1994, 12).[58]

Indeed, we have seen how the so-called secular Congress I used religion as a legitimizing ideology. It is not so much that religion has been neglected as it has been appropriated for different partisan ends. The question, as van der Veer notes, remains: Whose ideology gets privileged? To Madan, this is a prescriptive concern. To the social anthropologist, this is a methodological *and* a moral concern. There are multiple "crises of meaning" in rapidly modernizing societies. As we saw, these crises can take a benign or malevolent form; and as we will see later, even present in a medicalized form or symptomotology. For some, rationalizing and legitimizing eliteness is, as Geertz (1968, 1973) notes, a "spiritual" concern. Others, we have seen, must rationalize a loss of status under new political conditions. Yet for the many, the suffering caused by poverty and the stigma of ethnic discourses leads to other more immediate concerns. Recognizing this, a "culturalist" model of ethnic and religious mobilization is highly deficient if class and power are not taken into account.

To conclude this chapter I return to Kakar, who notes that individual self-esteem is inseparable from the "social self." As the self is formed socially, we invest great emotions in a cultural identity. Drawing upon symbolic interactionists, Kakar suggests that as we incorporate the cultural into our self-identity, we simultaneously protect that self- and group image by projecting what we "are not" onto other groups: "'We are' makes me aware of the other dominant group (or groups) sharing the physical and cognitive space of my community. The self-assertion of 'We are,' with its potential for confrontation with the 'We are' of other groups, is *inherently* a carrier of aggression, together with the consequent fears of persecution, and is thus always attended by a sense of risk and potential for violence" (1996, 189).

Kakar concludes, following Freud, that to maintain the good and moral vision of the "We are," bad qualities, particularly "animality," are projected onto the "Other." This is particularly true when the "We are" feels threatened by changing social conditions. This seems largely incontestable. But I have suggested that the "moral community," however it is imagined (religious, linguistic, or ethnic), can also serve as a tool to legitimate status and class positions that have been buttressed by statecraft and what the Comaroffs (2006, 2009) have felicitously labeled as "lawfare," capturing the inherent violence within the legitimization of ethnic privilege. "Lawfare," or the "use of legal means for political and economic ends" (2009, 56), involves the use of ethnic, linguistic, or religious categories within state bureaucracies to enhance or suppress their relative status. As the Comaroffs argue, "Lawfare . . . is endemic to the technology of modern governance. Democratic and authoritarian states alike have always relied on constitutions and statutes, on charters, mandates, and warrants, on emergency and exception—on the violence inherent in the law (Benjamin 1978; Derrida 2002)—to discipline their citizenry" (2009, 56). Moral discourses, we have seen, are shaped by class and status concerns—whether these take the form of conscious rationalizations or not. Moreover, these discourses, be they racial, religious, or ethnic, have been used politically to moralize an economic system in which there are obvious disparities. Those most stigmatized by ethnic discourses are—not coincidentally—the weakest and most marginalized members of society. It was, for instance, the Tamil poor who suffered the most during the Cauvery riots. This was also true of Muslims affected by the Ayodhya-related violence.

But, as we have seen, Bangalorean Tamils or Muslims are not passively constituted by discursive frames. Present sufferings are sometimes rationalized with moral, ecumenical, and millenarian notions of the better future. At the same time, celebrating identity can also reinscribe ethnic stigmas, producing sharper boundaries in what I have called, following Anderson, the serial imaginary. I am reminded of the swami in Bangalore who said, "If you pray for a better cage, then you will get a better cage." That is, religious or ethnic "freedoms" might remain within the discursive and material strategies of larger structures. In this context, Tamil or Muslim counters to linguistic and religious nationalisms expressed in Bangalore can certainly add fuel to the fire, confirming the presence of wholly different others within the city. The reciprocal sharpening of divides across boundaries that were once more permeable is certainly a cause for concern. Conversely, as we have noted, against the grain of monocultural or serial accounts of identity, everyday forms of plurality continue to exist in Bangalore and its wider region. It is to these linguistic and religious pluralities that I now turn in an attempt to demonstrate that politically/legally constructed identities are continuously undercut by the traces of past cosmopolitanisms within the region. These sources of plurality serve to modulate and ultimately deconstruct the more strident political projects and the violence they potentially engender.

CHAPTER 6

Local Pluralisms
Domlur, Ulsoor, Malleswaram, and Melkote

One Tamil academic at a prominent local research institute, an economic historian by discipline, explained that one of the interesting features of Bangalore's cultural landscape was the way in which "villages" were being incorporated at a rapid pace within the city limits.[1] As this process occurred, sometimes without the consent of those within the villages, an assertion of identity as well as a spatial claim was being performed through festivals. Though these festivals were religious in nature, they also celebrated the local temples, their deities, and the communities that sponsored them. In that sense, a revival of certain rituals associated with Tamil culture, such as a *kavadi* performance, might be an assertion of locality (Appadurai 1996) as much as one of linguistic or ethnic difference. What he encouraged me to consider was the ways in which spatial politics, given the expansive growth of Bangalore, emerged as a struggle between economic and specifically real estate pressures, such as those that drove the incorporation of villages into the metropolis, and local sentiments, lifeworlds, and practices.

These struggles, however, can be cast sometimes in linguistic terms, given the politics of the pro-Kannadiga movement. That is, as the city assumed its role as the capital of the Kannadiga-dominated state, the very reality that Kannadiga dominance was not naturally evident in Bangalore (Nair 2005, 2011), given its fluid and protean past as a multilinguistic city, brought various religious practices in different villages or neighborhoods under closer scrutiny by various groups allied to the pro-Kannadiga cause (Nair 2005). This chapter explores these enduring polyglot fluidities of identity in three Bangalore villages, as well as in an important pilgrimage center in the nearby region.

One such area of linguistic and religious pluralism was Domlur. Domlur was an ancient village that had become part of the Bangalore city limits long ago. Like Ulsoor and Malleswaram, old villages that I discuss later, Domlur predated the city and was marked by an ancient temple around which the village grew. A local art historian told me about the significance of this temple, owing to its Chola and thus Tamil origins. The art historian, who was a Kannadiga, emphasized the origins of the temple, as well as other Chola or "Tamil" sites in Karnataka in order to suggest that linguistic pluralism and complexity were ancient features of this Deccan region. Moreover, the language chauvinists were by extension working their standardization of Kannadiga identity against history, he claimed. While this particular academic was sympathetic to the literary aims of the pro-Kannada movement and wished to see the language flourish despite the onslaught of English-speaking jobs and industries in "cosmopolitan" Bangalore (see Nair 2005; Vasavi 2009), this, he felt, should not come in the form of an erasure of plural pasts that were also an important part of Karnataka's history. Yet, both the Tamil and Kannadiga academics separately mentioned to me that the "Tamils' origins had been covered up" in response to linguistic nationalism in Bangalore. Thus, I felt a strong desire to see this Chola temple within Bangalore's city limits.

Domlur was not mentioned in any tourist literature on Bangalore, despite its purported ancient temple. To my surprise, it was not a village in the conventional understanding of that term. Instead it appeared to be an urban neighborhood like many others in Bangalore. But unlike a planned urban neighborhood, Domlur was built with the temple at its center. Around it was a labyrinth of streets and homes radiating outward, as would be in a typical village or ancient city.

The temple, dedicated to Chokkanatha—also called Chockaperumal (Vishnu)—is not an architectural marvel at first glance. It lacks a tower gate (*gopuram*) or an impressive spire (*vimana*), though this could have been due in part to centuries of neglect. Large and broken stones with carvings could be seen lying on the ground before the temple, so it is possible that at one time the structure was larger. According to one published booklet about the temple, there was once a Someswara (Shiva) temple opposite this one, also built by a Chola king. The Shiva temple evidently had disappeared, though it was said that some of its carvings and stones had survived and could be seen in the Chokaperumal temple courtyard. The temple is marked by old Tamil inscriptions along its base. In one section, I could make out the word "Dombulur" in the old inscription. My colleague, a scholar of Tamil, quickly made the association of Domlur and Dombalur upon reading the word in context.[2] Evidently these inscriptions indicated grants and tax exemptions given by the Chola kings (Balasubramaniam n.d.). As was the case in other parts of southern Karnataka, Chola-built temples continued to be patronized by later kings of the Vijayanegara period. Indeed, even within the Domlur temple, as was the case in most shrines, inscriptions in Kannada are visible, indicating that Hoysala and/or Vijayanegara kings offered their continued patronage after the Cholas were no long sovereign. As Balasubramaniam puts it,

One happy feature that we notice in this connection is that though the Chockaperumal temple was built by Chola, the Hoyasalas and

Vijayanagara Kings patronized it. The Kannada Kings have preserved the temple. The identity of the temple has not been destroyed. One unifying factor was Bhakti, the respect for the Almighty which prompted every one to patronize the temple at different times for the past 1000 years. Years have gone by, but the ancient shrine remains. (9)

As Sastri (1975) and Stein (1994), among others, point out, the linguistically plural or polyglot nature of the Deccan's past afforded opportunities for political alliance building. Thus Chola kings, for instance, might incorporate Kannada inscriptions alongside Tamil ones. Conversely, a Ganga or Hoysala king might incorporate Tamil inscriptions within a shrine, particularly in ancient Mysore-area temples (southern Karnataka, inclusive of the Bangalore region). This linguistic cosmopolitanism was circumscribed and reinforced by a shared language of devotion, whether it be Vaishnavite or Shaivite (Ramanujam 1973, 1993). We see this feature of ancient shrines in a few other important sites that I discuss shortly.

The inner sanctum of the temple features attractive and what are apparently the original carved pillars, as well as what is believed to be the original idol or *murti* of Vishnu and SriDevi and Bhoodevi (different manifestations of Lakshmi), his consort. One of the priests directed me to the home of one of the primary trustees of the temple located a few steps off to the left of the structure. In a modest but comfortable traditional home, we met with the wife of the temple trustee initially. She, an elderly woman, promptly invited my colleague and myself into her home and offered us tea. When I explained my interest in the temple's history and current congregation, she gave a very detailed exegesis in eloquent literary Tamil. She explained that the *agrahara* (a residence where Brahmins reside) surrounding her home was supported primarily by Reddys, a Telugu merchant community to which she and her husband belonged. Reddys were powerful and large in number in Bangalore. She explained that the Domlur temple and the village more broadly had been controlled by Reddys for the most part, though there were strong Tamil and Kannadiga constituents in the community as well.

The village as a whole was very multilingual, as was the temple congregation. Her fluency in Tamil and that of her family members as well owed in part to their hailing from Tirupati, an important pilgrimage site in Andhra Pradesh but also quite popular among Tamils. Though they were a fourth generation—or having "four hundred years" of residence in Domlur, as she put it—they retained links to their ancestral homeland. Moreover, the language of Alvars, or Tamil Vaishnavite saints, was an important part of their religious heritage. The devotional hymns of the Alvars were still memorized and sung by members of the congregation. Indeed, the songs of the saints, Nammalvar and Andal in particular, were important. Thus, in addition to patronizing a religious or "Agama" school, the temple also sponsored classes in Tamil, Sanskrit, and Kannada. During Dussera, an important festival, they also sponsored a reading of Valmiki's *Ramayana,* a classic Sanskrit version of the great epic. Moreover, they were quite proud of the Chola origins of this particular temple. She explained that the Reddy community had been very influential and strong within the Nayaka dynasty, based in Madurai. During this time, Reddys spread throughout south India. She was proud of Domlur's multilingualism as well as its patronage of the old temple.

This woman was herself eighty years old. Her husband, retired but working for the temple as the head of its management, was in his mid-eighties and arrived as we spoke. He mentioned that there was once a Shiva temple of equal antiquity, most likely built by the same Chola king. Though the temple no longer exists, some of its stones, he explained, were kept in this temple's courtyard. He then turned to the important festivals that were celebrated within the temple, mentioning and describing Sri Ramanavani, Vaikuntha Ekadesi, and Navarathri/Dussera as three of the most important events that occurred. While Telugus and Kannadigas outnumbered Tamils, he suggested that in Domlur one could hear all three languages spoken by devotees at any given time. There were no language issues within the congregation, despite language pressures being mounted elsewhere in the city.

He proudly proclaimed that the "whole village is the temple *devasthanam* [committee]," regardless of one's mother tongue. Moreover, this is a sacred site, not only because of the generations of devotees who sanctified and energized the shrine with their devotions but also because it is blessed with yet another sacred temple directly opposite this one and adjacent to where the Shiva temple once stood. This temple, an ancient structure itself I was told, is from the Vijayanegara period (see Balasubramaniam n.d.). But the origins of this shrine added sanctity to the village. According to our guide, the elder Reddy, Anjaneya (Hanuman, the monkey god), had once visited Domlur. It was through the god's grace that his temple thrived. This in turn sanctified the Domlur Vishnu temple, making it a pilgrimage spot.

While this gentleman acknowledged that language politics had affected the administration of temples within Karnataka—and especially in Bangalore—the Domlur community was fiercely proud of its multilinguistic legacy. He went to great lengths to describe other ancient temples in the region that possessed similarly plural pasts. Within Bangalore itself, he mentioned three temples I was already very familiar with: Gavipuram, the Someswara Temple in Ulsoor, and the Venketeswara temple near the city market. These structures were built during different periods and under the patronage of different dynasties. Thus, the history of the temple is in a sense the best history available of the region. Temple inscriptions

Chola-era Tamil inscriptions at Domlur temple. The temple features both Tamil and Kannadiga inscriptions, with the former being the oldest and the latter occurring later in history.

recorded the deeds of various rulers, making it clear that religion crosscut regional differences in language to a large degree. These pluralisms could still be felt in certain places where the congregations were linguistically diverse, as in the case of Domlur. He underscored, too, the impact of Tamil Vaishnavism within the region, pointing towards the presence of Tamil-speaking Brahmins in places such as Srirangapatna, Melkote, and Sringeri. Also, the Cholas, he maintained, had built several important temples in the area, such as in Nandi and Devanhalli Hills, just outside Bangalore.[3]

I returned to the temple on another evening, wanting to witness worship (*puja*) amid its congregation. As was predicted, I heard several languages being spoken by devotees outside the temple. Within the temple's small sanctum, the priest spoke Sanskrit during his songs of praise to the deity (*archenai*). The worship included the singing of the 108 names of God (for Vishnu). This was followed by offerings (*naiveytiyam*) of sacred *tulasi* leaves (a kind of basil), coconut, holy water, fruit, and flowers to the deity. At the conclusion and climax of the ritual, the sacred camphor flame was waved before the image of God to the accompaniment of ringing bells. The camphor smoke, incense, and bells within a small enclosure were both stirring and powerful to the senses, producing a hypnotic effect to the devotees (and, perhaps, to the anthropologist). But there was nothing extraordinary about the service. It was quite orthodox and similar to countless others I had observed in India and Malaysia or had read about. After worship, *prasadam* (sanctified food) was distributed to the devotees. This consisted of banana, coconut, a sweet called a *ladoo,* and *malas* (flower garlands).

While in the temple courtyard, I spoke with the son of the elder Reddy man I had met previously. He praised his father's dedication to the temple, which he claimed had revived it by employing two priests full time, as well as upgrading and reinforcing the actual physical structure, adding lighting, staircases, and better parking. Because his father "took interest in the temple, all these things were done." His knowledge of Hinduism, too, was through his father's efforts. The son had returned from an IT job with Intel in Arizona after several years. Now he felt the need to be closer to his parents, though he maintained some interest in returning with his family to the United States at some point. He also spoke of an interest he had in "pranic healing," involving "seven spots" for prayer and meditation within the body.

Turning to other important sacred sites, a favorite and ubiquitous theme in discussions I had with people, probably as they assumed I was mainly interested in historic and religiously significant shrines, he mentioned Melkote, a famous temple town not far from Mysore and about one hundred kilometers from Bangalore. There, in Melkote, "the Brahmins [Tamil Iyengars] upheld the culture," he explained. As outlined in the history of the region in chapter 2, the legend that Ramanuja, a famous Tamil Vaishnavite saint and philosopher, had brought his followers to Melkote after being persecuted by a Chola Saivite king was still important. Ramanuja's legacy established the Vaishnava presence in Karnataka, and the Iyengar priests had left a deep imprint on the Brahminical culture of the region. But their capacity to uphold the old culture had consequences.

For this individual, the Iyengars of Melkote were "different and very conservative—like Hasidic Jews. They are too orthodox, I feel." The mention of Hasidic Jews betrayed his experience in the United States but pointed towards a reserve and distance from tradition, despite the rediscovery of his faith through the

Domlur temple. The Domlur temple, in contrast with the vestige of pure Iyengar culture that existed in Melkote, was more urbane and cosmopolitan, reflective of Bangalore's many linguistic communities. The congregation was not only linguistically mixed but also featured Reddys from the IT sector, north Indians, and middle-class Tamils, Telugus, and Kannadigas. But, of course, there was something special about a Chola-built shrine for the Tamils of the area. It was a place to take pride in, especially given the administrative switch to Kannada language in most temples in Karnataka, even when their devotees were predominantly Tamil, as in the case of Ulsoor, discussed later. He said, "lots of north Indians come. But Tamils, especially in the 'layout' [more suburban housing areas], come. Telugus and Kannadigas, of course [come]." Even between the two priests within the temple, there were differences in linguistic competency. The older and more senior priest was fluent in Tamil as well as Sanskrit and Kannada, though he came from Andhra Pradesh. A younger priest from Devanhalli, near Bangalore, knew Kannada and Sanskrit only. I witnessed a similar linguistic attenuation in a village near the Karnataka, Tamil Nadu, and Andhra Pradesh border, in the opening vignette to this study.

As I am not an art or architectural historian, it was not possible for me to ascertain the origins of some shrines that are purported to be either Chola, Hoysala, or of Vijayanegara origins. Sometimes, as in the case of Domlur, there was little controversy, and all sides agreed on the original patrons of a shrine. In other cases, however, one could hear different accounts, which varied in accordance with the proclivities of the speaker. Thus many shrines and temples were described to me as inaugurated by Cholas, Vijayanegara, Hoysala, or by Kempegowda, the "founder" of Bangalore. One might hear all these different theories for a particular shrine if one talked to devotees or temple officials. And while neither my role nor my competence is to interpret the truth of origins, I suggest that the various accounts reflect a more general truth of these southern Deccan shrines. That truth, quite simply, is the plurality of influences and additions that were made to individual shrines over time, depending on who was in power. This multiple or layered version of the past was literally imprinted in the temple or shrine itself. For example, I saw both Tamil and Kannada inscriptions upon the base of the Domlur shrine.

This plurality notwithstanding—for the purposes of making a different point—some proclaimed the singular origins of shrines in alignment with their political sensibilities. Recall the statement that "The Tamil origins had been covered up," that the academics had made. Thus, the reading of the past, not surprisingly, was shaped by contemporary debates over identity (Ali 1999; Thapar 2005). Even a cursory reading of the Internet blogs and tourist sites devoted to Bangalore's temples reveals a range of origin stories. For instance, the Gavi

Gavipuram temple has been described as being of both Chola (ninth to twelfth centuries) and Kempegowda (sixteenth century) origins. Reading Karnataka's state tourism Web sites, the emphasis, not surprisingly, is on the non-Tamil origins of places of architectural interest. The same is true for the great Someswara Temple in Ulsoor, to which I now turn.

Someswara Temple, Ulsoor

One of the more ancient architectural wonders in Bangalore is found in the old Tamil-speaking enclave of Ulsoor. This area, though close to the center of the city, was often described to me as the "Little Madras" of Bangalore, owing to the high concentration of Tamil speakers living there. In numerous shops and restaurants, Tamil could be heard more than Kannada. In numerous trips to Ulsoor over the years, I had come to feel comfortable approaching strangers in Tamil, which was not true in many other areas of the city.[4] The shops and homes and general street life in the area had a distinct Tamil ethos and aesthetic as well. While not totally dissimilar to Kannada-speaking neighborhoods, there were subtle and not-so-subtle reminders of difference. For one thing, signboards in Tamil, though not common due to the pressures described earlier, were more visible than in any other part of the city. Advertisements in Tamil were ubiquitous. Tamil film posters could be seen on most streets. And the style of wearing flowers in the hair among Tamil women was different than that of Kannadigas. A few Tamils I knew said they liked the Tamil Nadu–like feeling of Ulsoor. One often joked with me about the volume of music (film songs) blaring from shops that could always be heard in Tamil Nadu towns and cities. Conversely, a few Kannadigas told me that they found Ulsoor dirty and noisy, like "Tamil Nadu," with its narrow and crowded dusty lanes. In comparison, they said, Kannadiga areas were cleaner and more tranquil. Significantly, the Bangalore Tamil Sangam was located in Ulsoor, and, as I discuss later, the controversial statue of an ancient Tamil saint, Thiruvalluvar, was erected in Ulsoor and nowhere else in Bangalore.[5]

Ulsoor possesses one the largest and most ancient temples in Bangalore. Because it is somewhat hidden within a bustling but chaotic and crowded working-class part of the city, this temple is normally not within the itinerary of city tours for the scores of tourists who visit Bangalore. So, like the Domlur temple, it was by word of mouth that I discovered it. I had been told that there was an impressive "Chola" temple in Ulsoor upon my first visit to Bangalore in 1992. During that year, and in many subsequent trips to Bangalore, I had visited this temple (most recently in 2015). The temple was dedicated to Someswara, another name for Shiva. The first thing that caught my eye upon approaching it was its very large and ornate gateway tower, or *gopuram*. But upon entering the temple, the visitor or devotee beholds impressive and beautifully carved stone pillars, notable for their detailed depictions of deities, as well as animals such as horses. To my untrained eye, it appears as if the tower and stone pillars are of the same period. However, upon entering the main shrine, the *molosthanam*, it appears as if the inner sanctum of the temple might be older, based upon the different colored and

Someswara Temple, Ulsoor, an ancient temple that was expanded and modified by successive rulers in Bangalore.

textured stones and less ornate style. Like many other shrines in the region, this one appears to have been built in stages over multiple centuries. Surrounding the main shrine is a large and peaceful courtyard where shrines to other deities—primarily Shiva's two sons, Ganesha (Vinayagar) and Subramaniam (Murugan), and a version of the Goddess—draw worshippers.

Tamils from the local community were numerically dominant within the temple. Though it was possible to hear Telugu or Kannada, the majority of worshippers were Tamil speaking. A large percentage of people I spoke with about the temple over the years claimed it had been built during the time of Rajendra Chola I. It was at this period in history, during the early eleventh century, that the Cholas had built numerous temples in the Deccan, having conquered the Ganga dynasty. However, a sizable number of people also claimed that the temple had been built by either Kempegowda I or Kempegowda II. Most official local tourist literature I encountered emphasized the Kempegowda origins, not mentioning the Cholas at all. A quick survey of Internet sources and other semischolarly information on this temple was equally confusing. Many claimed the Chola origins, citing architectural styles, whereas others emphasized the more "official" story of Kempegowda's origins. And while I cannot stake a claim to one or the other version, the very fact that origins are contested, both in media accounts and everyday ones, is significant. Some Tamils, for instance, felt that Ulsoor was being rebranded as a Kannada neighborhood. They pointed to the official name change from Ulsoor to Halasuru, a Kannada word. While ostensibly about rectifying a British corruption of an old Kannada word, the name change was perceived by local Tamils as an attempt to rewrite history, marginalizing the Tamil presence. And conversely, to local Tamils, the purported Chola origins were something to be prideful of. In signifying a Chola presence, the Tamil speakers could make a claim for an ancient Tamil presence in Bangalore that was continuous in certain areas, such as Ulsoor.[6]

During visits to the shrine in more recent years, I had noticed a more pronounced and exclusive Kannada labeling of the deities and shrines. All signs were, in fact, in Kannada by 2009. Though I had not seen many Tamil signs earlier, the large and visible signs in Kannada were more pronounced. When I queried a priest within the temple about this, he explained that the management of all temples was controlled by Kannadigas. All temples in Karnataka, he said, were instructed to have signs in Kannada and to minimize the usage of other languages.[7] This was part of the overall plan to promote the state language by encouraging its use in public places. On the other hand, the proponents of the view that the temple was much older than Kempegowda received a boost when a purported "1200-year-old kalyani [temple pond]" was excavated in 2010 (*Times of India,* Bangalore online edition, April 30, 2010). The tank had been covered by earth for over one hundred years after the local British administration had ordered it closed, citing safety concerns. In any event, its restoration cast doubt on the notion that the original structure had been built by Kempegowda (also see Annaswamy 2003; Iyengar 2005). But, as was the case in numerous temples in south India, there was little argument that later rulers had renovated and expanded the temple.

I heard two priests give their own versions of the legend of the temple's origin, in effect harmonizing the two theories. The first priest, who spoke to me in Tamil, his mother tongue, said that the area surrounding the temple was "flooded at the time of Kempegowda I.[8] But Kempegowda had a dream in which God appeared and told him that there was an invisible *linga* [aniconic symbol for Shiva] inside the Ulsoor forest. He was instructed by God to construct a temple for the *linga*."[9] The temple would encompass this "invisible" or hidden *linga* and provide a proper and "bigger" *linga* that devotees could pray to. In this account, an original and invisible "*linga*" represents the discovery by Kempegowda of an original and powerful shrine of Chola origin. Indeed, he confirmed this interpretation when he stated that the backside of the inner sanctum, where the *linga* is found and expanded upon, "was built by the Cholas." Kempegowda in turn sponsored the construction of the *gopuram* and exquisitely carved pillars.

A second priest, this one speaking Kannada, provided his own reaffirmation of the Kempegowda legend. He explained that his forefathers and father had worked in this temple. He related that a secret "treasure" was discovered by Kempegowda in Ulsoor after a visionary dream. The treasure provided the resources necessary for building four temples in the four corners of Bangalore. These temples were thus built in Lalbagh Hill, Sivaganga, Gavipuram, and the Someswara Temple of Ulsoor. The priest explained that Kempegowda had built the four temples to safeguard the city of Bangalore. The Chola reference, however, was significantly missing in his account. That is, the source of the said "treasure" was not disclosed. Nor was there an attempt to link the Ulsoor temple to a miraculous but ethereal *linga,* as was the case with the Tamil priest. The Tamil priest's invocation of a real core to the later, more visible temple can easily be interpreted as a claim for Chola origins. On the other hand, the ubiquitous pattern in the folklore of most major temples references a subtle or invisible spiritual manifestation as the antecedent of the physical temple's emergence. Its sanctity, in these accounts, accrues from its divine rather than human origins.[10]

Two other points bear mentioning. Within the main shrine, along a dark corridor, is a row of statues representing the sixty-three Tamil saints, the so-called

Nayanmars, hailing from the eighth to the twelfth centuries. These saints were champions of *bhakti* and often transgressed normal everyday forms of social hierarchy with their ecstatic devotions. The representation of the Nayanmars provided further evidence of a strong connection with Chola Saivism. On the other hand, to the surprise of myself and my colleague, the Nayanmars in many instances had been renamed using Kannada names. But their iconography was unmistakable. These were the Tamil saints with new Kannada names. As it turns out, the exploits of these saints had long been heralded in Kannada Saivite devotional poetry (Ramanujam 1973). Thus, their incorporation into a Kannada lexicon did not translate into a modern appropriation. Rather, the sharing of a cultural fabric or texture was intrinsic to the cultural and historical mélange that had occurred in the Deccan, at the crossroads of various empires. A second and potentially more troubling observation was made in the main sanctum and in its outer walls, within the main shrine.

One colleague, a scholar of Tamil and Kannada folklore, upon looking closely at the stone walls, felt that chisel marks were ubiquitous and inexplicable. They were clearly not decorative. Upon close examination, he suggested that the chisel marks may have been an attempt, at some point in time, to render mute earlier inscriptions within the temple. As one might imagine is the case with the Domlur temple, the inscriptions in stone tell a story of royal patronage. These inscriptions, if they existed, would confirm and/or challenge local versions of the origin legend. But while the chisel marks are clearly visible, it was not possible to ascertain whether lettering underneath had been defaced, thus even mentioning a suspicion harbored by some is fraught with risk, for these marks could have been originary, bearing no connection to recent language politics. That said, the word "Halasaru" was written on the wall of the sanctum, in an apparent act of recent graffiti, suggesting that an activist had done so to make a point about language and place. At certain places, moreover, it does appear that the chisel marks cover previous writings, but in the dim of the dark corridor I could not be even modestly certain. But all the same, the suspicion that inscriptions are being defaced in order to mask a certain history is troubling in its implications. If historical revisionism could resort to defacement within a sanctified place, presumably for political reasons, then anything is indeed possible—even the unthinkable.

Waiting outside the temple on one hot afternoon, I spoke with a Telugu-speaking man named Narasimha living in Bangalore who frequented the shrine. Originally from Andhra Pradesh, he had moved with his family to Bangalore when he was a child. He explained that he had taken the day off to pray in the temple for a "better job." His pay at that time was a mere 100 rupees per day, which was not nearly enough to support his family. At present, he had fallen into hard times, though in the past he had played small roles in Telugu and Kannadiga films, he explained.

Describing his childhood, he mentioned that all of his childhood friends were in fact Tamils, owing to the fact that in his neighborhood, the Hindustan Aeronautics Limited area, not far from Ulsoor, was over 70 percent Tamil speaking. Thus growing up in a Tamil enclave, he "liked Tamils" and felt comfortable worshipping together with them. Ulsoor was his favorite enclave. In addition to the Someswara Temple, there was a famous and ancient eight hundred-year-old temple dedicated to Subramaniam (Murugan) nearby. We walked over to the Murugan temple hoping to see it together. But alas, we arrived just after noon, after the morning prayers had been completed. Thus we went for lunch together.

Narasimha described a Bangalore that was inextricably multilinguistic. As was the case in Domlur, it was said that Telugus were at least equal in number in the city to Tamils and Kannadigas. One prominent academic at a local university told me that Telugus now actually outnumbered other communities, though no census ever reported this.[11] What struck me, however, about this particular gentleman was that he felt comfortable in the multiplicity of language and culture of Bangalore. This was the plurality he had grown up with. There was no need for him to draw distinctions between Tamils, Telugus, and Kannadigas. Instead, the fluid boundaries that existed between them at the linguistic and cultural levels made Bangalore a zone of interactions and intersections, rather than one of competing or conflictual relations between communities. Like countless others I had met over the years in the city, his Deccan reality was quite different from that of the linguistic chauvinists who imagined, projecting backwards and forwards in time, a monocultural and monolinguistic community for the region.[12]

There was one prominent figure on the Someswara Temple that caught my eye. This is the mythical Yazhi (pronounced "yaalli"), which features the body of an elephant and the head of a lion. It is carved into the pillars of the temple. The Yazhi is found in most if not all of the prominent Chola temples within Tamil Nadu. Its association with Tamil and Chola culture is quite close, though not exclusive. The Yazhi can also be seen in Vijayanegara temple architecture. In a sense, the presence of the Yazhi serves as evidence for a shared cultural template that traversed divisions of region and language in the premodern era. While I am no expert in south Indian architecture, it appears that many iconographic and architectural features of Chola temples reappear at later times in successor dynasties, including, of course, the Hoysala and Vijayanegara periods (Sastri 1975; Stein 1994; Mitchell 1977). And that is not to suggest Chola origins of these features, as they have borrowed from their predecessors, the Pallavas, in some instances.[13] The symbol of the Yazhi is just one example of symbolic crossings that existed between empires. To the average devotee, the semiotic repertoire would have been not only comprehensible but captivating and motivating, given the preeminence of the devotional (Saivite or Vaishnavite) over and above the linguistic. It is this shared devotional space, I suggest, that makes any serialized version of monoculture resulting from the drawing of state boundaries in the modern age both impossible and troubling. The intertwining of the sacred landscape (Srinivas 2001) traversed linguistic and political divides throughout the history of the Deccan.

Thinking of Narasimha, I was reminded of a Kannadiga taxi driver I had the pleasure of spending a few days with as he drove my family and accompanying close friends from Bangalore to the famous temple town of Melkote, near Mysore. After visiting Melkote, we traveled on to Mysore and ultimately to Wayanad, Kerala, before returning to Bangalore. The driver, a middle-aged man, spoke fluent Tamil and mentioned that he too had grown up in a part of Mysore that was very multilingual. But in his case, it was the Tamil film hero that drew his admiration. He spoke of his love for Rajanikanth, the actor known for playing tough characters that champion the working class. Rajanikanth's working-class appeal and superb fighting skills had made him, arguably, the most famous Tamil film star since "MGR," who went on to serve as Tamil Nadu's chief minister.[14]

We spoke at length about Tamil films, his neighborhood growing up, his family, his business, and the local community. His pride in speaking several languages fluently (not uncommon in India, of course), including Tamil, Telugu, Malayalam, and, of course, his mother tongue, Kannada, was palpable. His linguistic pride was precisely in his multilingualism rather than in promoting one language at the expense of another. As a driver, especially at this Deccan crossroads, he passed into all four southern states quite often. Thus his own cosmopolitanism was reinforced by his travel and customers, who themselves hailed from different linguistic backgrounds. But his own childhood had made this fluid regional identity within southern Karnataka possible. Having friends and neighbors from all four language groups provided a rich context for his linguistic dexterity. And, as he explained, all his friends also spoke several languages. Therefore, code switching occurred rapidly and fluidly. But beyond code switching, he explained that a local mixed dialect also existed. His local identity was thus one of pluralism in a different sense. It was not tolerance of the other as much as a very porous or fluid emergent identity that represented informal borrowings. This local culture as a regional synthesis, of course, was probably forged over centuries of interaction. It follows that the notion of a monolinguistic state probably did not make much sense to such a person.

Kadu Malleswaram Temple

Like Domlur and Ulsoor, Malleswaram is an ancient neighborhood within Bangalore's city limits, in all likelihood much older than the city itself. This neighborhood is noted for its many temples, ashrams, and its overall Brahminical influence and ethos. On the other hand, it is also a thriving business district, popular with middle-class Bangaloreans for its modern amenities, artistic offerings, quiet and verdant side streets, and a pleasant recreational lake. Moreover, it is located quite close to a prominent university, the Indian Institute of Science, as well as the respected Ramaiah Medical College.

In the heart of Malleswaram, there is an ancient temple dedicated to Shiva. This temple, the Sri Mallikarjuna Swamy temple, is unimpressive from its entrance on the main road. Here one passes through a small door and into a spacious courtyard. Once inside, one realizes that this temple is actually quite large, straddling a hillside with many additional shrines and beautifully arranged *naga* stones.[15] At the base of the hill is a large *gopuram,* evidently a modern addition built in the traditional architectural style. The courtyard features elaborately carved pillars and shrines to Lord Shiva, the Goddess Parvati, and their two sons. There is also an image of Ardhanarisvara, the fusion of Shiva and Parvati within one body. According to Iyengar (2005), the workmanship and style of the images indicate Tamil craftmanship.

I met a couple of middle-aged men sitting behind a desk within the temple. My assumption that they were volunteers turned out to be correct. One of the men, a man named Balan, spoke at length with me, as well as guiding my visit to the temple. Over the next couple of years, and in three visits to Bangalore between 2009 and 2011, he enlightened me about certain aspects of the shrine. On my first visit, he and his colleague told me about a legend, not unlike the Ulsoor one we heard earlier, in which a *linga* was found to be existing naturally in the midst of the forest (*kadu*). Later, around eight hundred years ago, a wooden temple was built to house the *linga*.[16] Hence the temple became known as the Kadu Malleswaram temple. Balan was himself a Telugu but spoke fluent Tamil and Kannada. He claimed that, like others in Malleswaram, most people spoke the principal south Indian languages in this linguistically plural neighborhood. Inside the temple itself, one could hear all four southern languages, though Tamil, Telugu, and Kannada were most common. But his fellow volunteer on this day happened to be a Malayalam speaker, though he also knew Tamil and a smattering of English. As both men were decidedly not from the elite or middle-class backgrounds of many in Malleswaram, their command of English was weak. We were able to converse in Tamil, however.

The Malayali volunteer within the temple said that the structure of the temple was about "680 years old." But he added that it had been built by Sivaji, the great Marathi Hindu leader.[17] During Kempegowda's time, however, the outer walls of the temple had been built. Balan interjected that the inner parts of the temple, particularly its sanctum, were actually much older than indicated by his friend. He went on to suggest Chola origins to the shrine, which pushed its age closer to one thousand years. During my subsequent visits to the temple, Balan explained certain further aspects of worship there.

He came every day twice to volunteer, helping with the *archenai*,[18] and also answering questions that devotees might have. As "lots of people" (*neriya makkal varavattu*) come to the temple from all over, he tries to tell them about it. Balan worked part-time in real estate deeds but did not appear to be very successful, materially speaking. His clothes were simple and he possessed no phone or e-mail. Also, his knowledge of English was practically nil, suggesting limited formal education. On the other hand, his knowledge of Hinduism was extensive, in my estimation. He seemed to possess an encyclopedic knowledge of this particular temple and of other sacred shrines in the city. He often told me about famous pilgrimage spots in the region.

When I asked about the age of the temple, he claimed it is "ageless." But thousands of years ago, the sage Gautama had a vision of a *lingam* made of blinding light. That blinding light became the *lingam* that the temple was formed around. For a long time, it existed in a remote forest, hence its name, Kadu Malleswaram. But gradually, as it became very dangerous for people to travel to and from the temple, a small village grew up around it. The temple itself was built on a small hill, also indicated in its name: the Iswara (Eswaram or Lord Shiva) on the hill (*mall-*) in the forest (*kadu*).

Within the temple, as noted, one could hear lots of languages. It was emphatically multilingual. "One hears Tamil, Kannada, Telugu, Hindi, and Marathi within," Balan explained. Just as the history of the region bears the traces of all these languages throughout the successive reign of various empires, the present reality among devotees within her ancient shrines also bears these traces. The origins of the present structure were a bit unclear. While it was claimed that the inner sanctum was close to eight hundred years old, there were no visible inscriptions in Tamil, Kannada, or any other language. The only inscription found (as of yet) mentions a grant by the Maratha ruler, Ekkoji, from 1669, of a village for the purpose of worship within this temple, "as long as the sun and the moon exist" (Iyengar 2005, 147; Annaswamy 2003). Balan claimed that one raja about 350 years ago, perhaps Kempegowda or Ekkoji, had ordered the building of the outer walls and other structures. He also explained to me the significance of the *naga* shrines in the temple. There was a complicated forty-eight-day ritual for fertility that people underwent when they were having problems conceiving a child. Most of the *naga* stones were installed by devotees who were performing the ritual themselves.

Balan claimed that, as of 2010, there were no problems between groups in Bangalore. Whatever language tensions had existed as a result of the Cauvery water dispute and the kidnapping of Rajkumar had dissipated. And the installation of the Thiruvalluvar statue the previous year in Ulsoor had not caused riots, as threatened by extremist pro-Kannadiga groups.

Most of Balan's pilgrimages had been to Tamil Nadu. He had recently gone to Chidambaram, a major Saivite temple for a *kumabhisheck* (reconsecration of the temple and anointing of the deity) and *puja*. He had also gone to Rameswaram, a major pilgrimage site for both Shaivites and Vaishnavites. As it turned out, he often visited Salem, in Tamil Nadu, to see his sister. His kin were mostly in Tamil Nadu, despite his Telugu origins. Through intermarriage and residency, his family was also increasingly Tamil, in a sense. This helped explain his fluency in Tamil, though it was not uncommon to find people in Bangalore who were largely fluent in three or four of the south Indian languages simply through the multilingualism of their respective neighborhoods.

We often spoke a long time about Hindu philosophy when we met. He told me about the "stages of spiritual growth." He suggested that the majority of devotees only understood the "first stage of spiritual life," which is "idol worship." "They don't go further to ask where does this breath of life come from," he explained. Though working class and devoted to an orthodox temple, his leanings were philosophical and abstract. As I later discovered, his guru was the former Shankaracharya of Kanchipuram, perhaps the highest official authority for Hindus within India. This helped explain his intellectualist understanding of image worship, as the Shankaracharya, tracing its lineage through the great philosopher and saint Shankara, was a champion of Advaita or nondualistic philosophy.[19]

The Kadu Malleswaram temple had grown in recent years through the donations of many middle-class devotees. It now possessed a large *gopuram* and had been modernized to accommodate a growing clientele. Balan claimed that he received "a prediction" about the future successful renovations to the temple, such as the building of the *raja gopuram* (tallest tower). This, he said, was foretold by an astrologer in Tamil Nadu, and sure enough, the donations from devotees were forthcoming.

Another element of mystery lay adjacent to this temple, next to its newly built *gopuram*. In 1997 a property developer had planned to sell a plot next to the Kadu Malleswaram temple. When local residents asked first that the land be excavated to be sure it was not covering anything significant (recall the discovery of the tank adjacent to the Someswara Temple in Ulsoor), excavations revealed an underground temple and tank (*kalyani*). The temple was devoted to Shiva and especially his vehicle, Nandi the bull. Surrounding the tank and shrine to Shiva and Nandi was a stone-cut courtyard in miraculously good condition. Adding to the mystery, it was discovered that out of Nandi's mouth flowed a continuous fountain of water that landed directly upon the *linga* of Shiva. Thus a perpetual *abhisheckam* (anointing of the image) occurred. According to local legend, the source of the perpetual water is unknown. It was reported that some suggested the age of this temple exceeds seven thousand years (*Deccan Herald,* September 27, 2012, online edition). While highly unlikely, such claims are not uncommon in India. Antiquity is often made equivalent to divine power, attracting greater attention. In any event, this discovery had also, not surprisingly, reinvigorated worship at the Kadu Malleswara temple. Indeed, the large crowds at the newly discovered temple often flowed directly in to the neighboring temple and vice versa. Balan certainly took pride in both, explaining to me the story of the ancient *kalyani* as we walked around its damp courtyard.

Balan struck me as an interesting person for many reasons. In his late forties, he was unmarried and had dedicated his life to the temple and its devotees. He would spend most of his free time learning Hindu thought and traveling when possible to temples throughout the south. I suspected that he was underemployed and that the temple management provided some modest support for his volunteer work. I never failed to find him when I visited the temple during worship hours. But beyond his own personal spiritual odyssey, one might extrapolate a couple of generalities. Religion, particularly within the historic and important shrines in and around Bangalore, transcended language and ethnicity. A shared cultic landscape provided an index towards various historic presences (Srinivas 2001). These presences retained their traces through the contemporary acts of devotees. In this sense, religious sites become resources and evidence for and of a premodern pluralism's persistence against the monoculturalist fantasies of modern linguistic movements and organizations. Bound serialization, buttressed by maps, technologies of enumeration, and *bumiputra* privileges need not, paradoxically, harden around focal images of religiosity, as it is sometimes assumed. Rather, devotees such as Balan extended the imagined community to one tied by a tapestry of historical entangling and shared faith.

Melkote

I have already touched on Melkote when discussing the saint Ramanuja's arrival in the region in the eleventh century and establishment of Vaishnavism in the twelfth century under Hoysala rule (see chapter 2). Ramanuja is believed to have established the Cheluvanarayanaswami temple, a large and ornate structure in Melkote, a town about a forty-five-minute drive from Mysore (and less than two hours from Bangalore). Over time, the temple was richly endowed by kings in the Mysore region. Another big temple in Melkote, also associated with Vishnu, is the Yoga Narasimha temple, situated on a hill overlooking the town. One can see the Yoga Narasimha temple as one approaches Melkote, as it has a sizable *gopuram*. Melkote is an important pilgrimage center, attracting large crowds of pilgrims during certain festivals. Despite the antiquity and popularity of its temples, Melkote's large and ancient tank, surrounded by detailed and intricate sculptured pillars right in the center of town, is quite serene. Indeed, the impression

Ancient temple town of Melkote, noted for its Tamil-speaking Iyengar community dating back to the time of Ramanuja, an important Vaishnavite saint and philosopher.

I had of this important center for Vaishanavism was of its calm dignity, a jewel of ancient architecture and semiruined palatial pillars and tanks. An important Sanskrit academy is also located in Melkote. Even the *agrahara* surrounding the Cheluvanarayanaswami temple was tranquil.

After visiting the hill temple, I explored the Cheluvanarayanaswami temple. Having heard that an important Tamil community of priests presided over the temple (recall the Domlur resident's comments), I was interested in seeing whether the Tamil language and traditions were still honored. The homes surrounding the temple did in fact have Tamil lettering on their entrance gates, and I could hear the conversations of young Brahmins in the community as they all conversed in Tamil. These Tamil Brahmins were Iyengars.

When I arrived at the temple around 3 p.m., it was still closed.[20] To pass the time before the late afternoon prayers began, I struck up a conversation with one of the older priests who was resting in the shade of the outer pillars of the temple. He, a man most likely in his sixties, had spent his entire life in Melkote. As is the case in Domlur, the majority of priests in this temple had lived their whole lives never leaving the town, owing to their orthodoxy. The priest explained that there were only twenty families of Tamil-speaking priests remaining in Melkote. These families conversed primarily in Tamil. He went on to explain that many of the people in Melkote were Telugu speakers. The presence of Tamil was now confined to the priestly (Iyengar) community within the temples. Of course, living in Karnataka, the younger people in town also spoke Kannada fluently.

The priest then recounted how Ramanuja had fled the Chola king in Sri Rangam (near the town of Trichi in Tamil Nadu) and with the aid of a local king had built this temple. The temple, he explained, had been built with Hoysala patronage, but Ramanuja "did all this." By this he meant that Ramanuja's efforts and the sanctity of his personage had established the presence of Vaishnavism to the region.[21] Within the temple itself, Tamil inscriptions were visible on certain pillars in an older Tamil dialect from the twelfth century. As my colleague, Dr. S. Carlos, a linguist and professor of Tamil and Kannada literature, was accompanying me on this trip, he was able to decipher the inscriptions and identify their antiquity. Given that the priestly and monastic community surrounding Ramanuja comprised mainly Tamil speakers, it was not surprising to note the influence of the language within the temple. Indeed, we heard all of the priests at various shrines within the temple conducting their business and prayers in Tamil, not Kannada. On the other hand, we could see Kannada inscriptions within the temple in other areas. Again, given the Hoysala and later Mysore royal patronage, it was hardly surprising to see these inscriptions. After all, devotees would undoubtedly learn about the generous grants provided by royal figures as they circumambulated the large temple structure. In that sense, these inscriptions were a kind of permanent archive of important founders, patrons, and donors. The key impression I received in Melkote was of a polyglot and linguistically complicated town where Tamils, Telugus, and Kannadigas united in devotion to their god, rather than to particular linguistic allegiances. This undoubtedly is more the norm than the exception in Karnataka, if not all of India (Stein 1994; Pollock 2006; Nandy 2002).

Srinivas (2001) makes precisely this point in her detailed discussion of the Karaga *jatre* ritual in Bangalore. The Thigalas, an agricultural caste in the region, are primarily Tamil speaking originally, but they have strong allegiances with other Thigalas that are primarily Kannada speaking. Their ritual landscape crosscuts linguistic exclusivity and is organized around devotion. We will recall, too, that many believe that Kempegowda's grandfather hailed from a Thigala lineage in Kanchipuram, in today's Tamil Nadu (see Srinivas 2001). Indeed, Srinivas's important study goes further, demonstrating that Sufi and Hindu devotions were combined within certain temples associated with the Karaga *jatre* rituals and processions, further blurring not only linguistic but also religious boundaries. Thus, while communal and linguistic tensions have emerged in modern times as a result of statecraft and the serial forms of identification (Anderson 1998) it engenders, underscoring the persistence of permeable and blurred boundaries is, I suggest, not only politically useful as a means of critiquing the former but also empirically sound, ethnographically speaking (Flueckiger 2006; Gold 2014).

Through the various vignettes about sites of pluralism in and around the Bangalore region, this chapter has attempted to underscore that monolinguistic and indeed monocultural fantasies associated with a modern or serial rendering of ethnicity are countered by a "landscape of memory" (Srinivas 2001). Here I have only scratched the surface, as there are countless other regional shrines, both ancient and modern, that attest to both a plural past and present. But even in this small sample, the point can be understood. That is, the practices of multilingualism and nonexclusivity are part and parcel of the history embedded within the religious landscape of south India. Bangalore, despite the contemporary troubles that have been described earlier that culminated in the Cauvery riots, Ayodhya tensions, and Rajkumar's kidnapping, has not witnessed an escalation of linguistic or ethnic chauvinism, even with the more strident voices among the Kannada activists and the reciprocal Tamil response. This is not to deny that threats to the plural fabric of life are real, as we have witnessed earlier, but that, as Nandy suggests (2002), the conditions that allow oneself to imagine the other as an essential part of oneself continue to be met in Bangalore, thus mitigating against monoculturalist fantasies associated with the bound serial measurement of identity

(Anderson 1998). Though Bangalore, post-1956, became a linguistic capital of a linguistic state, the city remains largely at ease with its blending of languages.[22] This pluralism appears to contribute to communal harmony as well, as the strident voices of linguistic chauvinism are often tied to sectarianism—in this case, Hindu nationalism. Put another way, the imagining of bound serial identities leads to slippages and displacements as genealogies and plural practices are disentangled, be they linguistic or religious. Thus, it is no accident that the Shiv Seva of Mumbai (Hansen 2001) and the most strident voices within the Kannada movement are allied, or perceived to be allied, with Hindu nationalism.

In the next chapter, I briefly consider the case of statue politics in shaping a public imaginary in Bangalore. My focus will be on the politics of unveiling a statue dedicated to a famous Tamil poet, Thiruvalluvar.

CHAPTER 7

Statue Politics

Political *Darshan* and Urban Space

Thiruvalluvar's Statue

As we have witnessed, Tamils occupy a special position in Bangalore's landscape owing to both past and recent migrations. Though census numbers are not entirely reliable for reasons alluded to regarding the self-ascription of language speakers, I noted that Tamils are officially the second largest linguistic community after Kannadigas (Nair 2005). Further, owing to historical divisions between the Cantonment and non-Cantonment parts of Bangalore, the concentration of Tamils occurs in specific areas, particularly Ulsoor. The Tamil enclaves in turn have been somewhat resented by Kannadiga activists who sought to transform public space in Bangalore so as to display a more robust and visible and/ or audible Kannada presence. In this context, we can understand the opposition that occurred when the Bangalore Tamil Sangam decided to erect a statue of the ancient Tamil poet and ethicist, Thiruvalluvar.

As Nair (2005) points out, statues of Thiruvalluvar are ubiquitous in Tamil Nadu, as well as in parts of Karnataka heavily populated by Tamil speakers, such as the Kolar mining fields (near the Tamil Nadu border and close to Bangalore). The Bangalore Tamil Sangam obtained permission from the city's corporation commissioner to unveil a statue in Ulsoor, close to the Tamil Sangam building, in 1991. This aroused protests from the more militant of pro-Kannada groups, particularly the Kannada Shakti Kendra and the Rajkumar Abhimanigala Sangha, which we might recall from our discussion of the Cauvery riots. Again, as Nair cogently suggests, "the installation of the statue was seen as a deliberate re-territorialization of the Ulsoor area. The Bangalore Tamil Sangam president's unwitting remark that the statue could not be offensive as it was in a Tamil-dominated area served to further provoke those who had desired that Bangalore city should reflect 'Kannada culture and civilization'" (2005, 283). The installation of the statue, in short, was flaunting a Tamil identity in the eyes of the pro-Kannada activists. To many Tamil speakers, however, the protests were an unnecessary provocation against a linguistic minority, as well as against a poet and ethicist who transcended region and language. Nair's meticulous work demonstrates that while moderate and intellectual voices in the Kannada movement denounced the "destructive opposition" to the statue and noted that both Tamils and Kannadigas shared a common "Dravidian" cause (2005, 286; also see Vasavi 2007, 2009; Nagaraj 2009), the more militant groups drowned them out.

The protests grew more aggressive and generalized as the Cauvery water issue grew in importance in December of 1991. As the anti-Tamil riots broke out, the unveiling of the statue appeared doomed, particularly as then chief minister of Karnataka, S. Bangarappa, withdrew his support of the unveiling and sided with the anti-Tamil cause. To avoid riots and anti-Tamil violence, the statue remained veiled and covered in plastic for another eighteen years. The tensions surrounding the unveiling were exacerbated by the Rajkumar kidnapping, as well as by the annual tensions that surrounded the release of Cauvery waters to Tamil Nadu. The covered statue in turn galvanized Tamil sentiment in Bangalore and beyond as a symbol of Kannadiga extremism. This and the anti-Tamil violence associated with Cauvery and, later, the Rajkumar episodes contributed to a defensive reimagining of Bangalore's history (Nair 2005).

As I visited the city many times over the years between 1992 and 2015, I heard numerous stories—many recounted in this study—of the Tamil origins and/or domination of certain sections of town, dating back to the Chola period, the Thigala (see Srinivas 2001) presence, and more recently the organization of the Cantonment. Recall former Tamil Sangam president R. S. Maran's comment that he thought "he was living in Tamil Nadu" prior to 1956. And, of course, there are the stories about the Chola origins of several shrines, as well as the reimagining of Bangalore's founder, Kempegowda, as having a partially Tamil background and hailing from Thigala (Tigala).[1] Consider the following statement from a Bangalore Tamil Sangam–produced pamphlet entitled "A Mute Genocide," which chronicled the atrocities committed against Tamils during the Cauvery riots:

If driving the Tamils out of Karnataka was the sole objective of the State-organised violence[2] on Tamils, we have to drive in a point. The Tamils in Bangalore and Kolar districts are not alien migrants, as is being made out by the Kannada chauvinists. They are not like the Tamils elsewhere, who had either recently settled or those who were brought in as indentured labour during the British days to work in the coffee and tea estates of Chickmagulur and Coorg, or the iron industry at Bhadravati. In fact, Tamils of Bangalore and Kolar districts are the original inhabitants, and these areas were gradually colonized by others. The Hoysala country was divided among brothers in 1254. The Hoysala King Ramanatha inherited this region, and his inscriptions were mostly in Tamil. . . . The inscriptions found . . . in and around Bangalore are mostly in Tamil. . . . Bangalore district was known as Vikrama Chozhamandalam. There are still Cholanayakkanahalli and Choladevanahalli in the Bangalore district. Magadi town itself was founded by the Cholas in 1139. The tank on Palar at Bethanmangalam was built by Vijayaditya Chozhan. Most of the temples, like the ones at Domlur, Begur, Ulsoor, were all built by the Cholas and the Tamil Gangas. Kempe Gowda who founded the city of Bangalore in 1537 was a Thigala, who belonged to the Tamil Vanniyar caste. He hailed from Kanchipuram in Tamil Nadu. In fact, these Thigilar were the oldest and original inhabitants of Bangalore. Thigilar numbered 31,644 out of a total population of 307,124 in Bangalore in 1931. Out of the population of Bangalore Civil and Military Station and Bangalore City, which was at 189,485 in 1911, Tamils were 61,172, Kannadigas 33,612, and Telugus 47,423. These references are made only to make people understand how these historical facts are being overlooked in building up the anti-Tamil psyche. (Bangalore Tamil Sangam 1992, 39–40)

The defense of a Tamil historical presence seems important here. We might ask why this archive is critical to Tamils in light of political persecution. The obvious answer is that the arguments of the Kannadiga chauvinists had produced this defensive counter in order to deny the monolingual pretentions of the modern state. A less obvious answer, as we will see, can be found in an understanding of public space that has emerged in modern India, particularly in its cities (Vasavi 2007; van der Veer 1994). While it is possible to see continuities with past forms of political symbolism and statecraft, the move to linguistically defined states in 1956 heralded a new way to imagine what it meant to be a "son of the soil" in Karnataka. I return to this shortly. For now, what I have attempted to show in a limited way is the extent to which the city's and region's urban fabric cannot be claimed exclusively for use by any one linguistic community. In its own perhaps exaggerated manner, the Tamil Sangam's pamphlet had not made exclusive claims upon the city and region, though it tried to argue for autochthony through its emphasis on the "Thigilas" as well as the Chola settlements as a geographically contiguous part of the Tamil-speaking world. Rather, the pamphlet clearly indicated that Tamils were living alongside others for hundreds of years, going back to the time of the Hoysalas and beyond. That a Hoysala king, for instance, would use Tamil inscriptions for his subjects, who would have been conversant in both Tamil and Kannada in all likelihood, shows that in premodern times statecraft did not depend upon linguistic or ethnic homogeneity. Instead, the polyglot nature of the great Deccan empires was seen as a strength in their relationships with neighboring kingdoms (Stein 1994; Pollock 2006; Sastri 1975, 1949; Shulman 2016). And as noted, the ties that crosscut language through a shared religious imaginary produced a sacred landscape that confounded monolinguistic pressures (Srinivas 2001; Shulman 2016).

But it is precisely this failure to achieve linguistic hegemony among supporters of the more radicalized Kannada movement that has provoked violence and a stronger attempt to "occupy" Tamil spaces within the city. Many Tamils remarked to me over the years that areas such as Ulsoor, where Tamils were a clear majority, have had their Tamil orientation made invisible through the vandalism of shops carrying Tamil signboards, the muting of advertisements for Tamil films, and road signs appearing exclusively in Kannada, rather than in the four languages one could see in colonial times (English, Kannada, Tamil, and Urdu). The physical "Kannadization" of the city marked an absence or failure in the Kannada nation, rather than celebrating its hegemony. Thus, what I have called the dense fabric or pluralism also incites its obverse: an inscription and assertive public presentation of monolingualism. In this way of thinking, the physical archive of Kannada writing upon public spaces served, in Derrida's sense, as a "supplement" in order to efface the impossibility of its assertion (1995, 1976). Once again, Nair's (2005) commentary seems apt:

A new and more belligerent face of Kannada activism soon became evident in the occupation of public spaces both in a temporary and more permanent sense. If newer Tamil-dominated slum areas have been the target of rioters, older and more established Tamil localities have been the site of symbolic occupations. Poles supporting the Kannada flag mounted on tiled platforms that [depict] Kannada Bhuvaneswarai [goddess of Kannada] have proliferated across the city since 1982. . . . If red and yellow flags [Karnataka flags] are particularly numerous in areas which are dominated by Tamilians, such as Ulsoor or Murphy Town, they do not symbolize linguistic dominance: rather they serve to visually compensate for what is plainly an auditory absence. Thus, it was plaintively remarked at the height of the opposition to the Thiruvalluvar statue that the chance of street and area names did nothing to alter the popular references to older coordinates. . . . The attempt to produce a new linguistic cosmos that reflects the fullness of Kannada literary culture is defeated by familiar historical associations with place, and the sheer weight of habit. (280–281)

Flags were accompanied, I have been told, by threats of vandalism against shops that had signboards in Tamil. As discussed earlier, even the temples with clearly Tamil and/or multilinguistic orientations among worshippers were obliged to display signs exclusively in Kannada. This assertiveness in public space, of course, had the effect of inspiring the defense of Tamil as well. And, as some Tamils told me, it was important not to be intimidated by threats. One went as far as to suggest that Tamils must reassert their right to display the Tamil language upon signboards, given their large numbers. Another said, having visited Malaysia recently, that if Malaysian Tamils are proud to display the Tamil language, the same should be true of Bangalorean Tamils.[3] As traffic signs, buses, and signboards, including those on official buildings, became exclusively Kannada, the specter of the invisible Tamil presence continued to lurk. The Tamil presence is spectral precisely in the sense that boundaries between Tamils and Kannadigas are so very porous. The specter emerges only in the wake of serial forms of identification with their concomitant purifying of porous and permeable boundaries.

At long last, despite the recurring tensions surrounding Tamil use, as well as the annual rancor caused by the release of Cauvery waters to Tamil Nadu, the Thiruvalluvar statue was unveiled on August 9, 2009, to much public relief. The extremist voices were drowned out and no major disturbances ensued after the chief ministers of Karnataka and Tamil Nadu joined in the large public event. Conjoined to this unveiling—and perhaps a necessary condition for its happening—was the unveiling of a statue of Sarvajna, an important Kannada-speaking poet and ethicist, in Chennai a few days later. Ironically, after years of controversy the unveiling became a huge and happy event in the media and attracted thousands of attendees. The chief minister of Karnataka, B. S. Yeddyurappa, hailed the event as "a historic day and will be written in golden words. It's not just the unveiling of two statues, but the bonding between the people of Karnataka and Tamil Nadu" (*Times of India,* Karnataka edition, front page, August 8, 2009). At the actual unveiling, Yeddyurappa said to the assembled crowd and media, "The fostering of friendly ties between two states is a model for the entire country." He further stated that "Karnataka and Tamil Nadu share the heritage of friendly relations from ancient times. There have been ups and downs over the years. There is a growing public perception that the way we were able to resolve the issue of unveiling of the statues, which had remained most contentious for 18 long years is simply marvelous and most remarkable. This will surely go down as a model for solving other contentious issues" (*Times of India,* special section entitled "Beckoning development," August 23, 2009). For his part, the chief minister of Tamil Nadu, M. Karunanidhi, said that he "had decided 18 years ago, when the controversy erupted, not to attend any public function in Bangalore till the statue was unveiled. Today, my thambi [younger brother] Yeddyurappa, has made me break my vow with his gesture. On August 13th [the date for the Sarvajna statue unveiling], I will wait in Chennai to welcome him" (*Times of India,* Karnataka edition, front page, August 10, 2009). The two leaders were photographed laughing and smiling at one another before the large assembled crowd, purported to be several thousand strong.

The event occurred without major incident, despite threats of protest marches and strikes by Kannadiga activists. The leaders of the Karnataka Rakshana Vedike and the Kannada Chaluvali Tal Paksha held rallies in opposition to the unveiling, including one before the statue of Kempegowda. In addition to their grievance that the statue should not be unveiled at all, they protested that the invitations to the event were printed in Tamil as well as in Kannada. They also reiterated in a press statement that "unveiling the statue in Bangalore was one of the demands put forth by forest brigand Veerapan when he had held Kannada matinee idol Rajkumar hostage in 2001" (*Times of India,* Times City for Bangalore section, page 7, August 7, 2009).

Clearly, the opposition to the unveiling, unlike the official emphasis on state-to-state relations, remained concerned with the status of language in Bangalore. Invoking the bandit Veerapan and likening his demands to those made by Bangalore's Tamil community—and in particular the leadership of the Tamil Sangam—cast suspicion upon the local community more than pointing the finger directly at Tamil Nadu (though the Cauvery issue, obviously, was a state-to-state concern). The protest over the use of Tamil on the invitations, again, obviously pointed towards the problems of language in the city and region. Had there not been a sizable Tamil population in Bangalore, the insult posed by the Tamil language use would have been mute. The pro-Kannada activist Vatal Nagaraj, who was later placed under preventative police custody before the unveiling, went further and suggested that "the statue unveiling is being done due to the pressure of Tamils and it's a conspiracy" (*Times of India,* page 4, August 8, 2009). He and others accused the Yeddyurappa government of using the unveiling as an election ploy, suggesting in so doing of selling out Kannadiga interest to the sizable Tamil population in Bangalore.

Despite the opposition to the event by the groups mentioned, the unveiling was peaceful. Much of this had to do with the heavy police presence at the event and throughout Bangalore, estimated to be about three thousand additional officers. The "peacekeeping force" included sixty platoons of Striking Force; sixty platoons of Karnataka State Reserve Police; thirty platoons of Central Armed Reserve; one thousand Home Guards; forty-five assistant commissioners of police; two hundred police inspectors; five hundred sub-inspectors; and a thousand constables and head constables. The police commissioner said, "Overall it was a peaceful affair, thanks to the cooperation from the public and police force" (*Times of*

Unveiled Thiruvalluvar statue in Ulsoor.

India, Times City section, page 2, August 10, 2009). It should also be noted that fifty activists were arrested before their protests could even begin. Clearly, the deterrence of violence was due to preemptive and ample preparation.

More moderate Kannadiga voices among the intelligentsia, especially among those promoting Kannada literature and scholarship, were largely in support of the unveiling of the statues, as were official statements by local politicians from both the BJP (Yeddyurappa's party) and the Congress side. Kannada literary giant U. R. Ananthamurthy was quoted in the *Times of India* as saying, "Non-Kannadigas have also contributed a lot to Kannada. There is no meaning in protesting against the unveiling of the Thiruvalluvar statue." Chidananda Murthy, another noted scholar of Kannada literature, added that "the unveiling will further strengthen [the] centuries-old intrinsic relationship between Kannada and Tamil" (*Times of India,* Beckoning Development section, August 23, 2009).[4] These views were echoed by several others in the media, further marginalizing the more extreme groups that were in opposition to the unveiling.

Interestingly, most of the coverage of the event in the media focused upon the possibility and promise of improved interstate relations. This was certainly the emphasis within the two chief ministers' remarks. But some local Tamils were also given voice in the media coverage. Under the caption, "Tamilians rejoice," the *Times of India* wrote,

> The event was also a moment for many Tamilians settled in Bangalore. Bahnumathi Bhaskaran, who was at the venue with her husband, has been living in Bangalore for the last six years. "It is surely a great moment for us. And we thank the Karnataka government for making it happen. For long, we Tamilians in Bangalore have been among those worst affected during issues like the Cauvery water disputes and matinee idol Rajkumar's kidnap. Such an act will surely help bring more harmony between the two states and people in particular. It's truly a historic moment for all of us," she said. (Bangalore edition, page 2, August 10, 2009)

Another Tamilian, Mugilvannan, who interestingly dressed as Mahatma Gandhi for the occasion,[5] was quoted in the same article saying, "I'm here to express my gratitude to the Karnataka chief minister, his cabinet and the people who have made this programme possible. It has, indeed, brought both Kannadigas and Tamilians in Bangalore together."

The occasion was, not surprisingly, also utilized for political advertising. Ulsoor was filled with posters and banners of the chief minister. Opposition politicians followed suit. The posters of politicians were conspicuously placed together with posters of Thiruvalluvar so as to make the iconic association with the poet saint more potent. The mix of spiritual and political imagery was also conjoined to that other potent figure of the imagination, the film hero. Prominent posters of the Tamil film heroes Rajanikanth and Sivajiganesan were ubiquitous and always in close proximity to the political images. The mixtures of spiritual, film, and political iconography provided a visual apprehension of the event. That is, as Vasavi (2007) argues, politics has increasingly taken the shape of *darshan,* or the connectivity of sacred power established between the devotee and the deity through "seeing" (Eck 1981). This modality of politics is particularly potent in a Hindu context, as van der Veer (1994) has argued. Price (2013) also argues convincingly that this modality of "honor" politics is particularly pronounced in contemporary Karnataka.

I was in Bangalore during the unveiling and witnessed much of the anticipation, anxiety, relief, and eventual happiness among Tamil speakers I met. I also witnessed both the heavy surveillance in anticipation of strikes and other disturbances, as well as the political mileage that Yeddyurappa sought through a massive publicity campaign in which the press played no small role. If, as many more cynical voices suggested, the unveiling was simply a political gimmick to gain support in upcoming elections, it strangely also showed that the pro-Kannada populism of previous chief ministers, particularly when it came to opposing the unveiling of the statue, was not necessarily politically advantageous. Indeed, what Yeddyurappa had demonstrated, whether consciously or not, perhaps, was the large presence and influence of a Tamil-speaking constituency within the region.

I myself attempted to attend the unveiling function but could not find an auto rickshaw to take me on the morning of the event. As it had turned out, the auto rickshaw union in Bangalore had decided to back the strike called for by the more strident pro-Kannada groups. Nonetheless, I became attuned to responses of the unveiling from Tamils in Ulsoor and elsewhere. I now turn briefly to these observations.

Most Tamils I spoke with about the unveiling felt relief and some measure of happiness about it. Some hoped this represented a small shift in the political climate. That is, many Tamils, and to some degree Kannadigas, seemed weary by 2009 of the annual disturbances (e.g., strikes, processions, and vandalism) caused by the more strident pro-Kannada and anti-Tamil groups in the city.[6] This was nowhere more true than in Ulsoor, a Tamil-dominated part of the city and the site of the statue. Though Ulsoor had changed most of its signboards over the years to the Kannada language in response to political pressure and threats of vandalism, the Tamil language was still heard everywhere in this part of town. Just before and after the unveiling, the public display of Tamil on posters and billboards was more pronounced, as if to compensate for years of suppression. Again, not only were posters of Thiruvalluvar ubiquitous, but advertisements for Tamil films seemed more prominent than before. In years past, as noted, many Tamil businesses were reluctant to display large signs in Tamil owing to fears of vandalism. One shopkeeper in Ulsoor, a middle-aged woman whose shop lay just across the street from the statue of the poet, said, "There won't be any problems; why fear? All are Tamils around here." She said that she was very happy (*santosham*) about the unveiling. She had studied Tamil in her youth in a Catholic school in nearby Sivaji Nagar but had also studied English and Kannada. Citing the annual troubles over the Cauvery water, she mentioned that she did not want to send her children to a Tamil school, implying some risk or discomfort given the anti-Tamil sentiments brewing as a result of the water issue and Rajkumar's kidnapping. Further, in order to find a job or go to a good college, she said her children would have to study Kannada. Of course, Kannada was also taught in the Tamil medium school. It was more a desire not to be marked as Tamil. But with the unveiling, she felt that the times might be changing. Tamils could be openly Tamil, it seems.

A Tamil military officer I spoke with inside a temple in Ulsoor pointed out the importance of temples and *maths* (ashrams) in fostering a sense of Tamil identity. He, too, was both relieved and happy. Temples, he said, were "peaceful places" where the "atmosphere" can be enjoyed without fear. He went on to suggest that Tamil cultural heritage was preserved in temples without intimidation. Citing his own children's study of Bharata Natyam (south Indian classical dance), he said they maintained their "culture" and language in the environment and sanctity of the temple. Of course, classical dance and sacred temple culture were not solely for Tamils in Bangalore. But he emphasized that certain temples, festivals, and practices were important to Tamils and helped them maintain their sense of identity. Ulsoor had several such shrines. In addition to the Someswara Temple discussed earlier, he singled out another ancient temple in the vicinity dedicated to Lord Subramaniam that was very important to Bangalore's Tamil community. He also mentioned the temple to Annamma (a goddess) near Majestic, the central bus station in Bangalore, as having special significance to Tamils. Though I did not visit this temple, I heard many others mention this temple as holding particular significance to Tamils in the city. Interestingly, this temple is also very important to Kannadigas and Telugus, has been described as the most important temple to the goddess in Bangalore, and is associated with the large Thigala community (see Srinivas 2001).

The military officer had studied in Bangalore as a college student eighteen years earlier but had lived all over India as a "military man." Though not native to Bangalore, he had made it home over the years. He liked the "climate and food" of the city, as well as its strong presence of Tamil speakers and religious traditions. He mentioned that, indeed, there had been problems "caused by politicians," but that "people are more sensible and reasonable now about this," citing the unveiling of the statue. Even the politicians, he claimed, were "now more sensible." But turning to the topic of whether the historical Tamil presence in the city and region were more openly acknowledged with the unveiling, he said that "this was still a sensitive topic." He added, "It is a good project to pursue, but it is sensitive." Thus, the statue, despite his optimism, did not undo years of symbolic erasure of Tamil culture. Indeed, as we have witnessed among Tamil activists and scholars, it is this erasure that produces a defensive mindset. Repeating what one prominent local scholar of Tamil heritage told me, "the Tamil origins are always covered up" of several important temples in the city. But, as demonstrated in the subsequent description of a religious festival, Tamil cultural practices are not always suppressed or covered up. If there is erasure or suppression, it mainly occurs in public and political discourse, not in everyday practice.

While a defense of the Tamil historical presence has been noted throughout this study, the continued use of the language and of cultural practices, such as those found in rituals, demonstrates that both chauvinist Kannada pressure groups and the Tamil defensiveness expressed by some are at odds with the everyday fluid boundaries that continue to exist among Tamils, Kannadigas, Telugus, and others. It bears repeating that in many if not most parts of town, I found residents of Bangalore to be conversant or fluent in at least three languages of the region. Most commonly, these languages were Kannada, Tamil, and Telugu, though Urdu and Hindi were also widely spoken. This was true for workers, such as auto rickshaw and taxi drivers, as well as for many professionals.

Political *Darshan*

To conclude this chapter, one might ask why statues are such a significant site of political struggle. An influential academic and architecture scholar who runs an independent institute in Bangalore explained to me the significance as arising from traditional forms of community building around sacred sites and images. Several temples, *dargahs* (tombs to Sufi saints), and churches were important for both community recognition and sociality. Moreover, Bangalore has grown through the incorporation of outlying villages and communities. As villages such as Domlur were incorporated in the city, processions of sacred images were pivotal in establishing linkages between them and ultimately creating a landscape that was symbolically as well as politically entwined. The Karaga *jatre,* in particular, performed by the Thigala community and involving the goddess Annamma as the region's presiding goddess, created a unique public sphere that cut across language and local village identities (Srinivas 2001). Thus, even before the modern state and city were structured, there were practices of procession and *darshan* that enabled communities to imagine themselves within the region as possessing layered and multiple pasts, not unlike the arguments made by Nandy (2002) regarding the city of Cochin. This understanding of statue politics in past idioms and ritual practices is supported by van der Veer's (1994) important study of religious nationalism and the underlying cultural practices and memories that support it. This, of course, does not fully explain the contestation that takes place, but it provides a cultural explanation for it. The same local scholar mentioned above, however, went further in her explanation.

While incorporation operated at a symbolic level, drawing upon cultural memories, the instrumentality of religion in the valuable real estate of Bangalore, particularly given the massive investments in business, industry, and housing by "entrepreneurs," was palpable. She explained that corruption and party politics in the control of local spaces for development were significant. Temple and statue patronage was a means toward creating "political communities" around figures that resonated culturally and spiritually. Thus, statues, and even entire temples, would be inaugurated and even wholly patronized by one party or another, she claimed. "If on one side of the street a temple patronized by Congress is built, you can bet a BJP temple will be built on the opposite side of the street," she explained. Statues of religious figures, be they gods or saints, are powerful political symbols, given the traditional nexus between religious symbols and community building. Building a religious structure or statue "established civic credibility," she claimed.

I had heard similar comments from others in the city over the years. In a sense, this suggested that both cultural and instrumental elements gained some currency in explaining the symbolic struggles for space in Bangalore. The more difficult question to answer, however, is why certain figures or symbols become more contested than others. As we recall, the politics surrounding Vivekananda's centenary procession and popularity in Bangalore were complicated, as both secularists and Hindu nationalists claimed him as their own. Further, Vivekananda, as a national figure rather than as a Kannadiga or Tamil hero, crosscut linguistic identities. But in the case of Thiruvalluvar, he was unambiguously identified with Tamil culture, despite some attempts to cast him as a pan-Indian poet and ethicist. Thus, Bangalore's multilinguistic present was a festering sore to Kannada nationalists who dreamed of a capital city of Karnataka with a dominant linguistic majority.

A. R. Vasavi (2007) points to a new emphasis on spiritual imagery in the political imagination of Karnataka. She suggests that a spiritualization of public space has coincided with a retreat from addressing serious disparities between rural and urban Karnataka and that this has been enabled by the rise of Bangalore's and Mysore's middle classes:

In the absence of inclusive and mass movements and critical and class-engaged political organisations, the likes of the Karnataka Rakshana Vedike and its variations are on the rise. The recent attack on an "inappropriately dressed" lady customer at a seven star bar is a testimony to where the anger and angst of the threats of globalisation lie. In the theatre of the political and mass culture of the state, four emblematic figures have taken centre stage: the IT entrepreneur (celebrated as the new hero representing success and the potential of being a global power); the Naxal (anti-state and people therefore to be hunted down); the swami (the moral force in a time of unanticipated and un-understood change); and the fan (who seeks to uphold moral and cultural propriety as represented by a hero). . . .

If religious-regional- and fan-led organisations envelop the middle and working class people, the upper class and the rich engage with and have led to the rise of the new age spiritualists such as Ravi Shankar.[7] In their presence and prominence in the English media and in the circuits of the noveau-rich stress-management classes, country club stays and spiritual sessions, new age spiritual leaders espouse and celebrate the new India and Indians who will combine the material wealth of the west and the spiritual strength of the east. Focusing on the individual's inner needs, the new age spiritualists bring to the public discourse a negation of social and political orientation. Matching such spiritual inclinations and the rise of the political society of the masses is the establishment and increasing presence of the foundations set up by successful industries. Claiming to be working towards their corporate social responsibility and seeking to signal their engagement and contribution to the disadvantaged of India, these foundations are increasingly key players in the education, health, urban and planning sectors. (Vasavi 2007, 3079)

There is much said here in these important observations by a leading academic and former dean of the National Institute of Advanced Study in Bangalore. But the key point is that political *"darshan"* increasingly takes the place of political work.[8] *Darshan,* be it of a religious figure, a statue that embodies spiritual power, or a politician who embodies the spiritual or moral fabric of society—or is made to appear so, in any event—supplants and effaces a more progressive political mobilization around social problems and iniquities. Vasavi, like the unnamed academic I quoted earlier, sees this as a convenient and powerful method to deflect attention away from corruption and income disparity. She also points to the nexus between local Kannada chauvinist groups and Hindutva mobilizations:

Amidst the consolidation of a coalition that seeks to legitimise itself through darshans as development and its alliances with the leading industries, the mutts (monastic ashrams), and the dominant Hindutva brigade, is the consolidation of different types of political societies in Karnataka that draw on these trends. Caste associations, mutts, regional protection groups and fan clubs are the four key political societies that have emerged with voices and visibility. Caste associations, first initiated by the dominant castes and then followed by all the castes, continue to be key political and social actors working at multiple levels of mobilising political support, participating in education institution-building and acting as civil society organisations. . . . Fan clubs range from the clubs for film actors (although the primary one, that of thespian the late Raj Kumar's, Raj Kumar Abhimanigala Sangha is now dormant), police officers (for Sangliana to Subash Barani), to those for politicians (e.g., for D K Shivakumar of the Congress). The region and language protection groups fall within the umbrella and aegis of the "Karnataka Rakshana Vedike" (Save Karnataka Forum) and the Kannada Sena (Kannada army) that have sub-organisations such as the Karnataka Rakshana Vakkilara Vedike (Karnataka Protection Lawyers Forum). Espousing Kannada and Karnataka protectionism, these associations are visible in the periodic large-scale meetings they conduct, the campaigns they support and their visibility through flyers and billboards. The Kannada and Karnataka Rakshana Vedike have championed regional issues such as the state's rights to Cauvery water (over the water tribunal's allocation to Tamil Nadu), promoting Kannada, and to a range of issues at the district levels. Emerging periodically to demand or support their "hero" and his visions or mourn his death as during the death of the actor Raj Kumar, the film, police and politician fan clubs represent the aspirations and orientations of a marginalised people. In a city that is globalising on a blueprint that has little or no place for the non-globalised worker and citizen, the aspirations of the marginalised are directed towards laying claims on the *ideal of the representative hero who belongs in culture and language to them but is on a higher plane in terms of class and power*. (Vasavi 2007, 3078–3079, emphasis added)

Vasavi is thus arguing that a critical nexus exists that bundles various forms of parochialism within the identity politics in the region. The figure of *darshan* coming in the form of a cultural, religious, or linguistic "hero" provides an object of devotion for those marginalized or fearing greater marginalization in Bangalore's uneven economic growth. Rajkumar represents the crystallization and focalization of fear, anxiety, and hope in the heroic figure he embodies through the celluloid. The championing of Kannadiga issues such as Cauvery water and the use of language in Bangalore in turn becomes focalized around symbolic figures of *darshan* or its obverse, as the case may be. Thiruvalluvar is certainly a figure of adoration and, perhaps, *darshan* for Tamils in Bangalore and beyond. The aspirations for this statue and the eighteen-year struggle for its unveiling in Bangalore exceed rational explanation. It is clearly an important symbol. But one could argue, following Vasavi, that its unveiling acts as political *darshan*, or more accurately, it might represent the "anti-politics machine" (Ferguson 1994) that *darshan* magically accomplishes in her terms. That is, a more progressive or pressing political agenda for working-class Tamils in the region is obviated through the symbolic gesture and celebratory *darshan* of the image.

On the other side of the coin, resentment among some Kannadiga chauvinists suggests a phantasm generated by the *darshan* of the Other. Establishing visual rapport between Tamils and their object of devotion within city space lays claim to that space in a manner difficult to disrupt. Thus, in these terms, *darshan* politics generates anti-*darshan* agitation, as well. This seems to be the main point that both Vasavi and the unnamed scholar quoted earlier seem to be making: *darshan* politics is generative, even mimetic—it produces replications by rival groups, be they language chauvinists, political parties, or religious organizations. On the more elite side, the idiom of *darshan* within the adulation of swamis, gurus, and the patronage of various ashrams and mutts points to, in Vasavi's analysis, a "sacralization" of the public sphere as a means of avoiding or "seeing" the plight of the farmer or working-class urban poor. Thus, the rise of Hindutva politics, in her view, is directly linked to class politics and cultural rationalizations surrounding morality.[9] The superhuman qualities of the guru figure surmount the everyday, rendering it illusory and nonconsequential. And while this might seem reductionistic, recalling the discussion of devotees in the Ramakrishna Mission, there is perhaps more than some element of truth in this evaluation.

This argument might appear to be a restatement of a core Marxist and instrumentalist idea that religious iconography and ritual forms invariably infect politics—and vice versa—making invisible inequalities and powerful interests; but there is something particularly Indian about what is being said. The idiom or logic of *darshan* is a powerful means of creating community, as van der Veer (1994) and Hansen (2001), among others, have argued. Thus, understanding the figure of the hero as an object of *darshan* requires an understanding of cultural logics, not a reduction to power and interest pure and simple. Indeed, it could easily be argued that the leaders as well as the led are equally under the spell of *darshan* politics. And, furthermore, it is not always easy to tell just who benefits, in instrumental terms, in the excess of identification around figures such as Rajkumar, particularly when riots and violence destroy lives and property and further marginalize those groups advocating extremism. As witnessed in the twenty or so years this study covers, the strength of extreme pro-Kannada groups actually declined, allowing for the unveiling of the statue. Thus, the excess of identity surrounding a figure of *darshan* cannot be easily understood in materialist terms alone.

In this sense, other explanations are still necessary. To conclude this chapter, let us examine a more psychological and phenomenological understanding of extreme identity politics—or perhaps more benignly, monocultural fantasies of the nation. An essay on Kannada activism by Rajendra Chenni that appeared in the *Hindu* newspaper on Friday, November 4, 2005, began with the following academic framing of the problem:

> The irony of language-based identities is that they support aggressive and sometimes violent postures, nurture brash and intolerant attitudes; and in some of their bizarre public expressions flaunt a crude masculinity—but beneath these they are fragile and insecure. They cannot exist without constructing that "other" such as the language of another neighboring State; or a community of those who live in the same territory, but are not so "openly" loyal to the language of the land. . . . It looks as though, as it presents itself in the public space, a language-based identity is anything but self-sufficient. It always turns out to be an assertion of a distinctive identity which is ironically, always defined against the other which threatens it. If one were to go by the idiom and rhetoric used in the vociferous debates on Kannada in which the participants are the Kannada activist groups, one would be forced to conclude that Kannada is threatened by English. As though it was not a language and cultural tradition with over 2,000 years of continuous existence. (Friday Review, page 1)

The essay, which parallels arguments made by Kakar discussed in chapter 5, goes on to describe the challenge posed by Bangalore's globalization and large multinational presence, coupled with massive in-migration to the city in the professional spheres. As a result of this movement, the use of English has increased over time. Indeed, as the author notes, the IT industry has promoted English over Kannada in order to promote growth and investment. Insecure and parochial sentiments arise from outside pressures. But the author also notes that Bangalore was never the capital of Kannada culture, and by an "accident of history" it had become Karnataka's capital, despite its plural linguistic pasts.

Leaving aside the question of language policy and practice, the main analytical point—and one that I have subscribed to throughout this book, as well as in my previous work on identity politics in Malaysia (Willford 2006, 2014)—is that modern forms of nativism require a supplement in the form of an Other that threatens the integrity of the self. Kakar made a similar argument earlier. This threatened self, in turn, is forged in a narrow definition of that self's boundaries. Kannada chauvinism is fueled by a threat, in short, and as Anderson pithily suggests, "the nativeness of natives is always unmoored, its true nature is hybrid and oxymoronic" (1998, 62). In such an understanding, nativism, parochialism, and an excess of identification serve as symptoms of some form of displacement. Postcolonial theorists (e.g., Chatterjee 1986; Chakrabarty 2000; Bhabha 1994) have argued along these lines for some time about the vicissitudes of "derivative" identities, born out of the crucible of colonial denigration and postcolonial ambivalence engendered by class and status differences. The nation, at least its unitary ideal, in Chatterjee's (1993) fecund analysis, is generative of "fragments" deemed as threatening or backward. In turn, anthropologists such as Marshall Sahlins (1993) have critiqued the notion that identity-based politics among colonized peoples represents "inventions," "fictions," and "derivatives" created in response to the threat of the Other.

Recall Kapferer's (1988) insights on the ontology of hierarchy in this light. The parochialisms and purges of contemporary Sri Lankan ethnic politics, he argues, are inspired by deeply rooted principles of hierarchy. Sinhalese nationalism was rooted in an ontology of "hierarchy." Following Dumont (1980), Kapferer notes that the Sinhalese find their identity within the larger social body (holism). This "body" was arranged hierarchically in South Asia. Categories of good and evil or pure and impure were categorized and resolved through submission to a cosmic hierarchy. The Sinhalese state, according to this cultural logic, had a special role in upholding the cosmic order. In his analysis of collective violence in Sri Lanka, Kapferer shows how the "fury" of riots directed against the minority Tamil population in 1983 was instigated by politicians facing a political and economic crisis. A growing urban Sinhalese working class was made increasingly insecure by government policies of economic liberalization, reversing a commitment to state-sponsored socialist policies.

At the same time, a rise in sorcery rituals and a growing cult of minor deities among Sinhalese located their source of suffering in "evils" that threatened both the cosmic and personal spiritual order from within. Exorcism rituals, with explicitly violent references to the suppression of evil within or around individuals, restored the proper hierarchy in everyday life. The violence implied in the rituals was experienced as "regenerating" insofar as evil was purged or put in its proper place within the hierarchy. While Kapferer's insistence on cultural ontology was important by pointing towards the deeply rooted sentiments aroused by symbolism, his analysis of political instigation did not ignore the political and economic factors exacerbating violence. Similarly, Price (2013) examined how the machinations of party politics in Karnataka were framed and emotively tinged by the logic of honor and respect, rooted in notions of hierarchy. Seen in this light, the relationships between Kannadigas and Tamils, Hindus and Muslims, or any other coexisting groups in the region are not, historically speaking, stark zero-sum competitions for hegemony. Rather, complex negotiations between groups over time have been understood not so much as competing hierarchies but as disagreements over the positions in which the ontology of hierarchy orders social life. Tamils, in this light, must submit and "honor" the position of Kannada as the ascendant linguistic group. In this sense, civility and coexistence are not coterminous with equality. Of course, this culturalist perspective, while useful in understanding the emotive resonance of symbolic forms, is never sufficient, as I have noted throughout this study.

Looking at the psychology of ethnic, linguistic, or religious attachment, however, need not be seen as a stark choice between authenticity and invention. Rather, looking at practices over the *longue durée* that mark a region, such as this Deccan crossroads of southern Karnataka, reveals that modern serial identifications, particularly in their "bound" form that separates one community from another, clash with durable patterns of belief and practice, be they linguistic or religious.

As scholars working on Hindutva (e.g., Hansen 1999, 2001; Gassem-Faschandi 2012; Menon 2010; Jaffrelot 1999) or Sinhalese and Tamil conflict in Sri Lanka (Gombrich and Obeyesekere 1991; Thirangamma 2011) have shown, for example, the fluidity of religious traditions in South Asia makes it impossible to disentangle one religious tradition from another, despite the work of revivalists and reformers. Thus, as Chenni suggests, the sustenance of such movements derives from a supplementary source, the archiving of the Other's threat. As F. G. Bailey (1998) has argued, true believers always demand and, in turn, show a "need for enemies." Thus, I have argued that the psychology and phenomenology of identity attachments can be understood in the particular demand that modern statecraft and nationalism makes of its citizenry. And here, Anderson's less-heralded contribution to the study of modern identity is relevant.

As noted, Anderson (1998) identifies two modes of serial identification that develop within the politics of imagining community. "Unbound" serialism allows for a more expansive and inclusive form of community imagining. Though boundaries exist within the nation's idealized image, it is not exclusively defined by a linguistic region or cultic practice. On the other hand, "bound" serialism is framed around the bureaucratic measurement of types, facilitated by the census. Bound serial types are sustained in turn through a disentangling of identities that might be otherwise more complex, fluid, and permeable. But as I have argued (2006), these "types" of bound identities are themselves troubled by the displacements and disavowals that sustain them. This is not to imply that bound identities are a pure fiction or invention. Rather, it is to suggest that modern forms of state politics can engender a fetishizing of such types, precisely in an attempt to cover their contingent origins through law and statecraft (Comaroff and Comaroff 2009).

In the case of the article quoted earlier, the author locates the activist desire as a response to the rise of English. But what he does not mention is the other manifestation of this sense of threat that we have discussed—the Tamil Other as the enemy within. This is not wholly surprising. While English is clearly a foreign Other that threatens local culture and identity and can be labeled as such, the case of Tamil is quite different. Tamil is a local language, sharing a geographic space with Kannada and Telugu in Bangalore. In that sense it is more, not less, a threat to those imagining a "bound" measurement of Karnataka's cultural and linguistic identity. It is the intimacy of the Other, in short, that serves as a threat, precisely because this intimacy points to the impossibility of exclusivity. One could argue that the very real threat of English hegemony within a global sphere removes a more fundamental anxiety inherent within the post-1956 imagining of Karnataka and specifically the capital city of Bangalore arising from its linguistic pluralism.

Thus, as Vasavi (2007) argues, there is a convergence between the various forms of political *darshan* that marks contemporary struggles in Karnataka. Threats posed by neoliberal development are addressed through largely symbolic means, though the manifestations vary according to class position. Kannada activists expressing anti-Tamil sentiments might point the finger at the presence of the Tamil community and its demands for recognition in urban Bangalore. But their struggles cannot be disentangled from the spatial and class politics of Bangalore's economic development in which the working and lower middle classes are threatened by the more elite and English-speaking IT sector. Thus the transformation of Bangalore into a global cosmopolitan city, ironically, is generative of monocultural fantasies that suppress cosmopolitan or plural pasts.

Hansen (2001), in an important study of Mumbai's Shiv Sena and the rise of Marathi chauvinism more broadly has illustrated this principle ethnographically, while providing a psychodynamic explanation vis-à-vis the work of Jacques

Lacan. As in the case described here in Bangalore, though on a much larger and more menacing scale, a convergence of Hindu nationalist and regional identity politics occurs in the xenophobic rhetoric and violence of the Shiv Sena directed at linguistic and religious minorities. The Shiv Sena is, as Hansen describes, a pro-Marathi nationalist party that appealed to the insecurities of young Marathi males by asserting a hypermasculine identity in the face of perceived injustices and invasions into the body of the Marathi nation by minority others, especially Muslims and Tamils. It is also a study in political violence and its constitutive role in fostering community, in naming it, and elevating the "ordinary" (street talk) and making it center stage within the nationalist imaginary.

Hansen, following Lacan, points to the inherent instability in identification and thus to the impossibility of a singular identity. There follows a desire to overcome this contingency through an overidentification in nationalist fantasy. That is, the violent potential and overzealous nature of nationalist identifications are rooted not in primordial attachment but, conversely, in the emptiness of official identities. This, Hansen argues, helps us to understand Benedict Anderson's fundamental question as to why the nation evokes such a willingness to kill and die for.

As Hansen explains, the "Real" of urban modernity in India, in Lacan's terms, is an unspeakable violence that lies outside of the symbolic or ego-ideal of the nation (its idealized image). This Real produces anxiety and an attempt to cover, efface, and displace this feeling through symbolic displacement coupled with the pleasures of violent "masculinity" made respectable.

Giving violence its due, but in a kind of moralizing term against the threats to the nation, the Shiv Sena thinly veils its enjoyment in its hypermasculine acts of aggression against minorities. This, however, does not erase the contingent origins of their claims, thus—in Hansen's view, following Lacan and Slavoj Zizek—fueling a circular chain of violence in a futile attempt to defeat an adversary that is, ironically, necessary for the sustenance of the nationalist ideal. The "emptiness of gestures" by the Shiv Sena betrays their inauthentic and uncertain sentiments. "The continued and often violent assertion of this identity seems, however, to indicate that a shared Maharashtrian identity remains haunted by its own incomplete character" (Hansen 2001, 23).

In many ways, Hansen's study is a useful parallel and also resembles arguments I have made for Malaysia's fetish with ethnic types (Willford 2006, 2014). What has concerned me here, in addition to the roughly Marxist and psychodynamic explanations suggested, has been the deconstructive tendencies within pluralistic traditions to mitigate against such monocultural fantasies, be they cynical or carried by the actions of true believers. I certainly agree with Hansen and others that the excessive quality of nationalist and ethnic identification—that is, its irrational and exuberant (indeed, pleasurable) core—cannot be explained by political interest. On the other hand, what I have tried to document in this study is an enduring pluralism that confounds what I have called, following Anderson, "bound" serial fantasies of the nation. Unbound notions of a more diverse Karnataka may wax and wane according to circumstance, but they do persist and thrive in the "landscape of memory" (Srinivas 2001), literally enshrined in centuries of religious and linguistic practice. I would go further and suggest that monocultural fantasies are deconstructed from within by the archives of knowledge and practice that confound "bound" serial types. While these moments of recognition can generate anxiety and violence, as Hansen suggests, pointing to contingency, multiplicity, and fluidity between various identities, it need not necessarily be the case. As Nandy has shown (2002), the "self" can have multiple symbolic and linguistic referents in India under the right conditions, extremist voices notwithstanding.

As Derrida explains in several works (e.g., 2002, 1976, 1995), the supplement that sustains an originary act of violence—for instance, in the naming of the privileged subject of the nation—oftentimes reveals the limits of the originary violence through its feverish acts of justificatory archiving. The archive of the Other's lack will ultimately reveal the lack in the originary violence of distinctions and demarcations. Put in the context of this study, the more Kannadiga (or Tamil) chauvinism protests the wrongs by the Other, the more evidence comes to light of a complex intertwining of identities that have been arbitrarily rendered distinct through legal and bureaucratic measures.

Thus, the problem arises in the marking of modern boundaries and the identities that are supposed to be contained within them. This marking inevitably produces anxieties from within, and these in turn can prove volatile, and, coupled with the rationalizations of class and status privilege, exacerbate the fundamental or originary violence of naming. But thankfully, violence is not the only outcome. Despite the instantiation of "bound" types, the traces of alternative and more fluid identities persist and modulate more pathological and excessive forms of identification. This is not to deny the threat and reality of violence but to recognize the gravitational pull against it. And for this, we need to consider, with a measure of sober seriousness, the power of culture and the attendant weight of history in forging it. A regional Deccan culture persists because the logics of its practices bear more than a heavy trace in the present. One can state this without adopting an exclusively culturalist or idealist position. That is, this does not mean that past cultural practices were benign or disentangled from power (Kapferer 1988). The logic of any cultural practice operates materially as well as symbolically (if these can ever even be separated).

To conclude and to underscore this point, I turn to an essay by D. R. Nagaraj, a leading scholar of Kannada literature. Nagaraj, in analyzing the works of two leading Kannadiga "nationalist" writers, M. Chidanandamurthy and Alura Venkatarao, concludes that there are two kinds of nationalist thought in Karnataka. He quotes Chidanandamurthy from a famous novel: "The region that does not protect its self-identity has no future. Let us have respect for our other language brothers. But these other-language brothers are coming to Karnataka and turning it into their colony. If this is not stopped, Karnataka will be destroyed. . . . The Kannada people have to prepare themselves for such a struggle" (quoted in Nagaraj 2009, 31). Nagaraj explains that, to Chidanandamurthy, it was the challenge posed by Tamil that aroused his fear. He goes on to describe Chidanandamurthy's thought as "fear-centered nationalism" (33). In contrast, Nagaraj quotes Venkatarao from one of his famous novels: "In short, we should not forget that Karnataka is a much broader entity that Kannada. Not only the speakers of dialects, we should also not forget the minorities who speak other (neighboring) languages—in the construction of a united Karnataka this is a principle to be kept in mind" (32). Nagaraj describes Venkatarao's thought as "spiritual nationalism" that "culminates in self-confidence" (33).[10]

Here we witness in Nagaraj's analysis both the "bound" (fear-centered) and "unbound" (inclusive, plural) forms of nationalism demonstrated. Nagaraj concludes by suggesting there are actually three models to choose from for the people of Karnataka. First, one could "treat Karnataka itself as a separate entity, so see it as the sole, language-centered reality: a fear-centred nationalism." Alternately, one could reject the cultural reality of Karnataka and employ "other, abstract, non-linguistic, non-cultural, modern political divisions such as class, society, or administratively efficient divisions." And third, one could approach Karnataka as a "desirable expression of cultural nationalism. Karnataka is real. The whole world is subject to an ugly homogenization by the forces of modern capitalism. Karnatak-ness is one of the legitimate forms of protest against it." This is a "spiritual perspective." And to Nagaraj, this third option protects the idea of Karnataka in the midst of its challenges. He suggests that "hatred of the Other is not a solution. . . . The language of militancy is inappropriate against it" (2009, 41), clearly referring to the activities of antiminority agitations spearheaded by those inspired by "fear-centred nationalism." While concurring with Nagaraj's analysis, I would simply conclude by stating that to him, this is a moral and normative question: a choice for Karnatakans to make. I, here and throughout this study, have suggested that a history of pluralism and cultural complexity favors the third option, that of civility, against the other two. A final ethnographic vignette drives this point home by way of a conclusion.

But prior to this conclusion, I first explore a parallel between Nagaraj's fear-centered nationalism and troubled identities in a clinical context, where a "need for enemies" or a threatening Other also increasingly subsists within the psychosocial stresses of modern life. Though the symptoms may be debilitating on a personal level, rather than being threatening to erupt into social violence, we will witness a clinical corroboration to Kakar's argument regarding the fragility of the Self within the homogenizing forms of serial identities. This will also support the general thesis of Appadurai's (2006) that increasing uncertainties associated with an accelerated pace of change produce a demand for absolute certainty. The key question, and the one that is most difficult to answer, is precisely under what conditions do the phenomenological and psychologically compelling searches for certitude and cultural meaning tip the scales towards more pathological or violent manifestations? My conclusion will attempt to address this.

CHAPTER 8

The Psychiatric Troubling of Identity

This study has up until now focused upon religious and linguistic/ethnic forms of identity in modern Bangalore. The implicit and sometimes explicit argument has treated a modern troubling of identity, in the wake of linguistic statecraft and the markings of categories through bureaucratic means, as a symptom associated with various forms of social and cultural strain. That is, I have suggested that sociocultural and political changes have produced dislocations, both social and psychological, that in turn have produced new imaginaries of identity. I have argued that these identity assertions cannot be understood through instrumentalist or culturalist lenses alone. These emergent identities are, therefore, oftentimes troubled and anxious, betraying older forms of plurality within the selves of individuals and communities. But the tenacious hold of modern or serialized identity constructs is not the only form of troubling that has occurred in Bangalore, or in other large cities in India. A discourse surrounding an emergent "mental health crisis" in contemporary India has taken hold of the public imagination, as well, through a series of feature stories expressed within the print and electronic media. In this chapter, I discuss a more medicalized site of troubled identities in Bangalore. The point here is not to draw a straight line of equivalence between psychiatric symptoms and political/religious/linguistic attachments but rather to suggest that there are some overlapping features that have contributed to both forms of troubling. This exploration, therefore, also provides bridges between the instrumentalist, culturalist, and phenomenological and/or psychological themes reviewed at the outset.

I had the opportunity to spend hundreds of hours at the National Institute of Mental Health and Neuro Sciences (NIMHANS) during twelve months of fieldwork in 2014–2015.[1] Most of my time was spent discussing mental health concerns in today's India with psychiatrists, as well as spending much time in the outpatient and inpatient clinics at NIMHANS observing patients interacting with physicians. While observing hundreds of cases, I will only note a few patterns that I observed that are relevant to the present discussion.

First, it should be noted that there is still a significant stigma attached to bio-medical mental health treatment in India, though this has been slowly changing within the urban context due to outreach and education. NIMHANS has played a pivotal role in disseminating information about mental health, as well as dispelling popularly held beliefs about mental health that oftentimes involve demon-ologies. In the rural context, belief in supernatural causation is still quite strong, whereas in the urban and particularly middle-class sectors, these beliefs are slowly changing towards the biomedical and/or Ayurvedic or AYUSH explanatory mod-els.[2] One consequence of the stigma (Koschorke et al. 2014) still attached to men-tal health care has been a patient desire for quick pharmaceutical fixes rather than sustained forms of therapy, such as undergoing psychotherapy. Physicians oftentimes lament the structural position they find themselves in having to send patients home with ameliorative medications knowing that psychosocial stress, owing to various forms of social and cultural precarity associated with rapid urbanization and social changes, have been left unchanged. That is, doctors are often cognizant that a high percentage of a patient's symptom presentation is rooted in structural conditions that cannot be remedied in the fast pace of the clinic, given both the heavy patient loads and the commitments of time by the patients to stay and be admitted into the hospital. Another aspect of stigma that I encountered several times throughout the year concerned the concealing of a mental illness before marriage by one or the other party involved. The conse-quences of this deception could be felt in the marital complications that inevitably ensued, leading to greater psychosocial stress within the family.

Hundreds of patients come each day to NIMHANS' outpatient department (OPD), sometimes having traveled a long distance from other parts of the country. While the majority come from the tristate areas of Karnataka, Tamil Nadu, and Andhra Pradesh—and most from Bangalore itself—patients from north India are commonly seen and treated.[3] It is not uncommon for a doctor at NIMHANS to treat twenty-five patients or more in one OPD session that might last six or more hours. While residents and fellows do perform fairly detailed intake interviews, the attending psychiatrists must still review and query each case history before making a recommendation for treatment and follow-up visits. Given the combina-tion of this structural reality and constraint upon both patient and doctor time, as well as the stigma attached to mental health, patients and their families are often very eager to receive a "tablet" with the promise of symptom alleviation. Being admitted or recommended for extended care or psychotherapy sessions can raise the specter of revealing oneself as "ill" to the extended family and community, with consequences for one's social standing or that of one's family or community.

This is a profound problem doctors and patients deal with, but unfortunately I cannot dwell on it here.

The mainstream print media oftentimes highlights the nature of the stigma and necessity of combatting it to meet the demands of mental health care in contemporary India. Another theme that emerges ubiquitously in the media concerns the "crisis" of depression and burnout that is thought to be enveloping India's most vibrant urban centers. This discussion points to high stress levels within the competitive workplace and the breakdown of social institutions, such as the extended family, to mitigate against this modern-day malaise associated with urban life. Bangalore is thought to exemplify this crisis with its very large and itinerant IT working population, as well as its very large, low-skilled call centers and factories run by multinationals. At NIMHANS I was oftentimes told that Bangalore's suicide rate is the highest in the country, running in the tens of thousands annually, an astonishing figure.[4] I discuss this issue of burnout and depression later as one of the main patterns of clinical observation witnessed in the OPD.

There are two other patterns relevant to this study of troubled identities as they relate to sociocultural changes and new imaginaries. One concerns the changing relationship between gender roles and a modernist and/or reformed version of Islam. In short, as I elaborate later, women who had hopes for education and careers have increasingly felt their dreams and aspirations clipped by increasingly rigid patriarchal values associated with global Islam and, in particular, its Wahhabi-influenced modern variant.[5] These frustrated aspirations seem to have produced somatizations and/or possessions by forces unseen. The other pattern I observed in the clinic, according to psychiatrists I knew, was an increasing inability to think flexibly or contextually about categories of right and wrong, good and bad, and self versus other. Patients often presented with symptoms of feeling betrayed by significant others in their lives and a very rigid legalistic perspective when it came to judgments. This iron cage of thinking, to paraphrase Weber, was apparently increasing and was fostered by experiences of flux and rapid change in one's life. I attempt to illustrate these recurring patterns through a few case histories. But one can already note a parallel between these patterns and the sometimes overzealous attachments to particular religious and/or linguistic/ethnic identities discussed earlier.

Burnout and depression were evidently increasing at an alarming rate, according to clinicians that I knew, as well as in media discussions (see Upadhya and Vasavi 2008; Mukherjee 2008; D'Mello and Sahay 2008; *India Today,* March 2, 2015, 52–61; *Outlook,* July 20, 2015, 56–64). The high stress placed on employees of IT companies in order to remain competitive included working long hours exceeding the normal workday, as well as dealing with firm deadlines and job insecurities. Some of the patients who came to NIMHANS would complain of feeling numb, depressed, or inadequate at their jobs and in their home lives. Many, particularly younger employees far from their hometowns, felt cut off and isolated, suffering a lack of meaningful social connections. Others felt culturally estranged, working alongside individuals from all over the country, if not the world, with different language, culture, and food habits. Though all major IT centers and tech parks had food courts offering a range of food choices, the lack of home-cooked food was an issue for some. But it was in many instances a combination of the quotidian day-to-day life, requiring repetition and routine, coupled with the expectation of producing a certain product under the duress of time that led to a kind of burnout, exasperation, and what might best be described as an IT drudg-ery. In addition, familial expectations could also prove stress inducing, with hopes pinned on a recent college graduate's potential but oftentimes unrealized earning power. While many were drawn into the IT–related fields with hopes for upward mobility and the promise of novelty and creativity, those that experienced burnout and depression found that they were simply going through the motions of a set routine, becoming, in a word, automatons. Such alienation might not surprise most readers, but the specific cultural shape with which it presented in Bangalore is interesting to note, particularly as the search for meaning in this context might take the form of a heightened sense of religiosity. A couple of somewhat represen-tative case studies from the clinic help to illustrate the dystopias of modern life.

A young male IT worker with severe depression had been admitted into a ward at NIMHANS. He came to the OPD and requested that he be discharged when he met the doctor in his clinic. His signs of severe depression included a very flat or expressionless gaze, coupled with very slow bodily and head move-ments. He spoke slowly and deliberatively, but his intellect seemed unimpaired. In addition to presenting physical signs of depression, he consistently devalued himself vis-à-vis comparison to others he felt were more "successful" in their work performance. The patient, a young man in his late twenties, had reduced initiative and felt despair at the prospects of returning to work. At the same time, he felt his therapy at NIMHANS was not leading to any improvement in his outlook or energy levels.

The doctor felt his depression and his reduced initiative were strongly related. To address this, cognitive behavioral therapy, or CBT, had been tried during his admission. But the patient said to the psychiatrist that the CBT tried at NIMHANS "did not work." He felt as depressed as before and perhaps even more so, for hav-ing failed "even in this." The doctor mentioned to me later that this patient had been surrounded by "strong people" most of his life and felt a deep sense of inad-equacy as a result. The psychodynamic dimensions of these relationships were not probed in the psychiatric sessions in the OPD. Thus, whether he felt like a failure before embarking upon his professional career remained opaque. Certainly the pressures of the IT world had exacerbated whatever insecurities he suffered. His wife, who accompanied him to the session, did not offer any insights into her husband's depression. The husband, too, did not offer any indication that the wife played a role in his depression. She appeared worried for his safety, because since his admission into the ward and clinic she had witnessed her husband's downward spiral to apparent hopelessness.

The patient was emphatic that he simply wanted to be discharged after two years of continuous treatment at NIMHANS. Electroconvulsive therapy had been performed four times, and he had tried various medications for depression. But he had "no relief" after all of this. On the one hand, he expressed angry frustration that nothing was helping him; on the other hand, he felt even more agitated when, apparently, he was told that he "needs to participate and initiate more in therapy work." Evidently, in his present state of lethargy and depression, he had remained largely passive in therapy. But as a result of his half-hearted participation, he felt that the medical staff blamed him for his failures to find relief.

At one point, he cried in the meeting and said he would "just like to end it" (i.e., his life). The doctor cut him off and said emphatically, "No, no!" But neither did the doctor show any indication that he would actually discharge the patient. When the patient said he was more anxious and depressed after therapy, the doctor said that anxiety can be a "positive sign of progress being made towards recovery." This, from a psychodynamic perspective, made a lot of sense. The closer to a breakthrough that one comes, presumably the stronger the psychic resistance would be, Freudian theory predicts. But in this case, there was no insight on the patient's part that would suggest any movement. Rather, the vortex of hopelessness was palpable and impossible to break through, even for a moment. There were no smiles, jokes, or hopes expressed, other than a desire to terminate care and, perhaps, life. The patient was compelled to continue with the psychotherapy and was asked to return in a couple of weeks.

Young professionals are not the main clientele at NIMHANS. But there is certainly a high enough percentage of them to warrant this observation that the stress of working in Bangalore's hypercompetitive IT industry is exacting a toll on many young people. Heightened expectations for professional success tempered by the reality of social immobility in the costly city are conjoined to a profound loneliness and alienation within the city, as many of its young are living cut off from family ties and support networks (D'Mello and Sahay, 2008). This case is suggestive of this pattern, though there are many loose ends left unanswered. Specifically, the role of the support network (wife, parents, siblings, coworkers) in producing stress or its relief remained unclear (Kleinman 1991). One very powerful impression from his case centered on the question of accountability. In the past, or even persisting today in more rural or traditional contexts, psychic stress or agitation was attributable to malevolent agents, such as ghosts, demigods, or demons (e.g., Kakar 1982). But in this narrative, we see a patient struggling in his comparisons with other individuals. He is not adequate. He is a failure at work and even within the healing context of the clinic. This shifting of accountability onto the individual, of course, is related to the socioeconomic structures of mobility, individual initiative, and efficiency as prime values within the competitive IT workplace. The despair of perceived failure was thus also rooted in a self-perception of individual agency and capacity. Thus failure is a failure of an isolated individual, not a systemic or structural problem in this mode of self-blame. The despair of both being the cause of one's own illness *and* the ineffectiveness of biomedical remedies occurs because the social has been disrupted and the individual championed as a maker or breaker of destinies.

In another case, a well-educated man, perhaps in his late twenties or early thirties and working for an IT–related company, also presented with depression. He was articulate and spoke absolutely fluent English. Interestingly, in this case, he had much insight into his own predicament. The patient was quite well read in psychological literature and reflected, perhaps excessively, about his own state of mind. He was well groomed and dressed.

The patient reported a feeling of "falling back" with regard to his work performance. In the past, he had been very active with social advocacy work within a fairly prominent nongovernmental organization (NGO), in addition to his professional duties writing "scripts," which I understood to be narrative descriptions of IT–related products. As a result of his feelings of "falling back," he had reduced his workload, especially his extracurricular work with the NGO. He explained that while the work was not particularly taxing, having done it for years, he was finding it increasingly difficult to get work done.

On the one hand, he seemed to be a perfectionist, not letting simple tasks go without excessive time and effort. On the other hand, he said he found it difficult to focus on the task at hand. The psychiatrist treating him asked about whether he could discriminate between essential or important tasks such as taxes or visa application forms versus routine tasks that can be quickly expedited. The patient claimed that he still could; but, he admitted, he still took too many hours to do each task, whereas his colleagues could quickly master a task and, with that "template in the back of their minds," replicate it quickly. He, conversely, found that he could not internalize such "templates" and would have to revisit each task anew, which took far more time than was optimal within the competitive workplace environment. As a result, his boss had questioned his efficiency. This in turn only worsened his self-scrutiny and concern over his performance, exacerbating his depressive condition.

When pressed a bit further, the patient suggested that he was fine with short e-mails and other minimal tasks. But when writing a new script, he had problems. Part of the problem was the format of the script, which was "unforgiving" and would not allow for "extra words or ideas." He found it difficult to add and subtract words, though the templates were easy to follow. "I seem to forget processes," he complained, adding, "It is a problem of memory; I can't remember the last time." Here we see an almost Tayloristic and/or Weberian "cage of reason" within the imagined creative space of IT scripting impinging his need to express "extra words and ideas." Standardized and routinized, his work was alienating.

The doctor queried whether this inability to work efficiently with the standard templates was a memory or, perhaps, a confidence issue. The patient, barely taking time to answer, said he had already given this much thought and replied that he suffered a "lack of interest and demotivation. Finally, it leads to a feeling tired and overworked [sic]." So, the general impression here was of someone suffering significant depression associated with the routinization of tasks that not only required repetitions of labor but repetitions of thought that were stultifying in their mechanical precision. This coupled with a degree of perfectionism—apparently self-imposed—led to a depressed feeling of inadequacy. It was also possible that his proclaimed forgetfulness was a defense against a more radical conclusion: that he actually despised the mentally constraining work he found himself doing.

The doctor noted that CBT might prove helpful. He also recommended that the patient reduce his antidepressive medication, which he took to help with his sleep. The medication, the doctor suggested, could be contributing to his memory issues and lack of mental alertness. The patient was also told that his problem was a "time-management issue" that could, perhaps ironically, "take time to remedy." He went on to describe the patient's condition as a "personality attribute" for which there was no medicinal cure. The doctor put the responsibility, in this sense, on the patient to work on his personality disorder, rather than seeking a medicinal cure.

My impression was that while this doctor's assessment seemed quite plausible, the patient's inward-directed compulsions and paralysis probably would benefit from a more nuanced reading. Why did he lack confidence, and what were the social and familial dynamics that had wounded his sense of confidence? The patient struck me as an excessive worrier who might do well with psychotherapy, in a broader sense, than simply CBT. In more classical psychodynamic language, he was a slightly neurotic person, plagued by self-doubt, depression, and perhaps a degree of guilt that was unaddressed in his medical regime up to this point. This was a problem of OPD time management, as much as it was the patient's own time-management problem. With patients coming in droves to the OPD, nobody is really examined in a deep, time-intensive sense. The issues would only emerge with a psychotherapeutic regime. My impression, however, is that many patients do not ask for extended psychotherapy, finding it both time intensive and uncomfortable. In this case, the hyper-reflexive nature of the patient seemed to suggest that he might be open to such an exploration. His paralysis, even hysteria-like symptoms, with regard to work must be located beyond the present work conditions and whatever stress he experienced there. On the other hand, the CBT would interrupt the overly self-absorbed and self-analytical mode of the patient, whereas psychodynamic therapy would possibly strengthen the imaginary sense of failed self this patient described about himself. Indeed, I often heard the doctors telling their patients not to ruminate excessively upon themselves, their illnesses, or their predicament. Instead they were to keep busy with their thoughts focused upon tangible tasks. In this case, the patient had been told directly that he was responsible for his predicament, given his "personality attribute." As in the previous case, the shift towards individual accountability as a first step in finding a remedy seemed both promising and troubling. For in both cases, the paralysis of self-doubt in the workplace suggested a singular measure against which efficiency or success was measured. This same yardstick, in turn, seemed to reappear in the clinic, in both patient's and doctor's narratives of illness and remedy. These standardized and serialized yardsticks were, thus, both causes of stress and depression and apparently a road to recovery by becoming accountable for one's predicament. Sometimes, however, this shifting of accountability further atomized the individual from the environment and structures that impinged upon their sense of self-worth.

As noted throughout this study, one of the consequences of modernity in India has been a changing perception of religious plurality and diversity towards a more homogeneous, rationalized, reformed, and—in a word—*singular* form of identification. While I have explored this in the context of Hindu/Muslim boundaries, as well as Tamil/Kannadiga ones, similar boundaries have emerged that divide a more literal and stricter version of Islam from the rich panoply of South Asian Islam, with its many schools of thought and varied cultural influences. I do not wish to discuss reformed Islam per se but to suggest that a more legalistic and strict understanding of Islam has introduced, in many instances, constraints upon the professional and social aspirations of women. A clash has emerged between a modern, serialized form of conservative global Islam versus the more fluid ways the religion has been practiced in recent history, especially with regard to gender roles. Of course, numerous studies have been authored that explore this phenomenon. For present purposes, I only wish to show how these sociocultural changes manifested in a clinical context among women frustrated by the constraints they faced, particularly after marriage to a more orthodox and/ or reformist partner. Again, a couple of cases help to illustrate the dilemmas faced by women after marriage.

A thirty-year-old, disheveled, and slightly overweight Muslim woman came with her husband and young son to the OPD. Her age was betrayed by her middle-aged appearance, suggesting significant stress factors. She was a mother of two children. There was a large scar on her forehead from hitting her head against the wall repeatedly. It seems that she was unaware at the time that she was doing this until the blood "would flow." She was initially evaluated for possible seizures with an electroencephalograph and had an MRI done as well. But her neurological evaluations had been negative. This was more likely a case of "pseudo seizures" or psychogenic attacks.

The woman came from a fairly affluent background and used to be better presented in terms of physical appearance. After marriage and childbirth, she had suffered depressive episodes and seizurelike symptoms. The husband was a secondhand clothes tailor earning a very modest wage. The wife had moved downward, classwise, after her marriage to this man. The attending psychiatrist thought that the woman might be frustrated and depressed as a result of this downward trajectory in socioeconomic terms.

Before coming to NIMHANS, the woman had sought traditional healing at shrines associated with saints (*dargahs*). One was for a Sufi saint and the other was for a Wahhabi, or conservative Muslim reformer. While both shrines had religious authorities who specialized in healing, and both suggested that she was possessed by "devils," their respective prescriptions were different. With the Sufi *pir* (holy man) she was possessed by a *jiin* (unruly spirit), and he had her drink a whole bottle of rum (she claims to have never had a drink before this curing rite). But this did not cure her. The Wahhabi holy man discouraged this sort of behavior and wanted her to follow orthodox teachings in order to drive the devil out. This also did not work, apparently. When both exorcisms failed, she decided to try psychiatry (or actually, neurology first).

It was pretty clear that her seizurelike behavior was volitional and communicative. If there were actually seizures occurring, they would not fall into a pattern of a particular self-injury in the manner presented. Moreover, if she was having an epileptic seizure, she would not be able stop it upon seeing the blood from her forehead, which evidently she did.

The woman's appearance was sluggish, somnambulant, and somewhat uninterested in the doctor's evaluation. There was some marital pressure due to her illness, as well. But the family had upward aspirations of sending their son to an English-medium institution. He spoke English to the doctor, whereas the woman and her husband could only speak Hindi or Urdu.

It is hard to understand the compulsion to bang her head without considering the sociocultural bind she experienced. She, now a working-class Muslim woman, experienced economic distress as well as social marginality. There was, we heard, much discord with her in-laws, who felt she was a "bad" wife and mother. The woman was very sensitive to their criticism. Significantly, she had been more autonomous and "South Asian" (the doctor's words) in her liberal practice of Islam, sprinkled with Hindu and Sufi elements (Flueckiger 2006; Gold 2014). She had worked as a hairdresser and enjoyed her work and the financial freedom it afforded. But the family saw her as a "bad" Muslim woman when she recoiled against their views, having themselves adopted a more reformed or "purified" Islam. Her father, a Sunni, had not raised her as strict as her in-laws and husband now expected. So there were religious tensions being played out in this family that were indicative, the doctor suggested, of a wider canvas of religious tension in the country.

Being caught between models of appropriate religiosity in the wake of reformist pressures was a cultural strain that worsened the symptoms of many female patients, as their freedoms and aspirations were increasingly frustrated after marriage. This was not exclusively a Muslim problem: Hindu, Sikh, and Christian women also experienced similar dilemmas once moving in with their in-laws, as has been documented in numerous ethnographies on the patrilocal joint family in South Asia (Kakar 1981, 1982). But I noted a high percentage of Muslim patients, particularly from the working class, in the OPD suffering from this strain, suggestive of a more radical attenuation of social aspirations within this community. In addition, the socioeconomic position of Muslims was comparatively worse, thus perhaps exacerbating familial tensions. But it should be understood that this is not a reflection of Islam per se but a structural change associated with the spread and dissemination of a "purified" and, in the language of this study, "serialized" form of faith, not dissimilar to the effects witnessed within a more homogenized or reformed Hinduism (Menon 2010; Hansen 1999).

As mentioned, her primary symptom of head banging left a large scar on her forehead. While banging her head, she said, she "feels alive." But this frightened her husband, understandably. Sometimes she presented with hemiparalysis (paralysis affecting one side of the body) as well. Though neurological tests were done, they were all negative. Her paralysis, like her seizures, appeared to be psychogenic. Sometimes while banging her head, she would speak to the voices of "other people [who are] not me." After visiting the aforementioned *dargah* specializing in demonology and exorcism, she was found to be possessed by an "evil *jiin*." The *jiin* was originally thought to be the spirit of a sixteen-year-old girl who had committed suicide. But sometimes the *jiin* spoke as if he was the deceased brother of the woman, calling attention to some murder that had occurred. The sixteen-year-old woman evidently had been murdered. At other times, a brother of hers who had tragically died young possessed her. The *jiin* was speaking beyond the grave about an injustice that had been done. This empowered the woman by making her an arbiter of justice or, at least, its siren. Aside from frightening her family, she received attention and a degree of support, though it must have been also ambivalent, given the family's more orthodox orientation to Islam. Here the validation of a more syncretic and demonological system of belief and healing was highlighted by the woman. Her symptom and its treatment called attention to the clashing cultural models of Islam at play.

But beyond the cultural context, which was also marked by socioeconomic challenges, why did the woman identify with the symptom or *jiin*? Why the emphasis on murder? Why a sixteen-year-old girl? Was this woman around this age when she married? Was her injustice within the husband's family tantamount to a kind of murder (i.e., that of her youthful self and its aspirations)?

The hemiparalysis and hurting oneself also suggest a kind of inward-directed aggression that cannot find an external target. Again, this accords with Kakar's (1982) psychodynamic model of paralysis and masochism as a means to defend against the horrors of being unfilial. There is certainly, too, a strong cultural model that the *jiin* must be exorcized through the banging of an iron nail utilizing the forehead. This is powerful among both Hindus and Muslims with regard to dealing with malevolent spirits, such as in *pey, bhut, preta*,[6] and *jiin* possessions. It would be interesting to know whether she had harbored romantic feelings to anyone before her marriage had been arranged. In this light, could the deceased brother double as a disguised and abandoned lover? Could he have committed suicide? Or, conversely, could she identity with the suicide of another vicariously (Nabokov 2000)? Could this be one of those transient mental illnesses in which larger social dilemmas are enacted and identified with (Young 2007)?[7]

In another case, a middle-aged Muslim woman came to the OPD with her son. She suffered from a generalized "mood disorder." Apparently, she was quick to cry and often became "overly emotional." To the doctor she complained that she carried out "her duties like a machine" in the household. But her automatism was not due to the Kafkaesque world of industrial bureaucracy or, as we saw earlier, an

IT routine. Rather, it was due to her relationship with her husband's family, with whom she lived in the joint household that is still oftentimes the cultural ideal. She suffered "disagreements" with the family and had learned to cope in this very hostile environment. But now her situation was becoming precarious within the family, and she proclaimed that she could not cope any longer.

The family lived in Hyderabad. During her premarital life in Hyderabad, she enjoyed meeting people, visiting *dargahs,* and had a fairly rich and satisfactory social life. But the in-law family severely controlled and curtailed her movements after marriage. She was oftentimes left alone in the house and felt depressed as a result. The husband's grandmother, it seems, was very blunt in her disapproval of her daughter-in-law, repeatedly saying things such as, "You are not the bride we wanted." Due to this relentless verbal abuse, she "lost confidence" in herself. But, as mentioned, prior to the marriage in Hyderabad she had played an active role in social organizations and clubs. When the family shifted to Kolkata after marriage, these social contacts were lost. She felt alone and had little to do outside the house in Kolkata.

The woman complained of many bodily aches and pains to the doctor and residents. These were assumed by the medical team to be somatizations of her depression, as nothing in her tests suggested an organic disease. She also quarreled with a younger sister and felt estranged within her own family to some extent. Her son—who came along and who was taking her in within his household temporarily as she visited NIMHANS in Bangalore, where he resided—said he did not know what to make of her somatic complaints. Further, she did not "forgive easily." One odd symptom of her distress was that she would walk around the house completely naked. This transgression of all propriety suggested, perhaps, a shedding of an intolerable social identity—one that made her into a "machine."

She found some relief in visiting fakirs (Muslim holy men). But this was also somewhat restricted by her in-laws. She eventually found faith in something called NV Life, an online interactive self-help spiritual program headed by a charismatic "guru." This group used Skype as a medium with which to "heal people," evidently. She paid "lakhs of rupees" (hundreds of thousands of rupees) for the "healing hands" therapy offered by this guru. But she felt that the guru had damaged her nervous system by evil and/or fraudulent means. Her worsening condition, she insisted, was due to his malevolent touch. She harbored great anger towards the guru (who was a Hindu) and felt he ruined her life. While it was true that the loss of money and face might have been yet another cruel blow, her problems were deeper and more long-standing than being taken in by a false guru. This was clearly a displacement. We might speculate that her attraction to the guru was, in part, a reaction to the social constraint imposed upon her by the in-laws, who disapproved of her ways. But her own ambivalence towards the more syncretic and certainly nonorthodox religious/spiritual flirtation with NV Life might have contributed to her symptoms as a somatization of her guilty conscience. In any event, she was at once committed towards rediscovering an Islamic identity, as well as literally stripping herself of identity. As in the previous case, she was caught between the rails of reformism and the melancholy of lost freedoms.

My own psychodynamic speculation notwithstanding, the attending psychiatrist thought that one issue of concern might be the side effects of antidepressants. Ironically, one of the side effects of these medications, which the woman had been on for some time, could be mood disorders that also manifest in somatic complaints.

The sons were now trying to help their mother by bringing her to NIMHANS and letting her stay with them in Bangalore. They were quite troubled by their mother's condition, knowing that they had themselves kept some distance from her owing to her personality disorder and odd behavior, which caused them some understandable embarrassment. Particularly as these sons were working now in IT, they did not want their own careers compromised by having a mother with mental illness. "Out of sight and out of mind" had been a coping mechanism within the family. But now that her sons were faced with the oddity of her behavior, she provoked a guilty response among them. It is also possible that her desire to reconnect with family provoked a range of symptoms as she passively enacted, through somatization, her anger at familial abandonment over the years. Her literal stripping of identity was a weapon of anger—or the negation of the Other's desire in Lacan's terms—making palpable the otherness of a woman estranged from her own sons.

In the previous cases, it has been shown that a more standardized identity had taken root, either in the IT workplace or within a gendered religious persona, leading to frustrations and symptomatic depression, lethargy, and/or transgressive behavior. That is, we have seen a social message within the symptom in which a negation of the normative role—or in Lacanian terms, the "Other's desire"—has been negated. A refusal to follow the homogenous and routine drudgery of the lower-level IT world, or a refusal to accept gendered notions of religious orthopraxy manifested as a bodily symptom, or being labeled as pathological (or demonological) by others were symptoms *and* social messages. Another symptomatic manifestation of the demands of modern, serialized or bureaucratized life is, ironically, not to resist but to become or enact the Other's desire in excess. In that Kafkaesque reality, or trapped within an "iron cage of reason," individuals lose their ability to make reasoned choices. Instead, like automatons, they enact with a vengeance the "correct" mode of behavior and thought. They are the oversocialized selves that, as Freud reasoned, extinguished the ambiguities and gray areas of compromise that mark human life within its social context. Nonflexible and noncompromising forms of thought or a relentless legalism without reflexivity seem to increasingly flourish within contexts of increasing social stress (Appadurai 2000; Hansen 2001). These uncompromising and legalistic selves, in turn, are only sustained through themes of betrayal and the identification of perpetual threats to the identity being posited. In Derridean language, a "supplement" is needed in order to shore up the internal inconsistencies that inevitably arise from categorical definitions of truth and untruth, self and other, right and wrong.

One particularly insightful and influential psychiatrist that I often shadowed at NIMHANS described numerous instances in which religious reforms, identity politics, and homogenization of cultural identities in the public sphere had psychic consequences that manifested in the clinic. That a rich tapestry of cultural syncretism was now being separable by enumeration and made legible into categories of ethnic, linguistic, and religious difference was an alarming trend all across India, and particularly in Bangalore, the doctor suggested. He told me of examples in which the slightest insults were taken as "cosmological" and polarizing between Muslims, Hindus, Jains, Sikhs, and Christians. There was one story, in particular, in which a woman was spat upon along the roadside by a bus passenger. The husband was certain this was a religious insult, as she was a Muslim.

In other cases, the doctor spoke of low-cost housing and flats in which one lived, sometimes, surrounded by total strangers. This was an increasing fact of modern life in the city. In one such case, a Muslim family expressed a sadness that they could not "be themselves" as Muslims in a new housing complex. I asked the doctor if this troubled the family because they could not literally be themselves surrounded by the other's culture—an Other who in turn would find them wholly different from themselves. He said, instead, that it was because they had reached a "level of consciousness" in which they were so aware of themselves as being separate and different and thus requiring formal boundaries of difference, wholly separate from the other. Intimacy, in a word, was increasingly intolerable, given the political demands for difference and separation that marked contemporary representational politics in India. The plural and, for lack of a better word, syncretic fabric of Indian life was under siege and, with it, the need to maintain these boundaries with pathological forms of othering. This obsession with guarding the borderlines and assuming the nefarious desire of the other required, in turn, the supplement of betrayal, conspiracy, and potential violence to maintain itself (Hansen 1999, 2001; Ghassem-Fachandi 2012; Juergensmeyer 2000). As F. G. Bailey (1998) argued, there is "a need for enemies" in modern forms of statecraft.

So it was their self-perception of cultural chasms that really bothered him, see-ing firsthand the consequence of categorical thinking in the clinical context. The aforementioned doctor told me of a case, for instance, in which a man, a Jain by birth, saw conspiracies at every level of the government and media to besmirch his faith. It became his mission, indeed manic obsession, to discover and hence pro-tect his Jain faith from these conspirators. This paranoid identity was buttressed by the perpetual supply of threats that came in the form of these conspiracies and plots. Without these enemies, his imaginary sense of self—and with it, a sense of purpose—would be impossible.

Again, an illustration is helpful from a clinical context to drive this point home. A young man came with his mother to the OPD. He was articulate and appeared to be very intelligent. Upon entering the examination room before the doctor had entered, he asked me where I was from. When I said I was from the United States, he said that he had lived there for five years. He went on to pro-claim that Americans were much better behaved outwardly than Indians were. For example, Indians would "cut the queue" in any line and would not follow traffic rules. But, he then went on to say that Indians would "not hurt the heart," though their outward behavior was rude. That is, outward and inward behavior were not always the same or transparent, he suggested. While this seemed to be stating the obvious, the relevance of this statement became clear only a bit later in the clinical interview.

The attending psychiatrist made some general inquiries as to how he was doing, as he had evidently been seen for a few years by this particular physician. His mother complained a bit about his "compulsions," which to her seemed unrea-sonable. The young man would counter with statements that were disparaging and sharply critical of his mother.

He told the doctor that he was studying Tamil and law online and found these things interesting. It seems he had been cheated in some business venture in recent times and was learning the law to deal with this. The doctor inquired whether it was necessary to go to such lengths to deal with relatively minor "cheaters" within the workplace. He also seemed to connect seemingly unrelated events such as the need to study law in great depth with the minor cheating of some employees who were skimming bits of profits in the family business. His study of Tamil (he him-self was a north Indian) was inspired by an intense devotion to some Vaishnava texts and his desire to go "deeper" into the religious literature of a particular community. He was quite devout in his Hindu faith.

The psychiatrist asked the young man and his mother whether his acts were impulsive or well thought out. He asked further whether he did all his decision making alone or took into account what others thought or did. The doctor said that some semblance of family harmony was essential. It was clear that the patient was combative with his mother and father. At one point, the mother explained that he had told his own father that he "was just waiting for him to die." When the doctor asked how he could speak to anyone like this, much less his own father, the patient answered that as "everyone is going to die, it was not anything wrong." There was an air of intelligence and reason about the man, though tempered by a kind of self-righteous arrogance, as well. His use of Indian philosophical notions of transience and nonattachment, while in a literal sense, seemed pious; in this context, they sounded hollow and cruel.

The doctor explained it was important that he learn to have close friends and family members. The patient replied that his "Guruji is close to me." This was in reference to having a close confidant to discuss problems with. The doctor tried to explain that the "Guruji" is different, as he was a spiritual guide but not a close confidant to discuss personal problems with. The patient countered by saying that, in fact, his guru was "very close" to him and cared for him intensely. Thus, he said he could discuss anything with him.

The doctor was apparently worried that his frames of reference seemed to come from a rigorous if not overly legalistic mindset. While the literal father had flaws, his spiritual father was perfect, all knowing, and wise. This perfect oracle could be trusted, while the more human father could not. People, more generally, were untrustworthy and could compromise his sense of ego. There was, indeed, a hypervigilance regarding his own ego. This manifested itself in being overly critical of others as well as taking offense very easily to perceived slights and insults. It meant he would always search for the flaw in the other person with a legalistic zeal for vengeance.

It seems he, too, had elaborate delusions and psychosis that were fairly well controlled with medication. At one point, echoing the "Truman Show syndrome,"[8] he felt that the Howrah (Train) Station in Calcutta was an elaborate "set" that was made to watch him. Not helping matters was his personal history of student life in the United States.

While attending the illustrious and highly competitive Indian Institute of Technology, this individual wrote a letter to the University of Rochester explaining that he was "bored" by the lack of intellectual challenge there. The university asked for his dossier/portfolio and, upon examining his work, discovered that he was quite brilliant. But while he was studying in the United States, an undercover FBI informant had entrapped him by offering to help him get a fake ID. The hope was that with this fake ID he could stay on and work in the university library for a while after graduation. When he was caught in this dragnet, he was forced to leave the country, but not before he was arrested and put in a jail. But when the local DA and his appointed lawyer saw how he had been set up and that he was not on any list of terror suspects, he was released and charges were dropped, provided he leave the country. So he came back to India. But he understandably became more distrustful of others after this subterfuge. It was not known whether he had extensive delusions or paranoia while in the United States.

Regarding his orthodox and legalistic interpretations, it seems he followed astrological beliefs to the letter and believed that the stories about the god Krishna—for instance, when he lifted the mountain to save a village (a popular myth)—were actual historical events. His obsessiveness about religious ideas translated also into his handling of the family business, where he prosecuted all and anybody who would even slightly cheat on the factory floor. Even the merest infractions incurred his wrath, it seemed.

In one sense, he appeared to have internalized and fully identified with the symbolic, the "figure of the Law," in the Lacanian psychoanalytic sense. But his adherence to the law was not tempered with any sense of reflexivity or conscience. Rather, it was an almost mechanistic, machinelike reality that he would cling to. His guru, his faith, and his sense of categorical differences between cultures and peoples were incapable of nuance or areas of gray. The Indian psychoanalyst, Sudhir Kakar (1981, 1982), has theorized that a wounded sense of self results in a form of secondary narcissism in the Indian context in which larger-than-life heroes, such as gurus, politicians, and film stars, are put on excessively high pedestals. The devotee's full identification with their perfect leader in turn nurtures a weak sense of self. But, on the other hand, any threat to that perfected "father" or "mother" figure is perceived as the gravest insult.

In this case, the patient was not calling for preemptive violence or attacking a particular community per se. But the same structural logic seemed to appear: there are threats and enemies that must be prosecuted in order to maintain the rightness of things. In the political context of modern Bangalore, fascistic tendencies, I was told by some doctors at NIMHANS, were emerging out of this kind of wounded and fractured identity. In this particular case, the fractures were visible after a bad experience overseas, whatever the latent tendencies were that existed before being set up by the FBI.[9] The doctors were seeing it at NIMHANS, and the public paranoia or "fear" of minorities (Appadurai 2000; Kakar 1995) manifested itself in discourses about the looming threat of the Other, be they Tamils or Muslims, as we have already discussed.

Even NIMHANS was not spared the consequences of categorical or serialized political identities. Though a national institution, during the height of the intensified pro-Kannadiga movement in the late 1980s and early 1990s, patients who were Muslims, Christians, north Indians, and/or Tamil speakers had trouble with the intake interviews and registration forms when being admitted into the ward or OPD. These forms were quite deliberately and exclusively written in Kannada. The government of Karnataka had mandated this at this time, I was told. That official documents should promote only the Kannada language was the order of the day. Because of this policy, patient information on non-Kannadigas was severely compromised, one doctor complained to me. Thankfully, doctors at NIMHANS had later won the day, and this policy was reversed.

This brief digression into a clinical context is not offered to mark a direct correspondence between mental illness and the intensification of identity in other perhaps less pathological forms. But I did want to suggest that modern sociocultural and political changes produce a continuum of effects that can be witnessed in the tenacious or excessive hold of identity in the imagination, increased othering, and a categorical making of boundaries between what used to be more permeable and protean lived realities. This chapter has illuminated how the homogenized and rationalized world of IT, with its attendant stress on efficiency and production, contributes to workplace burnout, depression, cultural estrangement, and anxiety. In the case of Islamic "reform" and/or purifications, we saw how a collision of modern aspirations (e.g., to be a good Muslim and also a productive member of society) impacted upon women, rendering them sometimes "mad." And last, we observed how a totalizing and inflexible mindset was manifested in a rigid love of the law, but without its spirit.

The key link, therefore, between these psychiatric symptoms and the excessive boundaries that sometimes emerge between religious and ethnic and/or linguistic categories is a social (and perhaps legal) demand towards some kind of impossible and categorical singularity. These demands are, of course, buttressed by bureaucratic and material relations of power, and thus we must always seek to understand the instrumental forces at work *in addition* to experiences of anomie and a crisis of cultural meaning. The demand itself, however, often betrays its own insecure origins and impossibility given the more protean reality of lived and historical identities in this region, be they gendered, religious, or linguistic. At the same time, as Appadurai (2000) argued, "dead certainty" paradoxically takes root in moments of greatest social uncertainty. This ominous chord notwithstanding (thankfully), as indicated before and as follows in the concluding chapter, sites of pluralism still exist within a landscape of memory (Srinivas 2001, 2015; Taneja 2013) across Bangalore and the Deccan region. The following is a look at a religious site where the mentally and socially afflicted converge across boundaries of linguistic and religious difference. One might call this a site of "tragic civility." Then I conclude this study with a more optimistic and celebratory moment of civility in the form of a religious festival.

Visit to a *Dargah* in Chintamani

While the large numbers of patients in the OPD at NIMHANS suggested that a shift in attitudes and awareness about mental health was occurring, a large percentage of people afflicted seek spiritual healing believing their symptoms to be the result of evil or malevolent forces (e.g., Sebastia 2009; Kakar 1982). Sufi shrines marking the tombs of saints (*dargahs*) are believed to be particularly efficacious in this regard. *Dargahs* are sites not only of religious healing but also religious and linguistic pluralism persisting within the increasingly biomedicalized and polarized religious landscape (Flueckiger 2006; Taneja 2013; Gold 2014; Gottschalk 2000).

The day began with enormous traffic out of Bangalore. After getting out of town, the countryside opened up and was pleasant for our drive, about ninety minutes or so to Chintamani, a small city in Karnataka famous for its *dargah* called the Murgh Malla. Along the way, led by a doctor from NIMHANS,[10] we found a roadside restaurant and filled our stomachs with a midmorning snack of tea/coffee and hot *dosas* (similar to pancakes) with spicy sambar (spicy vegetable and lentil-based stew).

This *dargah* was about ten minutes' drive out of the town in an area surrounded by dramatic and strikingly beautiful hills laden with large boulders and interesting geographic features. There were several old Hindu temples upon these hills, suggestive of the syncretism of the area. There was a famous goddess temple nearby that also drew lots of pilgrims. One of the legends I heard, in fact, was that the saint entombed in this *dargah* had been blessed with a vision of the goddess and thus was able to heal people. There were palpable and strong Hindu-Muslim crossings here. Though in Karnataka, the area was also not too far from Andhra Pradesh and Tamil Nadu, and lots of devotees from both places came to the *dargah.*

As we entered the vicinity of the *dargah* we could see pilgrims from all over the place. Small shops surrounding the shrine sold images of the *dargah,* of the saint for which it was named, and for other figures such as Mahatma Gandhi and Tipu Sultan for tourist pilgrims. Incense and flowers were also sold to be given as offerings within the shrine. Small canteens lined one side of the shrine selling refreshment and meals. And while there was a large presence of Muslims, naturally, in this area near the shrine the atmosphere was not monoreligious or exclusive, as imagery of Hindu gods was also prominently visible.

After parking a short distance away in an official parking area, the doctor informed the administrative office of the shrine of our presence and interest in visiting the sacred space. The doctor, a psychiatrist, had been there before a few times and had brought residents/fellows to the shrine to illustrate local healing traditions for them. As a result of this familiarity, the officials gave us a VIP tour of the shrines, which gave us access to the two main mausoleums housing the saint and his wife, also believed to be holy, as well as access to certain residents of the shrine who suffered various maladies but had found some measure of relief living there.

When we entered the shrine under a large corrugated tin-roof area that provided shelter for hundreds of residents and pilgrims, it became obvious that we were a large attraction. It also became clear that many of the residents were mentally or neurologically disturbed or challenged. It was also apparent that the majority of those living under this roof were poor and without familial support. There was a fairly high percentage of elderly women living in the shrine, perhaps abandoned widows who had no place else to go once their families could no longer care for them. This was suggested by the psychiatrist. Some women laughed hysterically, in the colloquial sense of the term, possessing matted hair and unkempt clothes. One woman surprised me when she spoke fluent English and seemed to be educated, though her disheveled appearance betrayed her social circumstance. She specifically tried to engage in conversation with my anthropological colleague and me only to be told to be quiet by male officials working in the shrine. The sick and abandoned were lying on straw mats and blankets on the concrete floor of the shrine, leaving little room for walking.

As this was not a festival time, nor was it during evening prayers, the shrine was not overly crowded. But with the hundreds of residents living on the premises, I wondered what would be the effect of a large group of pilgrims, transient patients, or, as was often the case, possessed individuals who came for exorcisms. Indeed, I and the other medical anthropologist expected to witness exorcisms being performed, as this shrine was famous for driving out evil spirits (*pey, jiin, bhut*, etc.). But on this afternoon, only a more permanent population of people suffering from various mental and psychical illnesses could be found within the shrine.

Despite the Mental Health Care Act of 1987 (Sebastia 2009), which supposedly prohibits the housing of mentally ill within nonregistered mental health care facilities, it was clear that hundreds of patients did in fact live permanently or semipermanently within the shrine. Indeed, we were told by some patients that this was their last refuge and the place where they had found some peace (Sebastia 2009). Some of these individuals had traveled to the shrine themselves, making a pilgrimage as it were, to find a spiritual home. Others had been abandoned by their families who could not bear the costs of care or the stigma attached to mental health within their families. Within the shrine, they received the protection and healing power of the saint, as well as a roof and hot meals. It was clearly much better than the alternative of being on the streets, homeless, with nothing. The psychiatrist leading our team pointed out that though the human suffering here was so palpable and acute, these people at least had some of their basic needs met. Moreover, from the stories we heard, some had found their symptoms alleviated by their faith in the healing power of the shrine.

At the same time, many of the residents of the shrine were interested in speaking with the doctor—or, in some cases, their relatives were. He had brought a few of his business cards with contact information, and as he spoke with a few individuals he suggested they visit NIMHANS for treatment. He explained that the treatment would be free for those of little means, possessing a Below Poverty Line card.[11] But, alas, many of them, though interested in biomedical treatment or counseling, could not afford the journey by bus and were unsure how they could physically endure the trip. In one case, a man was hemiparalyzed and needed to be properly diagnosed but would find it impossible to make the two-hour journey by bus without extensive assistance. But the patient expressed interest in being seen by the doctor. In the cases of neurological conditions or other movement disorders, there was little by way of treatment that the psychiatrist could offer on-site. For a neurological intervention, therefore, it was necessary to visit NIMHANS. Among the psychiatric cases, it was clear that some of the afflicted were depressed, dissociated in some ways, speaking to themselves, and manic. But no medicines would be administered on this day. The goal was to encourage people to also seek biomedical care, if this was at all possible.

My attention, however, was directed at the perceived efficacy of the shrine. One man explained how he could not walk well and had been to several doctors near Mysore, his native place, before coming to this *dargah*. Now his symptoms had abated and he wanted to share this miraculous news. One older man could not even sit up, lying on his side with discomfort and pain. The doctor implored the family visiting him to get him treated at NIMHANS.

Among the more general audiences within the shrine, there was a fairly sizable group of people who were making a pilgrimage to the shrines of the saint and his partner, also deemed a saint. There were two separate shrines. Men and women were directed to go in separate shifts to view the tomb and elaborately decorated coffins. The heavy smell of incense greeted the devotee when entering either shrine. One had to bend low under a very low door to enter the shrine. The inner shrines were fairly simple, though some gold and silver had been added over time to the entrance. It was not unlike the sanctum of a Hindu shrine in some respects. After offering flowers and touching the cloth that draped the coffin, which had sacred verse written in Urdu, the devotee was blessed with holy water by a local *pir* (Sufi teacher), dressed in traditional clothing. The *pir* would dip a bushy frond on a long stick in the bowl of holy water and then sprinkle a bit on the head of each devotee as one left the shrine. A sacred gold flag also pointed towards the main shrine, as in a Hindu temple. While a majority of visitors were Muslims from the region, a fairly high percentage were Hindu. In fact, later I was told that this shrine was equally popular among the two main communities. This looked to my eye as an apt observation, as we passed by long lines of devotees from both faiths, as evidenced by their facial markings and clothing (Flueckiger 2006).[12]

I could not help but feel some sadness seeing so many abandoned and mentally unstable people in one place. This tempered the mood of a place thought to be sacred. But with the faith invested in the shrine by the visitors, I also felt that the power of suggestion must have worked as a powerful talisman and solace to those suffering from a range of illnesses or despair in their lives. Indeed, it struck me that those who resided might not actually suffer diagnosable disorders, but they had found a spiritual home that accepted them without condition. There was an unmistakable smell of urine as well as bird droppings under the large tin roof. Monkeys were also ubiquitous. Though I was told the area was cleaned daily, the poor and "mad" who resided there had little investment, apparently, in personal hygiene. And without a constant water source, one wondered how the people could bathe regularly. Bathrooms existed, but not on the scale needed for such a large and popular shrine. We were told that only long-term residents were supported by the generosity of various patrons of the shrine. A simple communal meal was offered to all residents twice each day.

I also wondered about patronage and other forms of financing needed to keep such a large shrine functioning. A few large and strategically located collection urns were there to capture donations. But this was not a shrine that VIPs normally visited. I suspected that the challenges of housing, feeding, and bathing this many people must have been overwhelming, given the actual resources available. The Murgh Malla *dargah* is like hundreds of similar shrines within the country that are believed to have the spiritual power to drive away the devils or spirits that cause madness. These shrines, be they Hindu, Muslim, or Christian, as some scholars have argued (e.g., Sebastia 2009; Kakar 1982; Raguram et al. 2002), are hardly marginal or peripheral to the care of the mentally ill within India, but their survival is in question given legislative and economic pressures. The point being made here is that not only are pockets of religious and linguistic pluralism surviving in the Deccan, but various approaches toward healing those troubled by various mental disturbances continue to exist and even thrive. The Murgh Malla, like a few other powerful shrines across the religious divide, if anything, achieve greater popularity in the age of televisual media. News of miracles today spread much more quickly, as do the images of particularly powerful healing shrines through the print and televisual media. These shrines, in turn, attract ever-larger numbers of devotees as their healing fame spreads and/or the sources of psycho-social stress in urban Bangalore and other places increase.[13]

The Kumaraswami Festival and Civility

The Kumaraswami Koyil (temple) in Hanumanth Nagar, an old and bustling neighborhood in Bangalore, sits perched upon a hill, an auspicious location for a temple dedicated to this deity. Kumaraswami, also known as Murugan, Subramaniam, Karthikeya, or Skanda, is most popular among Tamils. During the temple's annual festival for the god, thousands of devotees gather to offer their devotions. Many of them travel from various parts of Bangalore, as this temple has come to have great significance among Murugan worshippers in the area. The growing popularity of this temple and its festival is also due to the increasing emotional and symbolic significance that Tamils attach to this place in the shadow of the Kannadiga movement and its more strident anti-Tamil populism.

I observed the celebrations in August 2009. At the base of the temple, devotees gathered in preparation for their pilgrimage up the steps of the shrine on the hill. Between the houses, on the street outside the temple compound, a carnival atmosphere prevailed. Bright colors of sanctified food consisting of puffed rice and fried snacks (*prasadam*), pinwheels for children, toys, and brightly decorated *kavadis* lined the streets near the temple. Devotees dressed in red and yellow prepared for their offerings, which included, among other things, milk, fruit, and other auspicious items.The rhythmic chanting of the lord's name could be heard throughout the festival grounds: "*Aro-hara, vetri vel Murugan, aro-hara veera vel*" ("Hail the lord, victory to Murugan's lance, hail the lord's heroic lance").

A fairly heavy police presence was felt at the celebration as devotees were escorted in procession up the right side of the stairs to the shrine, while family members ascended on the left side of the stairs. The police presence may have been related to the fact that just that week the Thiruvalluvar statue had finally been unveiled, much to the protests of radical Kannadiga activist groups. Demonstrations against the statue and against Tamil interests had been threatened, as noted earlier, but nothing significant had materialized. At this particular festival, devotees I asked remarked that the composition of the crowd was mixed. Though attendees were predominantly Tamil, I was told that at least 15 percent of the devotees were in fact Kannadigas. The Kannadiga presence was felt in other ways, as well. Though most of the *pusaris* (priests) were Tamils, the signs within the temple were all in Kannada, which was an obvious political concession in response to the pro-Kannada movement. Though the crowd was harmonious and multilingual, thus indicating a fabric of urban *bhakti* within the landscape that crosscuts language, differences were manifest. For example, one man whom I interviewed together with his family came to this festival each year. He, a middle-aged Tamil man, shaved his head at the temple during the festival, as this is considered a meritorious act and sacrifice. He said he comes, in part, because this is the "Tamil god." Moreover, this is one of the few temples where acts of possession and self-mortification—more common among Tamils, he claimed—were performed. While I witnessed some *kavadi*-bearers who appeared entranced and had *vels* (lances) piercing their tongues and cheeks, he said that if I were to come in the evening the crowd of devotees would be exclusively Tamil. Also, he claimed that at night the acts of self-mortification were more ubiquitous.

This man came with his wife and two young daughters and said he would continue to bring his family for the festival, as this temple "is for the Tamil people because it is a Tamil God and is on the hill." And, he claimed, there was reason to celebrate, given the long-awaited unveiling of the Thiruvalluvar statue in Bangalore. He was extremely happy about the statue, which had been covered up in legal limbo for nearly twenty years. Now the two sides had come together (*raandu pakkum*), and he felt only happiness (*santosham maddum*). But he shared the view of other Tamils with whom I spoke: the victory was one for the Tamils in particular. Though he was glad that Kannadigas had not acted violently in protest, he continued to assert with pride that this is a Tamil temple and a Tamil-oriented festival. The truth of Kumaraswami worship, however, is that, though it is very popular among Tamils, it is also popular amongst Kannadigas. Thus, what we witness in this festival is a shared religiosity and a porous boundary between communities. There are many such shrines and traditions within the fabric of life in Bangalore, as we have seen (Srinivas 2001).

Another devotee, a young Tamil man aged twenty-five, explained his special relationship with the temple. He told me that he must carry *kavadi* at the temple for the rest of his life, in order to fulfill a vow he had made. He also performed the same vow at the most important Murugan shrine in Tamil Nadu, in Palani. He explained that he had a problem with a stammer in his speech. This caused him great anguish during his school years. But after carrying *kavadi*—and specifically after carrying the *vel* through his cheeks and tongue in a state of possession—his speech "became clear." In preparation for his offering, for forty days he would eat vegetarian food and practice abstinence. His diet consisted mainly of milk and fruit. The *kavadi* pole itself would be washed in cow urine first so as "to avoid

Devotee making *kavadi* offering to Lord Kumaraswami.

mistakes, and as it gives strength." He would then bathe in cold water. Sometimes he or his siblings would also offer milk, curds, or cheese sprinkled with rose water to the deity. When asked who carries *kavadis*, he said, emphatically, that it was "just Tamils" (*Tamil maddum*). But then he moderated his response to say that Kannadigas increasingly come for the festival, and some might even carry the *kavadi*. He then said that Telugus also carry the *kavadi* sometimes.

What became clear to me after witnessing the festival and speaking with devotees was that, while Tamils still outnumbered non-Tamils at this event, there was a plural character that transcended mother tongue. Signs were visible in Kannada, as was literature about the temple. Priests spoke both languages fluently, if not many more (Telugu, Malayalam, etc.). Though it was clear that many Tamils perceived this deity and this shrine as signifying a Tamil space within the symbolic landscape of the city, it was impossible to mark it as exclusive.[1] And although Tamil ritualism might be reviving in response to the perceived assertiveness of the more strident aspects of the Kannada movement, this revivalism takes shape within shared idioms that resonate across the artificial and arbitrary boundaries of identities crafted through the magic of physical boundaries and censuses.

Enduring Civility?

How can we understand the sharpening linguistic and religious divides in Bangalore and, with them, the imagining of communities somehow separate and unique, serially bound, as neat as a census and map would have us believe (Anderson 1998)? As Ashis Nandy has observed for Cochin, an old cosmopolitanism or pluralism still exists within the city grounded in what he calls the "tacit memories." These are found, he argues, in "an identifiable, communicable, 'unconscious'" (2002, 170). How are these tacit memories produced? Nandy suggests that certain myths resonate in the public imagination of Cochinites as a result of a shared civic culture that involves, among other things, the capacity to incorporate the Other's myths as one's own. Serialization of identities, in Benedict Anderson's sense, as fostered by mass media and census taking, has not occurred there in a bounded sense, though, arguably, an unbound and inclusive serial imaginary for Cochin takes hold in collective myths of the city's history, if Nandy is right. Bangalore exists, perhaps, somewhere in between the pluralism of Nandy's Cochin and the communal separateness in parts of north India, Sri Lanka, and Pakistan that grew out of enumeration of communities through censuses and map/boundary making. On the one hand, the Deccan's crossroads continues to bear the marks of a shared repertoire of culture, religiosity, and multilingualism. Polylingual Vaishnavism, Saivism, urban *bhakti* across linguistic lines, iconographic forms and architecture, and a common film culture are just some of the expressive and aesthetic idioms that are shared across communities.[2] There are many others (music, poetry, arts, drama). While I have emphasized shared aesthetics, one could also point to a shared sense of historicity that was/is replicated in particular modes of narrativization (see Rao, Subrahmanyam, and Shulman 2003; Shulman 2016). In short, the very weight of culture—a shared ontology in Kapferer's terms—mitigates against the worst forms of othering that might occur.

On the other hand, the birth of Karnataka in 1956 created the conditions of linguistic insecurity for today's Kannada speakers in Bangalore. The creation of a linguistic state with a linguistic capital along the tristate border of Tamil Nadu, Karnataka, and Andhra Pradesh was bound for complications, given the demographic complexity of the region. But, as I have shown, the city itself was redrawn by state making. 1956 incorporated the whole of Bangalore into the state of Karnataka. Prior to this it was bifurcated between the Madras Presidency and Mysore State. Thus, for much of its recent history, it was not regarded as an exclusively Kannada-speaking city at all but rather a multilinguistic city lying at the crossroads of empires, states, and borderlands.

Theoretically, how might we understand the productive demand for ethnic and linguistic singularity? As I have argued, the demand can be understood in instrumental terms. That is, the political claim obviously produces and is produced out of differentials of power. There are two main concurrent and overlapping arguments in this study. A "softer" thesis, one might say, has been that modernization with its attendant stresses and serialized or homogenized forms of identity have a productive relationship. Serial forms, thus, are both symptom and cause of troubled identities as a result of social and cultural strain. Geertz has specifically argued, for instance, that ideologies grow out of a search for meaning within contexts of intellectual or cultural strain. In the register of linguistic, religious, and even mental health, the search for certitude was driven by the forces of "uncertainty" (Appadurai 2006) ushered in by social, cultural, and psychological stress factors. But a "stronger" thesis sits embedded within this, pointing to specific triggers and instances of serialized identity making that, in turn, seemingly demand a perpetual archive of difference figured as the wholly Other that threatens the integrity of the Self (Hansen 2001). That is, the Self is now increasingly tethered to the collective, serialized form of identity, as the basis for its very survival. Herein lies the pathological or violent potential of such identifications.

While I have suggested throughout this study that the instrumentalist and culturalist explanations are still relevant and must be conjoined, the explanations for the passionate and irrational exuberance of identity attachments require a turn to both psychology and phenomenology. What of the feverish and irrational compulsion to difference that often marks the politics of difference in postcolonial spaces? What accounts for this passion? Paradoxically, I believe that differences take hold in the imagination precisely in the face of an impossible or absurd demand that is partially recognized by people as such. What I mean is that the "arche-violence of the law" (Derrida 1995), or the arbitrary demand, is perceived by subjects as arbitrary, not as natural. The retroactive work of naturalization is the product of an ethnographic "archive fever" (Derrida 1995). Dirks (2002) describes how modern statecraft, under these absurd conditions of effacing history and cultural sharing that have existed for centuries, is productive of a kind of "ethnographic state"; that is, in turn, endlessly obsessed with marking cultural, linguistic, and religious boundaries against the grain of culture and history. Grounding itself in conventions—or what I have called, following Anderson, serialized forms—provides an aura of retroactive historicity to the violence of the law and state. But, in circular fashion, it is in fact the more absurd demands for separation and difference that most threaten civility, as we have witnessed in Bosnia, Rwanda, and elsewhere. The postcolonial state, in short, requires a continuous source of exteriority through which to ground its authority and its decisions. The ethnographic archive of the state—an archive of difference—thus supplements and grounds an untenable ideology of ethnic or religious exclusivity out of a more porous past. Indeed, the excess of identification that often occurs where ideology appears most absurd and untenable suggests that the tenacious hold of ethnic and religious boundaries is contingent upon both the "irruptive violence" of the state and law—or what the Comaroffs (2009) have called "lawfare"—and of its supplement in the form of the archiving of difference.[3] Separation of types, in this case Tamils and Kannadigas or Hindus and Muslims, is not easy—indeed, it becomes absurd, and hence it is a dangerous political game. But even this deconstructive formulation offers a ray of hope. The law is ultimately deconstructible, as the archive that sustains its legitimacy becomes more spectral as it grows in authority and ubiquity. Justice and civility exceed the juridical.

Put in the terms of this study, the emergence of a linguistic and ethnic identification provides for an impossible demand upon the plurality of life in Bangalore. Genealogy and memory are contradicted by the demands of the state. But an ethnographic and historic archive reworks the historiography of the region, as conjoined to a political imperative. Kannadiga, Tamil, or Hindu chauvinism becomes plausible only in the face of its untenable narrative, given the rich pluralism of Bangalore's past and present.

The pluralism, again, is paradoxically generative of the chauvinism; and concomitantly, the chauvinism takes hold in the impossibility of its claim, as conjoined to the legalism of which it is generative. But for every claim of singularity, as buffeted by ethnographic and historiographic claims (the feverish archive of past empires, etc.), a counter is conjured. Further, the more absurd demands seem to emerge from specific political stakeholders and not from some sort of clash of cultural ontologies. As Nagaraj has argued, fear-centered nationalism comes from a particular source of ideology, but it can also, once institutionalized, lead to changing political subjectivities that exceed authorship. Under times of psychosocial or intellectual stress, these ideologies can take hold of larger segments of a population, producing xenophobic tendencies and the conjuring of threatening others.

The Murugan temple discussed here can never be exclusively Tamil, however much some Tamils imagine it to be so. For every example, the incorporation of the Other is also possible. In this sense, Nandy's thesis of incorporation and multiplicity, rather than communal identification, thankfully rings partially true for Bangalore as well, despite the sometimes polarizing trends in recent years. Even that most potent symbol of Kannadiga identity, Kempegowda, conjures the specter of his possible Thigala and Tamil-Kannadiga mixed ancestry. In viewing the city and region through the *longue durée,* a modality of cultural flow has miti-gated and continues to mitigate against the total serialization of modern identities. The same principle, we saw, held true for Hindu-Muslim boundaries. Though the events surrounding Ayodhya drove a wedge between communities, we witnessed Muslim participation in Hindu rituals and Hindu devotion at Sufi shrines. This, as Ann Gold (2014) suggests, is not just civility and toleration but the "sweetness and light" that continues to pervade daily life in contemporary India. Here the imagined primordial identity is, perhaps ironically, a deeply structured ontol-ogy (Kapferer 1988) or "landscape of memory" that binds not only Tamils and Kannadigas but also Hindus and Muslims. Civility not only remains possible but, thankfully, probable to continue given the force of culture and history against the force of law. But this civility is never guaranteed. The very same pluralism that mitigates against monocultural fantasies can also become its source through the irruptive violence of the law and statecraft. Thus, 1956 did set in motion the forces that frayed multiple and fluid identities through legal enactments conflating emergent geographies and linguistic space. Therefore, we can see that Bangalore is a good case to think through the problems of civility and difference. Here was wit-nessed both the violence of the law and the underlying civility that deconstructs it.

Glossary and Abbreviations

agraharam a Brahmin community
agraharas large joint houses where the temple Brahmins and their families live
AIADMK All-India-Anna Dravida Munnetra Kazhagam
arati waving of the flame before the deity
bandh general strike
BDA Bangalore Development Authority
bhajans devotional songs
bhakti devotion
BJP Bharatiya Janata Party
Bumiputra son of the soil
CBT cognitive behavioral therapy
dargah shrine associated with saints
darshan visual blessing; viewing or being viewed by the deity, sacred abode, or
  holy personage
devaram sacred hymns sung in Tamil
DMK Dravida Munnetra Kazhagam (Progressive Dravidian Federation)
gopuram temple gateway tower
HAL Hindustan Aeronautics Limited (industrial township in Bangalore)
Hindutva Hindu nationalism
Kannadigas Kannada speakers
Karaga Jatre an important Hindu festival honoring the goddess Draupadi
kavadi pole and arch carried on the back honoring Lord Murugan
linga aniconic symbol for Shiva
LTTE Liberation Tigers of Tamil Eelam (Sri Lanka)
Malayalis Malayalam-speaking inhabitants of the Malabar Coast of India
masjid mosque, Muslim place of worship
melas festivals
Mewaris Rajasthani merchants
moksha spiritual liberation

namaskaram reverential folding of hands in front of the chest or above the
 head
Nayanmars Tamil Saivite saints
NIMHANS National Institute of Mental Health and Neuro Sciences
OPD outpatient department
panchayat village council
pongal the Harvest Festival
puja act of worship, daily devotion
Rajyosatva Day Karnataka Statehood Day (or "reunification day")
RKM Ramakrishna Mission
RSS Rashtriya Swamisevak Sangh
sadhus wandering ascetics
samsara cycle of rebirth
VHP Vishwa Hindu Parishad
yatras processions

Notes

Introduction

1. I am inspired here by Deleuze and Guatarri's notion of "bodies without organs" and "rhizomes" that intersect and in a myriad of ways not predetermined by the homogenizing demand of mimesis, or what Anderson calls "serialization." Difference, to Deleuze, comprises more than a dyad that structures within an overarching linguistic structure of interaction but, instead, is the condition that allows unpredictable innovation and creativity.

2. While the synchronic and functional analysis of tribal societies did much to dispel Hobbesian myths of the "primitive," the societies studied were presented largely without history or agency (Wolf 1982). Also, the influence of Durkheim's ideological shadow upon these scholars meant that *consensus* was the norm of social life, whereas *conflict* was conspicuously absent in their anthropological accounts. Moreover, the placement of these societies within emerging nation-states was also given scant attention.

3. Bailey's model of action did not assume that all actors are motivated by a calculative rationality, though there were what he termed "political entrepreneurs" who pursued individual interests. It was these entrepreneurs, though not always economically motivated, who were the engines of social change at the village level.

4. To Dumont, the emergence of ideological contestation within Indian nationalism—to the extent that it posed challenges to the traditional caste-based hierarchy integral to the Hindu social structure—was a perversion of the cultural logic and ordering of Indian social life. It was the import of egalitarian ideas brought in through adopted models of the nation-state that produced communalism, separatism, and nationalist violence.

5. By focusing upon the structuring of difference, Barth offered a critique of the holistic continuity and seamless quality of cultural difference presented by Dumont. If the standardization of differences between groups results from an interaction between groups, the production of conventionalized ideologies occurs through the give and take of politics and economics within a social field.

6. Demarcations of ethnic difference were part of the British colonial policy or "indirect rule" in Africa. Ethnic groupings gathered salience under colonial rule because cleavages, perhaps already present, were widened along "tribal" or ethnic lines. Moreover, the boundaries between these lines were drawn within a political field that benefited from internal ethnic or tribal divisions. In India, for example, the jockeying between the Indian National Congress and the Muslim League for political rights occurred while the British were attempting to negotiate both a withdrawal from India and the formation of an Indian constitution. Similarly, in Malaya, the hardening of ethnic lines between Malays, Chinese, and Indians occurred in

part as a response to British legislation aimed at creating citizenship rights and privileges in a postindependence Malaya (Harper 1999).

7. Ultimately, the functionalism of Talcott Parsons finds its way into Geertz's formulation—that is, new structures of meaning must evolve gradually in order to coincide with the structural needs within modernizing states. Also, some Marxists accused Geertz of reifying the cultural constructs of elites, and thus his sense of power was "anemic" (e.g., Asad 1993).

8. While he agreed that nationalism is a particular construct produced through the structural apparatus of the state, Kapferer argued that the passions aroused by the deployment of nationalist ideologies could best be understood by locating the "cultural logic" that organized personality, culture, and practice within particular societies. Moreover, nationalism crystallized or encapsulated an ontology and gains its hegemony through its ability to make sense to a number of people.

9. Whereas Geertz employed a semiotic, phenomenological premise derived from Weber and Schutz when he viewed culture as an acted text (Daniel 1984), continuously being spun, habituated, and reinterpreted by social actors, Kapferer's model was inspired by French structuralist and poststructuralist theories. From structuralism, the ontology of a symbolic system establishes its *underlying principles*—its "logic" or code—which are generative of a social order born of its unique grammar. From this perspective, "Cultures are primarily systems of classification, as well as the sets of institutional and intellectual productions built upon those systems of classification and performing further operations upon them" (Ortner 1994, 380).

10. From poststructuralism, Gramsci, and Weber, Kapferer was interested in demonstrating the dialectic of action and structure in the production of particular arrangements of power and domination, with their sometimes violent consequences. Ontologies become hegemonic, in Gramsci's sense, through everyday social practices—they involve the "whole social process," or a dialectic between their material "base" and ideological "superstructure" (Femia 1987). From Bourdieu, Kapferer was interested in how ideologies (and ontologies) reproduce themselves through the agency of human actions shaped by structures of power.

11. The nation-state, according to origin myths, is encompassed by the kingship, which in turn is entrusted to uphold and submit to Buddhism: "In this unity of the whole is the integrity of the parts. Thus the nation or the people who compose a hierarchically interrelated social order discover their unity in the power of the state" (Kapferer 1988, 12). The logic of hierarchy, while a useful tool for the political elite through nationalist ideologies, was not "the constructive artifice of the dominant"—instances of the "big fix. . . . Nationalist ideologies, like many of the social theories that are engaged to fathom the world, *operate at depth*" (19, emphasis added).

12. To underscore his ontological argument, Kapferer employed the comparative method. In an analysis of racism in contemporary Australia, Kapferer argued that the egalitarian ideology of the nation was built upon the principle of "sameness." The individual must replicate the whole—and the whole must be the individual writ large. By this principle, if those not sharing the "egalitarian" premise (e.g., "Asians") are admitted into the state, the egalitarian ethos will be destroyed: "Nations must multiply likeness, not difference, otherwise national identity is weakened" (1988, 191). "Difference" is feared in Australia because the egalitarian ethos operates "at depth" as an ontology of self.

13. A useful starting point, prior to a consideration of anthropological usages, might be with Marx's and Engels's seminal statement in *The German Ideology*: "The class which has the

means of material production at its disposal, has control at the same time over the means of mental production, so that thereby, generally speaking, the ideas of those who lack the means of mental production are subject to it" (Marx and Engels 1947, 64).

14. He did so by describing religion as a system of symbols constitutive of "moods" and "motivations" that are "made meaningful" (Geertz 1973, qtd. in Asad 1993, 33). Such a formulation was too simplistic, Asad suggested, because it gives motivational weight and agency to the symbols themselves, failing to note the role that power plays in creating various truths.

In a discussion of British liberalism, "diversity," Asad argued, was to be tolerated so long as it did not critique the "core" (i.e., the elite) values of the nation. Therefore, diversity must remain "necessarily external" (1993, 246) to the national identity—that is, as a subordinate "tradition" being accommodated by a myth of liberal integration and universal "tolerance."

The liberal discourse of the British nation presupposed "equal respect for all cultures, but the realities of political power require the subordinate (less progressive) to adjust to the dominant (more progressive)" (1993, 252). This was the cultural policy administered in the colonies (see also Handler and Segal 1992) and became the ideology of British nationalism vis-à-vis the growing immigrant populations derived from the ex-colonies. Asad argued that the threat felt by the British liberal elite concerned the placement of different "cultures" in a subordinate position to that of the "progressive" and secular liberal humanism. We will find this point relevant when we look later at critiques of Indian secularism by academics, agitators, and activists.

15. Immanuel Wallerstein cast a large shadow upon Marxist anthropologists (Marcus and Fischer 1986; Ortner 1994). In his analysis of "core," "periphery," and "semiperiphery" sectors within the world economy, Wallerstein, following the lead of Andre Gunder Frank, argued that underdevelopment, rather than representing an earlier phase in sociocultural evolution, was systematically produced in the "periphery" with the emergence of a global economy and division of labor in the last four centuries (see also Wolf 1982). Wallerstein's analysis of ethnonationalist movements and of nationalism in general was consistent with the macro dictates of the world-systems model he proposed. Like Gellner (1983), Wallerstein argued that nationalism is invented for the purposes of political integration and to facilitate the workings of a capitalist—particularly industrialist—mode of production. Nationalism, Gellner suggested, functioned not only to enable the degree of standardization required for an industrialized economy but also mitigated against the psychosocial strains produced by modernization. That is, the acute suffering and increase in stratification initially produced by industrial capitalism would be assuaged by the new sense of horizontal solidarity fostered by the "self-deception" (50) of nationalism. Therefore, nationalism solidified the state politically by bringing disparate groups under a common loyalty.

16. Moreover, the threat to the bourgeois in the core countries was addressed through an expansion in the proletariat's purchasing power as a result of the expansion of the global economy engendered by colonialism. Ultimately, Wallerstein's perspective was avowedly instrumentalist: ethnicity and nationalism represent avenues for gaining or sustaining economic privileges for the exploiters and exploited alike.

17. Wallerstein inspired anthropologists to study the impact of the world economy upon local communities (e.g., Taussig 1980; Nash 1979; Ong 1987; Wolf 1982; Scott 1985; Marcus and Fischer 1986, 81). There were also critical voices, finding in the economically deterministic model an elision of the centrality and variation culture in human life (e.g., Sahlins 1994; Ortner 1994). To the latter, it was anthropology's role to note how modernity was "indigenized"

through particular cultural logics; whereas to the former, anthropology was, as Hobsbawm had indicated, a key player in unmasking the "invented" traditions from the "real."

18. Perhaps one of the most influential studies of local resistance to both capitalism and the nationalist politics and patronage that allow for its penetration into local communities was James Scott's *Weapons of the Weak* (1985). In this important work, the utility of a fieldwork-derived perspective was demonstrated through an analysis of "everyday forms" of resistance— of the variety that would go unnoticed by a purely historical or structural analysis of political economy. What emerged was a picture of peasant life in Malaysia that challenged notions of complete ideological domination. Scott's social actors were not passive recipients of "false consciousness." Rather, they, the landless farmers, actively resisted the policies of the government's "green revolution"—and its marginalizing effects upon tenant farmers—to the extent that they were able to do so. While some might find in his analysis a romanticizing of peasant agency, his study served as a useful corrective (or necessary complement) to overly deterministic and culturally insensitive models of political economy within the world system.

19. Arjun Appadurai, "Dead Certainty: Ethnic Violence in the Era of Globalization," in Meyer and Geschierre, eds., *Globalization and Identity* (London: Blackwell, 2000), pp. 305–324.

20. Slavoj Zizek, "Enjoy Your Nation as Yourself!" in *Tarrying with the Negative* (Durham, NC: Duke University Press, 1993), pp. 200–237.

21. While Chatterjee himself analyzed the fissures and "fragments" within the nation-state and, particularly, to the privileging of certain ideologies over others in the constitution of post-colonial social and cultural hierarchies within the public sphere, he was more ambivalent in his critique of the postcolonial nationalist imagination than he was in unmasking the ideological work done under colonial rule.

22. Sahlins's critique is outlined in two articles: "Cosmologies of Capitalism," in Dirks, Eley, and Ortner, *Culture/Power/History: A Reader in Contemporary Social Theory* (Princeton, NJ: Princeton University Press, 1994), pp. 412–455, and "Goodbye to Tristes Tropes: Ethnography in the Context of Modern World History," *Journal of Modern History* 65 (March 1993), pp. 1–25.

23. Sahlins, while in sympathy with scholars who analyze the deleterious social and economic impact of colonialism and capitalism and the erasures of indigenous social, political, and economic sovereignty in every section of the globe, argued that anthropologists and other cultural analysts should pay greater heed to the creative and resilient ways in which modernity is indigenized by distinct cultural logics. That is, he wished to avoid reducing cultural responses to modernity's acknowledged impact to a reflex of structural domination or the ethnographic and hence "double erasure" of cultural difference.

24. The risk of critique that Sahlins identified must be acknowledged. At the same time, however, there is a risk of valorizing the normative, given what it potentially obscures or silences. Perhaps, albeit in a more sophisticated way, Sahlins's analysis of distinct cultural logics possibly silences the anxieties and doubts that are not to be found directly in the cultural or symbolic order but in the gaps and silences that this order attempts to mask. This is precisely the argument that Gananath Obeyesekere makes regarding Sahlins's reading of cultural texts. See Obeyesekere, *The Apotheosis of Captain Cook: European Mythmaking in the Pacific*, 2nd ed. (Princeton, NJ: Princeton University Press, 1997). For Sahlins's response, see *How 'Natives' Think: About Captain Cook, for Example* (Chicago: University of Chicago Press, 1996).

25. At the same time, this is precisely what is being suggested, both rhetorically and methodologically, through a cataloguing of symptoms; and in the case of ethnographic writing,

through analysis of public discourse, private narrative, life history, historical archive, aesthetics, and participant observation, with all its potential for transferential relationships with one's subjects of study—that is, methods that are not uncommonly deployed by Freud himself in his voluminous writings. The intersubjectivity achieved through transference was believed by Freud to be a necessary stage in unlocking the patient's symptom. Obeyesekere (1991), in an essay comparing ethnographic practice with psychoanalysis, suggests that the two meet in their respective reliance upon transference and intersubjectivity that is obtained through it.

26. Zizek (1993) argued that those Nazis most implicated in heinous crimes during the holocaust were oftentimes those who had some degree of Jewish ancestry within their family lineage. According to Zizek, it was not so much a display of hatred and cruelty orchestrated to deflect suspicions of Jewishness but an excessive identification with the "Jew" representing the monstrous double within.

27. Liisa Malkki's terrifying book, *Purity in Exile* (1995), examined the profound uncertainty regarding ethnic boundaries and the haunting effect this had upon those who were asked to categorically demonize—and even kill—the ethnic Other (see Appadurai 2000 for an illuminating analysis of Malkki). Though Malkki did not utilize psychoanalytic theory, one can see in her ethnography ways in which her data supported the argument being forwarded here. The partial recognition of an official ethnonationalist identity's impossible closure—particularly where previously permeable and porous boundaries existed, as was the case between Hutus and Tutsis—produced terrible uncertainty about the Other within, the now-demonized presence within oneself.

28. The risk in psychoanalytic usage of creating a coherent structure that provides a lexicon from which diagnosis and cure are effected is particularly contagious, threatening to flatten difference within a machine/body with organs (Deleuze and Guattari 1987) or "regime of truth" (Foucault 1980). The risk of calling forth the symptom that it acts to diagnose is a recurrent problem, and one that Freud was well aware of given the transferential space between therapist and patient. Modern diagnostic categories oftentimes create the very somaticization they purport to describe (e.g., post-traumatic stress disorder, hysteria, chronic fatigue syndrome, etc.). Countertransference can occur within the archon's ethnographic practice (Derrida 1995), just as it can occur within the psychoanalytic encounter. Moreover, separating the normative evaluation from the diagnostic procedure has proven vexing, as Foucault and others have suggested.

29. Perhaps this is why Lacan states that "*desire is a metonymy, however funny people find this idea*" (1977, 175).

30. This phenomenological reading of the public sphere suggests that, to again deploy Anderson's ubiquitous "imagined communities" concept, the "imagined" dimension of public life betrays desires that resonate in a public imaginary and that in turn are generated by and achieve partial yet unstable resolution in a symbolic order. But lest the reader assume that the "culture and personality" school is being resurrected here—that "secondary institutions" (religion, expressive culture, myth, etc.) in the public realm are projective screens generated by "primary institutions" (family matrix, kinship, socialization practices, etc.)—as in the Freudian thought of Abraham Kardiner, Melford Spiro, Claude Devereux, Margaret Mead, and others, it is important to clarify that I am also pointing to *relations of power*, domination, and ideological distinction—that is, reasserting Marxian/Hegelian dialectics into the psychoanalytic read of the fractured subject (Sangren 2000).

31. On this point, see especially Siegel (2006).

Chapter 2: Bangalore in History

1. The city became officially known as Bengaluru, the Kannada spelling and pronunciation, in 2007. As most residents still call it Bangalore, I will follow suit.

2. There were many other smaller kingdoms vying for supremacy in the Bangalore region. The Kadambas and Gangas (both in the central and northern Deccan) were also of great importance (Thapar 1966).

3. Rama and Krishna are the most famous incarnations or avatars of Vishnu. Most Vaishnava temples in Karnataka, however, were built for Vishnu or Krishna.

4. As early as the sixth century, Tamil Vaishnava poetry spread into Kannada-speaking areas through the influence of the Alvars—Tamil-speaking *bhaktas* who, like their Nayanmar counterparts, preached of egalitarianism and personal devotion (Ramanujam 1993).

5. Legend has it that the city was originally a village named Bengaluru—the "town of boiled beans"—after a Hoysala king was offered boiled beans by an old woman when he visited her village while on a hunting exhibition. It is believed that Kempegowda founded the city upon the site of that village. Another legend that attempts to sacralize the city of Bangalore has Kempegowda's original fort collapsing several times. Kempegowda is said to have consulted priests who told him that a pregnant woman had to be sacrificed for the fort to stand. While Kempegowda was horrified by their suggestion, his daughter-in-law decided on her own to secretly sacrifice herself to the goddess by slitting her own throat. Upon hearing the news, Kempegowda was much grieved and ordered the construction of a goddess temple in her honor. The fort, evidently, did not fall again. The temple in turn, became a popular site for prayers (Venkatarayappa 1957).

6. There is some evidence of forced conversions within his capital, as well as during his attacks and conquest of the Coorg region. See Phillip B. Wagoner, "Tipu Sultan's Search for Legitimacy: Islam and Kingship in a Hindu Domain," review by Kate Brittlebank, *Journal of Asian Studies* 58: 2 (May 1999), pp. 541–543.

7. Hyder Ali planned and built the still-existing Lal Bagh, a famous botanical garden within the heart of the old city, as well as rebuilding Bangalore's old fort.

8. The village was named Nagarvalpalya. The area was also surrounded by Defence Department lands, particularly land controlled by Hindustan Aeronautics Limited (HAL). An entire township for HAL employees and families had predated the rise of the IT industry and the dramatic growth of these middle-class enclaves being described here (Heitzman 2004; Nair 2005).

9. The eastern side of the city has a very high proportion of Tamilians.

10. Viewing or being viewed by the deity, sacred abode, or holy personage. The act of *darshan* bestows grace upon the devotee (Eck 1981).

11. The Ramakrishna Mission and Self-Realization Fellowship, known locally as the Yoga Satsanga Society of India, were also popular local movements with nearby branches in Ulsoor and Indira Nagar, respectively.

Chapter 3: Rajkumar's Abduction and a Dispute over Water

1. The Sangam is the leading Tamil organization in Bangalore dedicated to promoting its language, literature, and fine arts. The Sangam has become increasingly politicized in response to the various pro-Kannada movements' anti-Tamil sentiments.

2. The Cantonment was closer to the border of the Madras Presidency, but the Mysore State's boundaries encompassed it.

3. These numbers vary from census to census. According to a recent book by A. Ravindra (2012), Kannada speakers comprise 31 percent of the population, followed by Tamils at 27 percent. Telugu, at 17 percent, is the third most-spoken language in the city. Though the numbers vary in different census accounts, all confirm the truly multilingual reality of Bangalore.

4. Exactly one year later, violence again erupted in Bangalore, this time over the Ayodhya controversy. My fieldwork in Bangalore took place between July 1992 and February 1993, again briefly in 1995, 2003, 2005, 2008, 2009, 2010, and twelve months between September 2014 and September 2015.

5. The *kavadi* is a pole and arch that is carried upon the back of the devotee in order to honor Lord Murugan, the son of Shiva, and an ancient Tamil deity (Hart 1975). It is associated with an act of penance performed by the demon-devotee, Idumban, after he had unwittingly insulted the Lord (Clothey 1978). The *kavadi* can be quite simple or complex and ornate. Moreover, the carrying of the *kavadi* is often accompanied by simultaneous acts of self-mortification. In some cases, the *kavadi* is attached to the flesh of the devotee through sharp spikes (Willford 2006).

6. The popular film icon Rajkumar was a leader in the Kannada revival movement. He presided over rallies demanding that Kannada be made the compulsory language for all administrative jobs in Karnataka. His roles in movies often cast him as a Hoysala or Vijayanagara hero—potent symbols of Karnataka nationalism and pride. In this sense, he was the Kannada counterpart to MGR (M. G. Ramachandran), the Tamil film star turned politician, who often portrayed Chola or Pandyan heroes.

7. The Indian People's Human Rights Commission (IPHRC) was formed in 1987, consisting of human rights activists, academics, and lawyers from different parts of India. The IPHRC has organized the Indian People's Human Rights Tribunal, which consists of ex-judges of the supreme and high courts of India. Both are based in Bombay. The commission takes up cases in which there are suspected significant violations of human rights by the state. They gather evidence and publish reports on such cases.

8. Numerous atrocities are chronicled that contain anecdotal evidence combined with selective media reports in this pamphlet. But it is impossible to verify their numbers against the nonpartisan IPHRC's own detailed report.

9. Of the total estimated loss of 170,119,002 rupees in damages, the governments of Tamil Nadu and Karnataka paid to the victims compensation of only 2,246,810 rupees (IPHRC 1992, 75).

10. For example, there were reports in the media that Bangarappa had granted lucrative liquor licenses to political supporters while simultaneously preaching temperance to Kannadigas. Also, he was accused of living opulently at the expense of state taxpayers.

11. The Dravida Munnetra Kazhagam (Progressive Dravidian Federation) was formed on an openly secessionist, anti-Hindi, anti-Aryan platform. Since first capturing power in 1967, the party has softened its opposition to the federal government. The party was at the time of this writing holding power in Tamil Nadu under the leadership of M. Karunanidhi. Karunanidhi's rivalry within the party with MGR led the latter to form the breakaway All-India-Anna Dravida Munnetra Kazhagam in 1972. Both parties claim to carry on the legacy of the Tamil movement, but the AIADMK also claims greater loyalty to India. Both parties have alternated rule in Tamil Nadu for the last thirty years. In fact, both parties have participated in national and mostly

Congress-led coalitions. At the time of these events, Jayalalitha, the leader of the AIADMK, was in power. In 1997, however, the DMK returned to power and Karunanidhi assumed the position of chief minister.

12. These are temporary cinemas that are housed in tents.

13. Thiruvalluvar was the author of the *Tirrukural*, a classic Tamil religious and moral text.

14. There are, however, numerous statues of Wodeyar rajas—the patrons of Kannada arts and culture in the Mysore State since AD 1399—as well as statues of Kempegowda I, the purported founder of the city.

15. Interestingly, she is not a Tamil-born Indian herself. It is said that she is a Kannadiga-Brahmin. She did, however, become a Tamil film icon, starring opposite MGR many times, with whom she is said to have had a long-standing affair.

16. This figure is also disputed. As reported in *India Today*, the Karnataka government claims that only 17,700 were forced to flee to Tamil Nadu. The rest, they claim, simply went home for *pongal*—the Harvest Festival.

17. Usually done secretly, these posters are pasted upon walls and poles in public places. This is a common form of political advertising in India, though often illegal. No one would dare display a poster in front of a private residence or shop, fearing the reprisals of pro-Kannada groups.

Chapter 4: The Kannada Movement and Tamil Revival

1. It is sometimes referred to as the "Gokok Agitation" after a report issued by a minister of that name suggested that Christian Kannadigas were discriminated against in churches dominated by Tamils (Nair 2005). Gokak argued that Kannada should replace Tamil as the language of worship. This report stirred other Kannadigas to make more general observations about the status of Kannada in public spheres in Bangalore.

2. He is referring to the suicides that followed the death of MGR, a film icon and Tamil Nadu's chief minister.

3. On this point see Kakar (1981, 1982), who argues, following psychoanalytic theory, that the personality structure of most Indians emphasizes a "narcissistic" relationship with an idealized figure who serves as a parental surrogate. This surrogate represents a desire to overcome the lack inherent within the parent-child relationship and establishes a fantasy image through which the self is aggrandized. As Kakar argues, the grandiose valorization of gurus and political leaders in turn enhances the individual's sense of worth through a complete identification. This disposition is supported by religious ideals of *bhakti*, or unlimited devotion, as a means of spiritual progress.

4. Andhra Pradesh and parts of Kerala were also part of the Madras Presidency prior to the creation of linguistic states.

5. On this point, see D. R. Nagaraj (2009). Nagaraj critiques the nationalistic thought produced by some Kannadiga writers organized around a purported ancient humiliation of Kannadigas at the hands of Tamils. This fear-based nationalism, to Nagaraj, is divisive and produces a need for enemies in order to sustain it, hence sparking a cycle of violence and victimization. I return to Nagaraj's point towards the end of this study.

6. Ironically, I heard that Rajkumar lived in a big house in Madras and only traveled to Bangalore to make pro-Kannada speeches or to accept awards from different Kannada arts

associations. Later, Rajkumar did move to Bangalore as his politics became more strident and pro-Kannadiga (Nair 2005).

7. This is an imagined age in the sense that the Vijayanagara Empire, though vast, was more linguistically and ethnically complex than the Kannada movement would have it. The same holds true for the Cholas (Sastri 1945; Stein 1994).

8. It was suggested to me that these motifs and arches were inspired by the epic films of Rajkumar and MGR, respectively, rather than necessarily representing accurate historical depictions of architectural style. In that sense, their film versions were "hyperreal," in Baudrillard's (1981) sense.

9. Bangarappa's pro-Kannada posturing could not save him in the end, as scandals and a perception of widespread corruption eventually led to his resignation in December 1992. Congress I Party leaders (his party) asked him to step down for the "best interests of the State and Party."

10. On this point, but focusing on the role of nationalist literature in Karnataka, see D. R. Nagaraj (2009, 37–38).

11. Some Kannadigas in Bangalore use this term to refer to their community as the legitimate "sons of the soil" in Karnataka.

12. She was a famous British Theosophist and activist in the Indian nationalist movement. Between 1910 and 1920, Besant's movement was active in Madras, where she befriended a number of Tamil Brahmins. Her pan-Indian and pan-Hindu sentiments were perceived by Tamil non-Brahmins as pro-Brahmin. The Justice Party, a non-Brahmin party opposed to her brand of Sanskritically imagined Indian nationalism, arose and gained momentum in opposition to her activities in the "Home Rule" movement: "The *Dravidian* printed headlines like 'Home Rule is Brahmana's Rule.' Pamphlets appeared questioning her integrity and that of her Brahman colleagues. . . . She refused to introduce interdining in the organization she sponsored because she regarded the Sudras as mere 'younger brothers'" (Irschick 1969, 51).

13. Many Tamils, of course, mark the beginning of resistance to Aryan hegemony in the south with the rise of Saivite *bhakti* movements between the sixth and ninth centuries. They cite the sometimes explicit rejection of caste distinctions by the Nayanmars (Tamil Saivite saints).

14. In Tamil Nadu today he is simply known by the honorific title "Periyar" ("great man"). He is famous for his agnostic views and for saying, "He who created God is a fool, he who propagates God is a scoundrel, and he who worships God is a barbarian" (quoted in Ryerson 1988, 91).

15. Subramania Bharati, Bharatidasan, Maraimalai Adigal, and even the former chief minister, Karunanidhi, wrote poetry, novels, and film scripts that glorified Tamil and critiqued social injustices suffered by the downtrodden—often at the hands of Brahmins.

16. In contrast, I was told that Madras, the capital of Tamil Nadu, did not have a particularly strong pure Tamil movement at that time. In spite of the man's claim, I found that the movement has less salience in Malaysia, where there is very little Brahmin presence. The literature associated with the movement is popular among Malaysian Tamils; the political threat, however, is perceived to come mainly from Islam, not Brahminical Hinduism. At the same time, the lack of success among the ashram-based movements among the working class is, I have argued, partly due to a consciousness of their Brahminical and hence elite orientation and control (Willford 2006).

17. A famous saint and founder of a school of Vedantic philosophy.

18. Jainism is a religion, like Buddhism, that does not revere the Vedas.

19. The story of Ramanuja and the Hoysala king notwithstanding, Lal (1986) suggests that many settled in Bangalore during Vijayanagara times.

20. Once when speaking to a Tamil Iyengar, she told me that I should first "study Sanskrit, the Mother of the Tamil language," in order to better understand Tamil. Later, when telling of her comments to my Tamil tutor—a non-Brahmin—he remarked, "only Brahmins believe that Tamil is Sanskrit derived."

21. The Saiva Brahmins, known as Iyers, did not escape criticism of the Tamil movement. But the harshest criticism was leveled against the Vaishanavas, due in part to a perception that the *Ramayana* was an anti-Tamil text.

22. These impressions were recorded in the year following the Cauvery riots, 1992.

23. A popular dish in Karnataka, but less so in Tamil Nadu, except among *adivasis* in the Nilgiris.

24. The yellow chord or *thali* is the string that all married Hindu women wear. The string usually has a gold pendant that signifies the union of the couple. Tamil women were thought to wear the yellow (*manjal*) string in a particular way that could identify them as Tamils.

25. This dispute and riot is discussed in the next section.

26. The Tamil newspaper *Thina Thanthi*—a pro-DMK paper that originated in Tamil Nadu—had a local branch in Bangalore. I was told that the popularity of the newspaper among Tamils was increasing in recent years, particularly after the Cauvery riots. I was also informed that its Bangalore office had been vandalized and threatened by extremist pro-Kannada groups.

27. While in Kuppam in Andhra Pradesh, about two hours from Bangalore by train, I met a Tamil writer who spoke of the latent power of the Tamil communities in Southern Karnataka, particularly in Bangalore. He said that once the Tamils "had united" and "pushed back" against the perceived discrimination, the Kannadigas would cease with their belligerence towards Tamils. Here, similar to the sentiments expressed earlier, courage and bravery were all that was needed to raise the Tamils out of their cowed status.

28. Many Muslims were drawn to the Tamil movement due to a shared opposition to Brahminical Hinduism. Also, the Sangam age is imagined by ideologues, though not by scholars (Hart 1975, 1979), to have been a caste-free, aniconic, and monotheistic society—a culture and society that is congruent with the teachings of Islam.

29. This is the perception of many Tamils and Kannadigas I spoke with in Bangalore, although there is no statistical data that I know of to validate it. It is, however, socially relevant that this is the case.

30. Two of the accomplices were eventually tracked down in Bangalore, where they committed suicide before being captured. The police, together with special agents from New Delhi, questioned members of the Tamil Sangam, but no charges were ever filed.

31. This seems to be happening in the other economic juggernaut, Mumbai, as well. Tamils, Bangladeshis, and Muslims, in general, have been popular targets for extremist political leaders. Most notoriously, the Shiv Sena, or Shiva's Army, under the leadership of Bal Thackery, argued that Mumbai's problems were due to the increasing presence of these groups in the city (Hansen 2001).

Chapter 5: "What? Legitimacy? Just Use Vivekananda in the Name of the Movement"

Author's note: I thank Dr. Sudha Sreenivas for suggesting this title. Originally from a paper I delivered at UC Berkeley in 1993, I have edited it to fit within this section of the chapter. She encountered this comment in an Internet chat room dedicated to a discussion of the Hindu revivalism in India and abroad.

1. One might also put Subhas Chandra Bose and Dr. Ambedkar in this category of revered modern Indians. Ambedkar, however, renounced Hinduism and converted to Buddhism.

2. In any shop selling prints of the gods, one will find his print, that of Ramakrishna, and that of Satya Sai Baba, the most popular contemporary gurus in the Hindu world (Srinivas 2015). I found this to be true in Madras, Bangalore, Kuala Lumpur, and Singapore. To see the influence of Vivekananda's thought in Malaysia, see Willford (2006).

3. While I only report here about India and the United States, the centenary was also marked by celebrations in Malaysia, Singapore, Fiji, and the UK, among other places.

4. The links between the two organizations are described in *The Brotherhood in Saffron*, by Anderson and Damle (1987).

5. This is the government-controlled national television network.

6. The *Deccan Herald* was and remains the most popular English-language newspaper in Karnataka.

7. The *Hindu* was and is the most popular English-language paper in Tamil Nadu. They have branch offices in other major cities in the south, including Bangalore.

8. Aurobindo was, like Bose, a Bengali Indian nationalist who, early in his career, advocated armed resistance to British rule. Later, however, after going into exile in the French-controlled Pondicherry, he became an "otherworldly" mystic and philosopher—and in so doing, became one of India's most famous religious teachers in this century.

9. Sarvarkar was the founder of the Hindu Mahasabha, and Golwalker was an important RSS leader.

10. The Ramakrishna Mission, the organization founded by Vivekananda, did not align itself with any political party trying to capitalize on the centenary celebrations. It supported the Parikrama, as did the RSS and VHP, but it also expressed no open hostility to the Congress I usurpation of it.

11. Comparatively speaking, this is not unlike the Malaysian government's efforts at promoting "true" and progressive Islam to fight both "Western decadence" and the "backward" Islam propagated by Islamic opposition parties (Willford 2006).

12. Tamil Nadu has a low rate of Hindi literacy due mainly to the DMK's anti-Hindi agitations and legislation.

13. The RSS and VHP were banned after the destruction of the Babri Masjid in Ayodhya, since it was determined that the two organizations had encouraged the act that triggered communal rioting. The ban was lifted several months later.

14. The mainstream media had, for the most part, also blamed the BJP and allied organizations for the escalating religious tension.

15. Sister Nivedita was one of Vivekananda's most important disciples. This Irish-born woman was to play an important role in the Swadeshi movement.

16. Fox (1990) discusses this "defensive" attitude and the feelings that "Hinduism is endangered" amongst the Hindutva followers.

17. The VHP has a large Indian-American following. Swami Chinmayananda, the organization's founder, was very active in the United States teaching Hinduism to expatriate and second- and third-generation Hindu youth.

18. This was later changed to "Global Vision 2000" after a business threatened to sue the VHP of America for using its name.

19. The Dalai Lama had actually accepted the invitation to come to the conference before backing out due to political pressure, the VHP maintained. The BJP claimed that the Indian government put pressure on him not to come. Nowhere was it claimed that President Clinton had accepted the invitation.

20. See Fox (1990), Embree (1990), van der Veer (1994), McKean (1996), Vanaik (1990), Anderson and Damle (1987), Madan (1997), and Kakar (1996) for discussions on Hindutva or Hindu nationalism in India.

21. Nehru also wrote of Vivekananda's influence upon him in his *Discovery of India* and *Autobiography*. He also delivered guest lectures at the RKM in New Delhi. These lectures have now been published by the RKM. While an agnostic, he admired the swami for his call for social reform and "socialism."

22. I also interviewed swamis in Madras and Mysore during my stay in 1992–1993. On an earlier trip in 1989, I stayed two weeks at the New Delhi ashram and almost one month at the Ramakrishna Mission Institute of Culture in Calcutta, where I interviewed swamis, devotees, and gathered historical materials on the movement for my MA thesis. I also conducted field-work with monks and devotees in Malaysia (Willford 2006).

23. All RKM temples are dedicated to Ramakrishna. Usually a statue of the sage sits in the sanctum and is the focal point of worship. A shrine for Vivekananda sits to the left, and Sarada Devi (Ramakrishna's wife) sits to the right of the Ramakrishna icon.

24. RKM publications were also easily found in Malaysia and Singapore in Indian enclaves or within RKM ashrams. In North America, the RKM centers are called Vedanta Societies. Each Vedanta Society has a bookstore that also sells their publications. The Vedanta Press, a North American branch of the RKM, also produces books, which are then sold in both Vedanta Societies and commercial bookstores.

25. He was using "you" synonymously with "myself"—thus accusing Indians of being self-centered.

26. The Congress split at one point into two parties. Congress I has, however, inherited the mantle of the Congress legacy.

27. One example in recent times that infuriated many Hindus was the Shah Bano divorce case. In this case, Islamic divorce laws were upheld by the Supreme Court. As a result, the ex-husband did not have to pay alimony to his ex-wife—in violation of Indian law. Feminists and Hindus were outraged by the granting of "special rights" to Muslims (van der Veer 1994).

28. I mentioned the Vivekananda Kendra earlier. The Divine Life Society and Sai Baba movement also adhere to and were inspired by Vivekananda's principles of social reform and service to the poor. There are many such organizations that have followed the RKM's lead in these areas. Most attract a middle-class clientele, who through their membership and service aim to give something back to society.

29. This, of course, is an ancient concern—since the time of early Buddhism—in Indian society. The question of reconciling social dharma with the individual pursuit of enlightenment (*moksha* or nirvana) consumed the writers of Hindu epics and most famously was resolved within the *Bhagavad Gita*.

30. A sacred city associated with the youthful Krishna; today it is the headquarters for the Hare Krishna (ISKCON) movement.

31. A summary of the events leading up to the demolition of the mosque is provided in van der Veer (1994). A collection of scholarly interdisciplinary papers on the controversy can be found in Gopal (1991).

32. It was suggested by many critics of the government that the demolition was allowed to take place in order to discredit the BJP.

33. The official number was thirty-eight, but the rumored total was over fifty.

34. Most Muslims felt that the police overreacted to Muslim protests of the Ayodhya mosque's destruction. So-called rioting in these areas, they said, consisted mainly of police firings upon "peaceful demonstrators." The suspicion that Indian police were, by and large, pro-Hindu was not new. Reports of police abuses against Muslims have been made in Bombay—particularly during the Ayodhya crisis—and Hyderabad (Kakar 1996; van der Veer 1994). In 1995, a controversial Tamil movie entitled *Bombay* took up the theme of police corruption and complicity in anti-Muslim rioting and the clandestine response by Bombay's Muslim mafia.

35. Ayyapan is popular among Tamils and Malayalis. Iconographically similar to Murugan, the youthful deity is said to be the son of both Shiva and Vishnu. According to the myth, Vishnu appeared once in the form of a woman, Mohini, seduced Shiva, and produced a child as a result of their union. Some have speculated that the Ayyapan cult was formed in order to reconcile tensions between Saiva and Vaishnava Hindus in the Tamil-speaking south (Daniel 1984).

36. Indeed, she later joined forces with the BJP to help put that party into power in 1998. She also threatened to break the BJP-led coalition unless Prime Minister Vajpayee (BJP) dismissed the DMK government in Tamil Nadu, led by Karunanidhi, a longtime champion of Tamilism. She claimed that the DMK was "corrupt." This, however, was not without precedent. Rajiv Gandhi had dismissed an elected DMK government in Tamil Nadu in the 1980s and helped the AIADMK (at that time allied to Congress I) assume power.

37. It was reported that V. P. Singh—the former finance minister to Rajiv Gandhi, who later replaced him as prime minister after he "uncovered" a financial scandal within Congress I—had attended this conference and was arrested for allegedly praising Prabhakaran.

38. Waheed's "grandmother's grandfather" had converted to Islam after being cured by a Sufi (Islamic mystic).

39. This is an Iyengar (Brahmin) stronghold.

40. This is the most populous state in India, and it was under BJP rule at the time of the Ayodhya crisis. The state government was dismissed by the central government when it failed to prevent the destruction of the mosque (Ayodhya is in Uttar Pradesh).

41. These states, all in the north, comprise the region known as the "Hindi belt."

42. Actually, the BJP and its political predecessor, the Jana Sangh, has always been committed to the cause of promoting Hindi as the national language. It would be accurate, however, to say that Sanskrit is much valorized by the Hindutva parties, as witnessed in various slogans and symbols used to invoke national identity. In that sense, Sanskrit is a great "unifier" and classical substratum to contemporary diversity in the vernacular linguistic traditions in India. The Tamil movement, of course, rejects this notion as "Aryan Brahminism."

43. He is referring to the popular Richard Attenborough film.

44. Sadly, a decade later, horrific communal violence was witnessed under BJP rule in the state of Gujarat. For an excellent if not horrifying account, see Ghassem-Fachandi (2012).

45. The BJP-led coalition has formed a strategic partnership with, among others, the AIADMK, led by Jayalalitha. Anti-Muslim or anti-Christian rhetoric, coupled with excessive "Arayan"-Brahmanic–sounding discourse would surely threaten this coalition.

46. The book is still out on the current BJP-led government. On the face of it, two years into Narendra Modi's tenure as prime minister, the BJP has not pursued high-profile communal

causes, such as the destruction of mosques built over purported temples or even the building of the temple for Rama in Ayodhya. On the other hand, many on the left among the intelligentsia have complained about an insidious project of Hindutva coming in the form of press intimidation and the replacement of mainstream academics with party sympathizers at various universities, think tanks, and other institutions of national importance.

47. "Aware of the links between industrial expansion and militarism, the Swatantra Party, like the Congress of the 1980s, found in militant Hinduism a congenial ideology. . . . Supported by the Forum for Free Enterprise, a body of Bombay corporate heads, and the All India Agriculturalists' Federation, a body representing the interests of rich farmers, the Swatantra Party was conservative, elitist, and capitalist" (McKean 1996, 35).

48. Backward castes are those traditionally associated with "untouchability"—that is, the rural laborers who are not landowners. Intermediate castes are those upwardly mobile groups that have joined the ranks of the urban petit bourgeoisie or have become landowners (Vanaik 1990).

49. McKean (1996) notes this in her study but focuses on another institution modeled closely after the RKM, the Divine Life Society. In both cases, the philanthropy and ecumenical rhetoric attract educated and influential members of society—including politicians.

50. Sanskritization is Srinivas's concept (1966) to describe the upward cultural mobility of certain castes. By emulating Brahminical norms and practices (i.e., abstinence from alcohol and meat), a previously lower-status caste is able to gain respect and recognition as a "clean caste."

51. Vanaik mentions how pro-Kannadiga groups and the Shiv Sena in Bombay have ties to local politicians and the police.

52. To compare with Malaysia yet again (Willford 2006), one might draw a parallel between Hindu nationalism and the politics of ethnicity (and Islam) in Malaysia. In both cases, political support was solicited through an appeal to values and the need to "protect" the corporate identity of the group against a perceived threatening other.

53. This was not always the case, of course, as pan-Dravidian aspirations did emerge across the southern regions. In the case of the Kannada movement and its relationship to Dravidian politics, see Vasavi (2009).

54. Indonesian and Indian Muslims have also found it advantageous to assimilate with the politically dominant Malay community in Malaysia, in effect becoming Bumiputras.

55. While Foucault became increasingly obscure and aphoristic in later works, particularly in the quote above, his *History of Madness*, an early and great work, chronicled the haunting exclusion of madness within Cartesian reason. Similarly, Marx, in *The Grundrisse*, speaks of the betrayed "guilty conscience" of the bourgeoisie in the work of ideology (1978, 254).

56. Kakar (1996, 148–149) elaborates:

The cultural group, which brings the "primordiality" related to shared myths, memories, values, and symbols to the fore, thus assumes a vital healing function. One of its most important aspects is to replace feelings of loss with those of love . . . Experientially, it is a reordering and opening up of the inner world of the individual to include members of the group who, in turn, open up to include the individual in their psychological space, a mutual affirmation which lies at the heart of love. In cultural groups, the shared ego ideal may not be the figure of a single leader but many historical and mythical figures from the group's tradition, its ideals and values, and even its social and intellectual traditions.

57. Both Madan and van der Veer are highly critical of Gellner's framework for nationalism and modernization, which, like earlier modernization theories, insists that standardization of education, bureaucratization, and a need for greater individualism go hand-in-hand with scientific inquiry, industrialization, and secularism.

58. A more detailed criticism of Madan can be found in Bailey (1991).

Chapter 6: Local Pluralisms

1. The academic was Dr. Narendra Pani at the National Institute for Advanced Study (NIAS).

2. The scholar was Dr. S. Carlos, retired professor of Tamil and Kannada literature from Bangalore University and Dravidian University, Kuppam.

3. The Shiva temple at the base of Nandi Hills, called the Bhoganandishwara temple, is a stunningly beautiful architectural marvel. It features Chola, Hoysala, and Vijayanegara artisanship and is incredibly large and ornate. Like the temples described, this one clearly grew organically throughout the centuries, as various empires ruled the region. During my visit to this temple in 2015, I was told by an officiating priest within its walls that the layers of construction from these three empires were more or less seamlessly integrated. The aesthetic beauty of this temple suggests that the later artisans had tremendous respect for their forbearers, less concerned about linguistic or regional identity than a shared cultic space.

4. Austin Town is another area with a very high percentage of Tamil speakers.

5. Ulsoor has both a congested working-class area and a well-planned and middle-class area on opposite sides of its famous lake. In recent years, it has been gradually gentrified by new businesses, hotels, and luxury apartment complexes, leading to the demolitions of some homes and neighborhoods, particularly on the working-class eastern side of the village. The Bangalore Metro also runs right through the heart of the old city.

6. One might also hear that this area marks a contiguous space with the heart of the Tamil-speaking world, noting the proximity to Tamil Nadu, its status within the Cantonment as falling under Madras Presidency rule, as well as the ancient Chola presence.

7. The nearby Subramanian (Murugan) temple, also ancient, had signs both in Tamil and Kannada in 2014. But this temple, popular among Tamils, appeared to be an exception in my observations of various temples in the city.

8. Though to Kannadigas, Kempagowda was the Kannada-speaking founder of the city, some Tamils told me that he was a Tamil chieftain in the employ of the Vijayanegar emperor. It is not my intent to investigate this claim. Its significance, like that of the claim for Chola origins, spoke more to a desire to complicate the idea of Bangalore's Kannadiga origins and dominance. We might recall this discussion with regard to Kempegowda's contested origins and whether he is of Tamil or Kannadiga descent.

9. This is a common origin narrative for Saivite shrines, particularly in the Tamil context (see Shulman 1980), even as far away as Malaysia (Willford 2006).

10. It is important to note, however, that another popular theory of any temple's sanctity arises from the collective energies generated by the devotions of its devotees.

11. When I asked how this could be the case when all the censuses had Telugus listed third, after Kannada and Tamil, I was told that a high percentage of Telugus were counted as Kannadigas, having assimilated well. Telugu is quite linguistically close to Kannada, and thus,

I was told, the Telugus have chosen to identify themselves as Kannadigas for practical reasons, similar to what we saw with regard to the Iyengars.

12. This was also true for my regular taxi driver in Bangalore during 2014–2015. Though Kannada was his mother tongue, he grew up in an area where Tamil and Telugu were also widely spoken, and he was fluent in these three languages. He enjoyed watching Tamil films and felt entirely natural conversing across the linguistic divide. He told me on more than one occasion that to him, Bangalore was a city where "all the languages" of India are heard and are mutually intelligible. Though a bit of an exaggeration, the point he was making was important: that the city he grew up in was multilingual and diverse.

13. The Yazhi can be seen in the Kailasanatha temple in Kanchipuram, which is believed to be of Pallava origin, dated to the eighth century.

14. Rajanikanth, ironically, is of Marathi origin, though he grew up in Bangalore and spoke both Kannada and Tamil fluently. Working-class Kannadigas that I met also adored him, claiming him as one of their own, a "Bangalore boy." Moreover, prior to his acting career he had worked as a bus conductor in Bangalore, a sign of modest origins.

15. The *naga* (serpent) stones are prayed to for fertility, healing, and protection.

16. Iyengar (2005, 147) relates a more specific legend surrounding the *linga* and temple: "A family from outside Bangalore camped on a high rock in Malleswaram and in order to cook food, used three stones lying nearby. To their surprise, the rice was found cooked even before the firewood could be lighted and upon close examination they realized that one of the stones was in the form of a Linga. This was gifted to the residents of the area who built a small Mantapa to house the same."

17. Shivaji was a great seventeenth-century Hindu king in the Deccan, famous for his military successes against the Muslim sultanates and for establishing an independent and vast Maratha kingdom that encompassed the Bangalore region.

18. These are songs of praise directed at the deity that simultaneously involve blessings directed at the sponsor of the ritual. In contemporary south Indian Hindu temples, one either purchases an *archenai* ticket or, more informally, makes a small offering to the officiating priest. In response, the priest beseeches the deity to provide blessings for the sponsor of the *puja*.

19. Of course, there are risks of making a distinction between intellectualist or textual and popular religiosity in underscoring this point. As many scholars have demonstrated (e.g., Fuller 1992; Eck 2012), there are many Hindus who interpret temple worship differently. On the one hand, there are those who view images as symbolic representations and worship on the whole, as pneumonic in nature, focusing the mind on higher truths. On the other hand, there is an orthodox belief as well that through the devoted invitation of devotees, the image, through the grace of the deity, inhabits the immanent spirit, bringing it quite literally into life. Both positions are accepted, and thus the distinction between idol or image worship and abstract philosophical positions becomes blurred. To many devotees, this difference in interpretations is not paradoxical, as they can simultaneously hold both views to be true (Eck 1981, 2012).

20. Temples in India (and in other places where Hindus live) generally close from noon until four or five in the afternoon. Thus, the most important times for prayer are generally early in the morning and from early evening into the night.

21. It is worth pointing out that some contest this narrative, pointing to Chola-built Vaishnava shrines in the Bangalore/Mysore region, such as the aforementioned Domlur temple. Thus, the notion that Cholas banished Vaishnavas and were sectarian Saivites is not totally accepted by academic historians of the region (Srinivas 2001; Professor Shettar, pers. comm.).

22. Tulasi Srinivas (2006) notes two other factors that contribute to relative pluralism within the urban shrines, including the Kadu Malleswara one discussed above. First, she points out that certain more orthodox shrines appeal to the emergent middle-class and upper-caste orientations of its worshippers, rather than to regional linguistic identities. In a study of middle-class–oriented temples in Malleswaram, she notes that the successful temples, and the priests who run them, are able to incorporate middle-class sensitivities with regard to hygiene and technology. In addition, the spectacle of a procession, aided by the technology of lighting, for instance, makes them more attractive to middle-class devotees. That worship is part spectacle is not a new idea in Hindu practice, as the concept of *darshan* through ritualized processions is quite ancient. But innovations on the ground, aided by technology, have intensified both the spectacle and the belief in the efficacy of the temple's power to help its devotees. The next chapter considers the political dimensions of the modern emphasis on spectacle within urban religiosity.

Chapter 7: Statue Politics

1. Tigala is a variant of Thigala, the form of spelling I have used.

2. This pamphlet, which was released by the Tamil Sangam in 1992, chronicles not only individual acts of violence and vandalism but also cites evidence that the state government of Karnataka played an implicit if not explicit role in instigating the violence. It cited several prominent newspapers, including the *Deccan Herald* and *Frontline* (a news magazine), that suggested the state government had been "Tamil baiting" for political purposes. And it quoted the state's Janata Dal leader and former chief minister Ramakrishna Hedge as saying, purportedly, that the violence was "blatantly organized by the [Karnataka] Government to divert issues" (Bangalore Tamil Sangam 1992, 1).

3. The politics of language use in Malaysia is quite different. The display of Tamil language in Tamil enclaves is not perceived to threaten the hegemony of the Malay-dominated state (see Willford 2006, 2014).

4. Chidanantha Murthy, sometimes spelled as Chidananthamurthy, at one point was more critical of the Tamil presence and failure to learn Kannada in Bangalore, as also underscored by Nagaraj's analysis (2009) at the end of this chapter.

5. It is not uncommon to see Mahatma Gandhi look-alikes at public events in recent years. Much like people dressing up as Uncle Sam or Abraham Lincoln, the appearance of Gandhi is probably a patriotic act either individually inspired or sponsored by those holding public events, such as political parties or local officials.

6. In 2015 a strike was called by pro-Kannadiga groups to protest against the government of Tamil Nadu for its opposition to a hydroelectric dam in Karnataka that might affect the flow of the Cauvery river into Tamil Nadu. The strike paralyzed the entire city for hours, to the exasperation of businesses and taxis. Even public transportation (buses, metro, and taxis) joined the *bandh*.

7. A popular religious teacher among Bangalore's middle class and globally. He is based in Bangalore.

8. *Darshan*, to simplify a complex idea, means literally "seeing" and "being seen." In Hindu thought, the visual connection between devotee and the object of devotion establishes a two-way rapport. It is believed that the deity's immanent presence within the object or person beholds the devotee, imparting a visual blessing, for lack of a better word. And the devotee's visual beholding of the deity enhances devotion or *bhakti* to the chosen ideal (Eck 1981).

9. It is worth noting, too, that the Tamil Sangam, in their own partisan study of the Cauvery riots entitled "A Mute Genocide," pointed the finger for anti-Tamil violence and pro-Kannadiga chauvinism at the RSS and BJP:

There are certain hidden hands behind the violence on Tamils. A bird's eye-view will do to trace the subtle role played by the BJP and its mentor, the RSS. . . . The Minister of State for Kannada and Cuture, Mr. S. Ramesh's statement that the 'violence had been orchestrated from BJP strongholds such as Kamakshipalaya' (*Deccan Herald*, 17–21, 1991) would also confirm this. BJP's role in the chauvinist violence is quite visible. . . . It is also no secret that the BJP is fanatically involved in the opposition to the unveiling of the statue of the great saint philosopher-poet Thiruvalluvar in Bangalore. . . . Its failure to win the Bangalore North constituency in the last Parliament elections and its candidate's personal grouse that the Tamils, by and large, had refused the vote for BJP's communal politics may have provided the necessary impetus to their crusade against the unveiling of Thiruvalluvar's statue. (1992, 20–21)

10. Nair (2011) describes early debates surrounding the creation of a Karnataka based upon language, as opposed to geography and religious identity. Some leaders had warned that the southern part of the state, being multilinguistic, would feel alienated by a more exclusive linguistic nationalism.

Chapter 8: The Psychiatric Troubling of Identity

1. This was part of a larger project on mental health in urban and rural south India that I am working on as a separate book project.

2. NIMHANS has a large AYUSH (Ayurvedic, Yoga, Unnani, Siddhar, and Homeopathy) unit, though biomedicine is their main focus of research, training, and care.

3. Patients come from all parts of the country. I saw a number of patients from northeast India, particularly Bengal and Assam.

4. Karnataka is also thought to have a very high suicide rate among farmers who have incurred debts they cannot pay off given neoliberal agricultural policies.

5. Wahhabi or Wahhabist Islam refers to a strict or "fundamentalist" reading of Sunni Islam that prohibits, among other things, the veneration of saints, versions of Sufi mysticism that violate doctrinal texts, and interreligious or syncretic practices. It is named after an influential reformer and revivalist, Muhammad ibn Abd-al-Wahhab, who lived in eighteenth-century Arabia.

6. These are other names for particular kinds of ghosts that afflict people by possessing them. In the case of *bhuts* and *pretas*, the untimeliness and injustice of the deaths caused their haunting presence. *Pey* seems to be a particular south Indian and Tamil variant associated with the suicide of young women and thus a troubling of patriarchy (see Nabokov 2000, for an excellent exploration of these themes).

7. Young argues that societal dilemmas that have traction with a larger public can suggest vicarious identifications. For example, people might confess to crimes they did not commit (such as a wartime atrocity) if the said crime has captured the public's imagination due to the "ecology" of an illness taking root within public discourse. Obeyesekere, in his classic book, *Medusa's Hair* (1981), called these resonances "personal symbols" that produce an intersection between a public concern and a personal or private motivation. Following Young and

Obeyesekere, one could argue that debates within the Islamic community about reform and the need to purge "devils" and unorthodox practices could resonate among those who—while not necessarily consciously worried about such proprieties—unconsciously identify with the "worst" or most evil of transgressions.

8. This is a syndrome in which people believe that the world is watching them, staging events and sets only to spy on their thoughts and actions. The name "Truman Show" comes from a movie of the same name in which the main character, played by Jim Carrey, discovers that his whole life is being watched by hidden viewers and that the town he lives in and his own house comprise one big movie set. Many psychiatrists attest to the fact that while this syndrome—a delusion of reference and a possible psychotic state—is universal, its cultural context can vary. In a provocative book about the impact of popular culture and diagnosable illness, Gold and Gold (2014) suggest that the film itself, as a powerful part of popular culture, proved suggestible, leading to a temporary spike in this syndrome within North America.

9. The patient's family had a history of bipolar disorder and schizophrenia, independent of the individual's unfortunate experiences living in the United States. But, as the doctor put it, the incarceration and betrayal this man experienced in the United States might have been the straw that broke the camel's back.

10. A psychiatrist, his filmmaker spouse, and another medical anthropologist based in the United States.

11. These are issued as a form of welfare by the government and provide access to free medical treatment and medications within government hospitals. NIMHANS, being a national institute, fell into that category and treated thousands of patients without charge annually.

12. We saw dozens of women with a *pottu* (Tamil) or *bindi* (Hindi) on their foreheads, the "third eye" characteristic of Hindu women. Muslim women were often partially veiled, and Muslim men wore traditional headgear.

13. As Vasavi (2012) argues, the precarity of smallholder farmers in rural south India has never been greater, given structural iniquities associated with the liberalization of the economy, contributing to the crisis of farmer suicides. Many of the "patients" within the *dargah* came from surrounding rural areas, and thus the agrarian crisis in India quite possibly also made healing shrines more relevant within the local social imaginary.

Conclusion

1. In this sense, it is not unlike the shrine of Kataragama, also to the same deity, in Sri Lanka. While ostensibly this Hindu god is paramount to Tamils there, it is also claimed by Sinhala-speaking Sri Lankans. Though there are certainly political dimensions to the appropriation and counterappropriation of the deity, the larger truth is that a shared idiom of *bhakti* unites the two communities (Gombrich and Obeyesekere 1991).

2. While I have highlighted temples and Hindu devotional traditions, there are also several Sufi and Christian shrines that similarly draw devotees from across linguistic boundaries. Shulman (2016) demonstrates the literary conventions and repertoires that the principle south Indian languages shared across religious and sectarian boundaries and over an eight hundred-year period.

3. Or, in Lacanian terms, the lack within the Other's demand, perversely, is the very source of its power to subjectify. Suturing that lack through a hysterical and compulsive identification with the Other completes the circle of power.

REFERENCES

Agamban, Giorgio
2005 *State of Exception*. Trans. David Attel. Chicago: University of Chicago Press.

Ali, Daud, ed.
1999 *Invoking the Past: The Uses of History in South Asia*. New Delhi: Oxford University Press.

Ananthamurthy, U. R.
2010 "Response to Gokak." In Narendar Pani, Sindhu Radhakrishna, and Kishor G. Bhat, eds., *Bengaluru, Bangalore, Bengaluru: Imaginations and their Times*, 202–210. New Delhi: Sage.

Anderson, Benedict
1991 *Imagined Communities*. London: Verso.
1998 "Nationalism, Identity, and the Logic of Seriality." In Benedict Anderson, *The Spectre of Comparisons*, 29–45. London: Verso.

Anderson, Walter K., and Shridar D. Damle
1987 *The Brotherhood in Saffron*. New Delhi: Westview Press.

Annaswamy, T. V.
2003 *Bengalaru to Bangalore: Urban History of Bangalore from the Prehistoric Period to the End of the 18th Century*. Bangalore: Vengadam Publications.

Anonymous: "A Hindu Monk"
1972 *What Every Hindu Ought to Know*. Bangalore: Sahitya Sindhu.

Appadurai, Arjun
1991 "Global Ethnoscapes: Notes and Queries for a Transnational Anthropology." In Richard Fox, ed., *Recapturing Anthropology*, 48–65. Santa Fe, NM: School of American Research Press.
1996 *Modernity at Large: Global Dimensions of Globalization*. Minneapolis: University of Minnesota Press.
2000 "Dead Certainty: Ethnic Violence in the Era of Globalization." In Meyer and Geschierre, eds., *Globalization and Identity*, 305–324. London: Blackwell.

2006   *The Fear of Small Numbers.* Durham, NC: Duke University Press.
2013   *The Future as Cultural Fact: Essays on the Global Condition.* London:Verso.

Aretxaga, Begonia

2008   "Madness and the Politically Real: Reflections on Violence in Postdictatorial Spain." In Good et al. eds., *Postcolonial Disorders,* 43–61. Berkeley: University of California Press.

Asad, Talal

1993   *Genealogies of Religion: Discipline and Reasons of Power in Christianity and Islam.* Baltimore: Johns Hopkins University Press.

Babb, Lawrence, and Susan S. Wadley, eds.

1995   *Media and the Transformation of Religion in South Asia.* Philadephia: University of Pennsylvania Press.

Bailey, F. G.

1960   *Tribe, Caste, and Nation.* Manchester, UK: Manchester University Press.
1963   *Politics and Social Change: Orissa in 1959.* Berkeley: University of California Press.
1991   "Religion and Religiosity: Ideas and Their Use." *Contributions to Indian Sociology* n.s. 25: 211–231.
1996   *The Civility of Indifference: On Domesticating Ethnicity.* Ithaca, NY: Cornell University Press.
1998   *The Need for Enemies: A Bestiary of Political Forms.* Ithaca, NY: Cornell University Press.

Balasubramaniam

n.d.   *Domlur Chola Temple.* Bangalore: Meera Balasubramaniam.

Bangalore Tamil Sangam

1992   "A Mute Genocide: A Report of the Gory Incidents of Violence on Karnataka Tamils during the Black December, 1991." Bangalore: Bangalore Tamil Sangam.

Barth, Fredrik

1959   *Political Leadership among Swat Pathans.* London: Athlone Press.
1969   "Introduction." In Fredrik Barth, ed., *Ethnic Groups and Boundaries: The Social Organization of Culture Difference.* Oslo: Scandinavia University Press.

Baudrillard, Jean

1981   *Simulacra and Simulation.* Trans. Sheila Faria Glaser. Ann Arbor: University of Michigan Press.

Bayer, Jennifer

1986   *Dynamics of Language Maintenance among Linguistic Minorities: A Case Study of the Tamil Community in Bangalore.* Mysore: Central Institute of Indian Languages.

Benjamin, Walter

1978   "Critique of Violence." In Walter Benjamin, *Reflections: Essays, Aphorisms, Auto-biographical Writings*, 277–300. New York: Schocken Books.

Bhabha, Homi

1994   *The Location of Culture*. London: Routledge.

Bourdieu, Pierre

1977   *Outline of a Theory of Practice*. Cambridge: Cambridge University Press.

Brass, Paul R.

1990   *The Politics of India since Independence*. Cambridge: Cambridge University Press.

Chakrabarty, Dipesh

2000   *Provincializing Europe*. Princeton, NJ: Princeton University Press.

Chatterjee, Partha

1986   *Nationalist Thought and the Colonial World: A Derivative Discourse*. Minneapolis: University of Minnesota Press.

1992   "A Religion of Urban Domesticity: Sri Ramakrishna and the Calcutta Middle Class." In Chatterjee and Pandey, eds., *Subaltern Studies 7*, 40–68. Delhi: Oxford University Press.

1993   *The Nation and Its Fragments: Colonial and Postcolonial Histories*. Princeton, NJ: Princeton University Press.

Chenni, Rajendra

2005   "Is It Capital Punishment? The State Finds Itself in an Unprecedented Situation Wherein a Linguistic Identity Is Threatened by Technology. And This Time the Adversary Is the State Capital, Bangalore." The *Hindu*: Friday Review, November 4, page 1.

Clothey, Fred W.

1978   *The Many Faces of Murugan: The History and Meaning of a South Indian God*. The Hague: Mouton.

Coedes, G.

1968   *The Indianized States of Southeast Asia*. Kuala Lumpur: University of Malaya Press.

Cohen, Abner

1996   "Ethnicity and Politics." In Hutchinson and Smith, eds., *Ethnicity*, 83–84. Oxford: Oxford University Press.

Cohn, Bernard S.

1955   "The Changing Status of a Depressed Caste." In Marriot, ed., *Village India*, 53–77. Chicago: University of Chicago Press.

Comaroff, John L., and Jean Comaroff

2006   "Law and Disorder in the Postcolony: An Introduction." In Comaroff and Comaroff, eds., *Law and Disorder in the Postcolony*, 1–56. Chicago: University of Chicago Press.

2009   *Ethnicity, Inc.* Chicago: University of Chicago Press.

Copjec, Joan

1994   *Read My Desire: Lacan against the Historicists.* Cambridge, MA: MIT Press.

Daniel, E. Valentine

1984   *Fluid Signs: Being a Person the Tamil Way.* Berkeley: University of California Press.

1996   *Charred Lullabies: Chapters in an Anthropology of Violence.* Princeton, NJ: Princeton University Press.

Datta, Damayanti

2015   "The Great Depression." *India Today*, March 2: 52–61.

de Certeau, Michel

1984   *The Practice of Everyday Life.* Berkeley: University of California Press.

Deleuze, Gilles, and Felix Guattari

1987   *A Thousand Plateaus: Capitalism and Schizophrenia.* Minneapolis: University of Minnesota Press.

Derrida, Jacques

1976   *Of Grammatology.* Trans. Gayatri Chakravorty Spivak. Baltimore: Johns Hopkins University Press.

1995   *Archive Fever: A Freudian Impression.* Trans. Eric Prenowitz. Chicago: University of Chicago Press.

2002   *Acts of Religion.* London: Routledge.

Deshpande, Satish

2000   "Hegemonic Spatial Categories: The Nation-Space and Hindu Communalism in Twentieth-century India." In Partha Chatterjee and Pradeep Jeganathan, eds., *Community, Gender, and Violence: Subaltern Studies 11*,167–211. Delhi: Oxford University Press.

Dickey, Sarah

1993   *Cinema and the Urban Poor in South India.* Cambridge: Cambridge University Press.

1995   "Consuming Utopia: Film Watching in Tamil Nadu." In Breckenridge, ed., *Consuming Modernity: Public Culture in a South Asian World*, 131–156. Minneapolis: University of Minnesota Press.

Dirks, Nicholas

1993   *The Hollow Crown: Ethnohistory of an Indian Kingdom*. Ann Arbor: University of Michigan Press.

1994   "Ritual and Resistance: Subversion as a Social Fact." In Dirks and Ortner, eds., *Culture/Power/History: A Reader in Contemporary Social Theory*, 483–503. Princeton, NJ: Princeton University Press.

2002   "Annals of the Archive. Ethnographic Notes of the Sources of History." In Brian Axel, ed., *From the Margins: Historical Anthropology and Its Futures*, 47–65. Durham, NC: Duke University Press.

D'Mello, Marisa, and Sundeep Sahay

2008   "Betwixt and Between? Exploring Mobilities in a Global Workplace in India." In Upadhya and Vasavi, eds., *In an Outpost of the Global Economy: Work and Workers in India's Information Technology Industry*, 76–100. New Delhi: Routledge.

Dumont, Louis

1970   *Homo Hierarchicus*. Chicago: University of Chicago Press.

Eck, Diana L.

1981   *Darsan: Seeing the Divine Image in India*. Chambersburg, PA: Anima Books.

2012   *India: A Sacred Geography*. New York: Harmony Books.

Embree, Ainslie T.

1990   *Utopias in Conflict: Religion and Nationalism in Modern India*. Berkeley: University of California Press.

Eriksen, Thomas Hylland

1993   *Ethnicity and Nationalism: Anthropological Perspectives*. London: Pluto Press.

Femia, Joseph V.

1987   *Gramsci's Political Thought*. Oxford: Clarendon Press.

Ferguson, James

1994   *The Anti-Politics Machine*. Minneapolis: University of Minnesota Press.

Flueckiger, Joyce

2006   *In Amma's Healing Room: Gender and Vernacular Islam in South India*. Bloomington: Indiana University Press.

Foucault, Michel

1980   *Power/Knowledge*. New York: Pantheon Books.

Fox, Richard G.

1990   "Hindu Nationalism in the Making, or the Rise of the Hindian." In Richard Fox, ed., *Nationalist Ideologies and the Production of National Cultures*. 63–80. Washington, D.C.: American Ethnological Society.

Freitag, Sandria

1989   *Culture and Power in Banaras: Community, Performance, and Environment, 1800–1980*. Berkeley: University of California Press.

Freud, Sigmund

1997   "The Uncanny." In Sigmund Freud, *Writings on Art and Literature*, 193–233. Stanford, CA: Stanford University Press.

Fuller, C. J.

1992   *The Camphor Flame: Popular Hinduism and Society in India*. New Delhi: Viking.

Gambhirananda, Swami

1983   *History of Ramakrishna Math and Ramakrishna Mission*. Calcutta: Advaita Ashrama.

Geertz, Clifford

1968   *Islam Observed: Religious Development in Morocco and Indonesia*. Chicago: University of Chicago Press.

1973   *The Interpretation of Cultures*. New York: Basic Books.

1979   "Internal Conversion in Contemporary Bali." In Lessa and Vogt, ed., *Reader in Comparative Religion*, 444–454. New York: Harper and Row.

1983   *Local Knowledge: Further Essays in Interpretive Anthropology*. New York: Basic Books.

Gellner, Ernest

1983   *Nations and Nationalism*. Oxford: Basil Blackwell.

Ghassem-Fachandi, Parvis

2012   *Pogram in Gujarat: Hindu Nationalism and Anti-Muslim Violence in India*. Princeton, NJ: Princeton University Press.

Gherovici, Patricia

2003   *The Puerto Rican Syndrome*. New York: Other Press.

Giddens, Anthony

1971   *Capitalism and Modern Social Theory*. Cambridge: Cambridge University Press.

Gold, Ann Grodzins

2014   "Sweetness and Light: The Bright Side of Pluralism in a Rajasthan Town." In Chiara Formichi, ed., *Religious Pluralism, State and Society in Asia*, 113–137. London: Routledge.

Gold, Joel, and Ian Gold

2014   *Suspicious Minds: How Culture Shapes Madness*. New York: Free Press.

Gombrich, Richard, and Gananath Obeyesekere

1991   *Buddhism Transformed.* Princeton, NJ: Princeton University Press.

Gomez, Terence, and K. S. Jomo

1997   *Malaysia's Political Economy: Politics, Patronage, and Profits.* Cambridge: Cambridge University Press.

Gopal, Sarvepalli, ed.

1991   *Anatomy of a Confrontation.* New Delhi: Penguin Books.

Gottschalk, Peter

2000   *Beyond Hindu and Muslim: Multiple Identity in Narratives from Village India.* New York: Oxford University Press.

Gupta, Akhil

1997   *Postcolonial Developments: Agriculture in the Making of Modern India.* Durham, NC: Duke University Press.

Hallowell, A. Irving

1955   *Culture and Experience.* Philadelphia: University of Pennsylvania Press.

Handler, Richard, and Daniel A. Segal

1992   "How European Is Nationalism?" *Social Analysis* 32: 1–15.

Hansen, Thomas Blom

1999   *The Saffron Wave.* Princeton, NJ: Princeton University Press.
2001   *The Wages of Violence.* Princeton, NJ: Princeton University Press.

Harper, T. N.

1999   *The End of Empire and the Making of Malaya.* Cambridge: Cambridge University Press.

Hart, George L.

1975   *The Poems of Ancient Tamil: Their Milieu and Their Sanskrit Counterparts.* Berkeley: University of California Press.
1979   "The Nature of Tamil Devotion." In Madhav Deshpande and Peter E. Hook, eds., *Aryan and Non-Aryan in India,* 11–33. Ann Arbor: University of Michigan Press.

Heidegger, Martin

1977   "The Age of the World Picture." In Heidegger, *The Question Concerning Technology and Other Essays,* 115–155. William Lovitt, trans. New York: Harper Torchbooks.

Heitzman, James

2004   *Network City: Planning the Information Society in Bangalore.* New Delhi: Oxford University Press.

Herzfeld, Michael

1982   *Ours Once More: Folklore, Ideology, and the Making of Modern Greece.* Austin: University of Texas Press.

1997   *Cultural Intimacy: Social Poetics in the Nation-State.* New York: Routledge.

Hobsbawm, Eric

1983   "Introduction: Inventing Traditions." In Hobsbawm and Ranger, eds., *The Invention of Tradition,* 1–14. Cambridge: Cambridge University Press.

Huntington, Samuel P.

1996   *The Clash of Civilizations and the Remaking of World Order.* New York: Touchstone, Simon and Schuster.

Hutchinson, John, and Anthony D. Smith, eds.

1996   *Ethnicity.* Oxford: Oxford University Press.

Indian People's Human Rights Commision (IPHRC)

1992   *Cauvery: What Language Does She Speak . . .?* Bombay: IPHRC.

Irschick, Eugene F.

1969   *Politics and Social Conflict in South India: The Non-Brahman Movement and Tamil Separatism, 1916–1929.* Berkeley: University of California Press.

1994   *Dialogue and History: Constructing South India, 1795–1895.* Berkeley: University of California Press.

Ivy, Marilyn

1995   *Discourses of the Vanishing: Modernity, Phantasm, Japan.* Chicago: University of Chicago Press.

Iyengar, Vatsala

2005   *Temple Heritage of Karnataka.* Bangalore: The Commissioner, Dept. of Hindu Religious and Charitable Endowments, Government of Karnataka.

Jaffrelot, Christophe

1994   *The Hindu Nationalist Movement in India.* New York: Columbia University Press.

Juergensmeyer, Mark

2000   *Terror in the Mind of God: The Global Rise in Religious Violence.* Berkeley: University of California Press.

Kakar, Sudhir

1981   *The Inner World.* Delhi: Oxford University Press.

1982   *Shamans, Mystics, and Doctors.* Delhi: Oxford University Press.

1988   *The Analyst and the Mystic.* Chicago: University of Chicago Press.

1996   *The Colors of Violence.* Chicago: Oxford University Press.

Kapferer, Bruce

1988   *Legends of People, Myths of State: Violence, Intolerance, and Political Culture in Sri Lanka and Australia.* Washington, D.C.: Smithsonian Institution Press.

Kaviraj, Sudipta

1991   "The Imaginary Institution of India." In Partha Chatterjee and Gyanendra Pandey, eds., *Subaltern Studies 7: Writings on South Asian History and Society,* 1–39. Delhi: Oxford University Press.

Kleinman, Arthur

1991   *Rethinking Psychiatry: From Cultural Category to Personal Experience.* New York: Free Press.

Koschorke, M., R. Padmavati, S. Kumar, A. Cohen, H. A. Weiss, S. Chatterjee, J. Pereira, S. Naik, S. John, H. Dabholkar, M. Balaji, A. Chavan, M. Varghese, R. Thara, G. Thornicroft, and V. Patel

2014   "Experiences of Stigma and Discrimination of People with Schizophrenia in India." *Social Science and Medicine* 123 (issue C): 149–159.

Lacan, Jacques

1977   *Ecrits: A Selection.* Trans. Alan Sheridan. New York: Norton.

Lal, Sam Mohan

1986   *Convergence and Language Shift in a Linguistic Minority: A Sociolinguistic Study of Tamils in Bangalore City.* Mysore: Central Institute of Indian Languages.

Lawrence, Bruce

1989   *Defenders of God: The Fundamentalist Revolt against the Modern Age.* New York: Harper and Collins

Lutgendorf, Philip

1997   "Imagining Ayodhya: Utopia and its Shadows in a Hindu Landscape." *International Journal of Hindu Studies* 1(1): 19–54.

Madan, T. N.

1997   *Modern Myths, Locked Minds: Secularism and Fundamentalism in India.* New Delhi: Oxford University Press.

Malkki, Liisa

1995   *Purity in Exile: Violence, Memory, and National Cosmology among Hutu Refugees in Tanzania.* Chicago: University of Chicago Press.

Marcus, George E., and Michael Fischer

1986   *Anthropology as Cultural Critique: An Experimental Moment in the Human Sciences.* Chicago: University of Chicago Press.

Marx, Karl, and Friedrich Engels

1947   *The German Ideology.* New York: International Publishers.

1978   *The Marx/Engels Reader.* New York: Norton.

Mayaram, Shail

1997   "Rethinking Meo Identity: Cultural Faultline, Syncretism, Hybridity or Liminality." *Comparative Studies of South Asia, Africa, and the Middle East* 17(2): 35–45.

2003   *Against History, Against State.* New York: Columbia University Press.

McKean, Lise

1996   *Divine Enterprise: Gurus and the Hindu Nationalist Movement.* Chicago: University of Chicago Press.

Meeker, Michael

1979   *Literature and Violence in North Arabia.* New York: Cambridge University Press.

Menon, Kalyani Devi

2010   *Everyday Nationalism: Women of the Hindu Right in India.* Philadelphia: University of Pennsylvania Press.

Mitchell, George

1977   *The Hindu Temple: An Introduction to Its Meaning and Forms.* New York: Harper and Row.

Moore, Sally Falk

1993   "Introduction: Moralizing States and the Ethnography of the Present." In Sally Falk Moore, ed., *Moralizing States and the Ethnography of the Present,* 1–17. Arlington, VA: American Anthropological Association Monograph Series.

Morris, Rosalind

2000   *In the Place of Origins.* Durham, NC: Duke University Press.

Mukherjee, Sanjukta

2008   "Producing the Knowledge Professional: Gendered Geographies of Alienation in India's New High-tech Workplace." In Upadhya and Vasavi, eds., *In an Outpost of the Global Economy: Work and Workers in India's Information Technology Industry,* 50–75. New Delhi: Routledge.

Nabokov, Isabelle

2000   *Religion against the Self: An Ethnography of Tamil Rituals.* Oxford: Oxford University Press.

Nagaraj, D. R.

2009   "The Nature of Kannada Nationalism." In A. R. Vasavi, ed., *The Inner Mirror: Kannada Writings on Society and Culture,* 31–42. New Delhi: Book Review Literary Trust.

Nair, Janaki

1996   "'Memories of Underdevelopment': Language and Its Identities in Contemporary Karnataka." *Economic and Political Weekly* 31(41/42): 2809–2816.

2000   "Language and Right to the City." *Economic and Political Weekly* 35(47): 4141–4146.

2005   *The Promise of the Metropolis: Bangalore's Twentieth Century.* Delhi: Oxford University Press.

2011   *Mysore Modern: Rethinking the Region under Princely Rule.* Minneapolis: University of Minnesota Press.

Nandy, Ashis

2002   "Time Travel to a Possible Self." In Ashis Nandy, *Time Warps,* 157–209. Newark, NJ: Rutgers University Press.

Narayan, Kirin

1989   *Storytellers, Saints, and Scoundrels: Folk Narrative in Hindu Religious Teaching.* Philadelphia: University of Pennsylvania Press.

Nash, June

1979   *We Eat the Mines and the Mines Eat Us: Dependency and Exploitation in Bolivian Tin Mines.* New York: Columbia University Press.

Nash, Manning

1989   *The Cauldron of Ethnicity in the Modern World.* Chicago: University of Chicago Press.

Nataraj, V. K.

2001   "Kannadiga-Tamilian Nexus in Bangalore." *Economic and Political Weekly* 36(5/6): 503–504.

Niranjana, Tejaswini

2000   "Reworking Masculinities: Rajkumar and the Kannada Public Sphere." *Economic and Political Weekly* 35(47): 4147–4150.

Obeyesekere, Gananath

1981   *Medusa's Hair: An Essay on Personal Symbols and Religious Experience.* Chicago: University of Chicago Press.

1984   *The Work of Culture: Symbolic Transformation in Psychoanalysis and Anthropology.* Chicago: University of Chicago Press.

Ong, Aihwa

1987   *Spirits of Resistance and Capitalist Discipline: Factory Women in Malaysia.* Albany: State University of New York Press.

Ortner, Sherry

1979   "On Key Symbols." In Lessa and Vogt, eds., *Reader in Comparative Religion: An Anthropological Approach,* 92–98. New York: Harper & Row.

1994   "Theory in Anthropology since the Sixties." In Dirks, Eley, and Ortner, eds., *Culture/Power/History: A Reader in Contemporary Social Theory,* 372–411. Princeton, NJ: Princeton University Press.

Pani, Narendar

2010   "Imaginations of Bengaluru." In Narendar Pani, Sindhu Radhakrishna, and Kishor G. Bhat, eds., *Bengaluru, Bangalore, Bengaluru: Imaginations and Their Times,* 1–30. New Delhi: Sage.

Parsons, Talcott

1966   *Societies.* Englewood Cliffs, NJ: Prentice-Hall.

Pemberton, John

1994   *On the Subject of "Java."* Ithaca, NY: Cornell University Press.

Pollock, Sheldon

2006   *The Language of the Gods in the World of Men: Sanskrit, Culture, and Power in Premodern India.* Berkeley: University of California Press.

Prasad, M. Madhava

2000   "Where Does the Forest Begin?" *Economic and Political Weekly* 35(47): 4138–4140.

Price, Pamela

2013   *The Writings of Pamela Price: State, Politics, and Cultures in Modern South India.* Delhi: Orient BlackSwan.

Raghuran, Sunaad

2001   *Veerappan: India's Most Wanted Man.* New York: Ecco/Harper Collins.

Raguram, R., A. Vekateswaran, Jayashree Ramakrishna, and Mitchell G. Weiss

2002   "Traditional Community Resources for Mental Health: A Report of Temple Healing from India." *BMJ* 325 (July 6): 38–40.

Ramakrishna Mission

1989   *Ramakrishna Mission Relief Services 1968–1988.* Howrah, India: Ramakrishna Mission.

Ramanujam, A. K.

1973   *Speaking of Siva.* Baltimore: Penguin Books.

1993   *Hymns for the Drowning: Poems for Visnu by Nammalvar.* New Delhi: Penguin Books.

Ramaswamy, Sumathi

1997   *Passions of the Tongue: Language Devotion in Tamil India, 1891–1970.* Berkeley: University of California Press.

Rao, Gopinath T. A.

1916   *Elements of Hindu Iconography.* Delhi: Motilal Banarsidass.

Rao, Velcheru Narayana, David Shulman, and Sanjay Subrahmanyam

2003   *Textures of Time: Writing History in South India 1600–1800.* New York: Other Press.

Ravindra, A.

2012   *Bangalore Multiplicity.* Bangalore: Atmaram Gangaram, Gangaram's Gallery.

Rostow, W. W.

1960   *The Stages of Economic Growth: A Non-Communist Manifesto.* Cambridge: Cambridge University Press.

Rutherford, Danilyn

2012   *Laughing at Leviathan: Sovereignty and Audience in West Papua.* Chicago: University of Chicago Press.

Ryerson, Charles

1988   *Regionalism and Religion: The Tamil Renaissance and Popular Hinduism.* Madras: Christian Literature Society.

Sahlins, Marshall

1976   *Culture and Practical Reason.* Chicago: University of Chicago Press.

1993   "Goodbye to Tristes Tropes: Ethnography in the Context of Modern World History." *Journal of Modern History* 65 (March): 1–25.

1994   "Cosmologies of Capitalism: The Trans-Pacific Sector of 'the WorldSystem'." In Dirks, Eley, and Ortner, eds., *Culture/Power/History: A Reader in Contemporary Social Theory,* 412–455. Princeton, NJ: Princeton University Press.

Said, Edward

1978   *Orientalism.* New York: Vintage.

Sangren, P. Steven

2000   *Chinese Sociologics.* London: Athlone.

Sastri, Nilakanta

1949   *Dravidian Literatures.* Madras: S. Viswanathan.

1975   *A History of South India.* Madras: Oxford University Press.

Schönbeck, Oluf

2012   *All Religions Merge in Tranquebar: Religious Coexistence and Social Cohesion in South India.* Copenhagen: NIAS Press.

Scott, James

1985   *Weapons of the Weak: Everyday Forms of Peasant Resistance.* New Haven, CT: Yale University Press.

Sebastia, Brigitte, ed.

2009   *Restoring Mental Health in India: Pluralistic Therapies and Concepts.* New Delhi: Oxford University Press.

Sen, Priyardarshini

2015   "The Grey Side of the Moon: Why Is the 'Mentally Ill' Label So Safe for Abuse in India?" *Outlook,* July 20: 56–64.

Shulman, David Dean

1980   *Tamil Temple Myths: Sacrifice and Divine Marriage in South Indian Saiva Tradition.* Princeton, NJ: Princeton University Press.

2016   *Tamil: A Biography.* Cambridge, MA: Belknap Press of Harvard University Press.

Siegel, James T.

1998   *A New Criminal Type.* Durham, NC: Duke University Press.

1997   *Fetish, Recognition, Revolution.* Princeton, NJ: Princeton University Press.

2000   "Possessed." In James T. Siegel, *Rope of God,* 336–422. Ann Arbor: University of Michigan Press.

2006   *Naming the Witch.* Stanford, CA: Stanford University Press.

Singer, Milton

1972   *When a Great Tradition Modernizes.* Chicago: University of Chicago Press.

Srinivas, M. N.

1966   *Social Change in Modern India.* Berkeley: University of California Press.

1994   "Reminiscences of a Bangalorean." In M. N. Srinivas, *Bangalore: Scenes from an Indian City,* 6–27. Bangalore: Gangarams Publications.

Srinivas, Smriti

2001   *Landscapes of Urban Memory: The Sacred and the Civic in India's High-Tech City.* Minneapolis: University of Minnesota Press.

2015   *A Place for Utopia: Urban Designs from South Asia.* Seattle: University of Washington Press.

Srinivas, Tulasi

2006   "Divine Enterprise: Hindu Priests and Ritual Change in Neighborhood Hindu Temples in Bangalore." *South Asia: Journal of South Asian Studies* 39(3): 321–343.

Stein, Burton

1994   *Vijayanagara*. New Delhi: Cambridge University Press.

2010   *History of India*. London: Wiley-Blackwell.

Subrahmanyam, Sanjay

1999   "Recovering Babel: Polyglot Histories from the Eighteenth-Century Tamil Country." In Daud Ali, ed., *Invoking the Past: The Uses of History in South Asia*, 280–321. New Delhi: Oxford University Press.

Tagliacozzo, Eric, Helen F. Siu, and Peter C. Perdue

2015   "Introduction: Structuring Moments in Asian Connections." In Tagliacozzo, Siu, and Perdue, eds., *Asia Inside Out: Changing Times*, 1–22. Cambridge: Harvard University Press.

Taneja, Anand

2013   "Jinnealogy: Everyday Life and Islamic Theology in Post-Partition Delhi." *HAU: Journal of Ethnographic Theory* 3(3): 139–165.

Taussig, Michael

1980   *The Devil and Commodity Fetishism in South America*. Chapel Hill: University of North Carolina Press.

1987   *Shamanism, Colonialism, and the Wild Man*. Chicago: University of Chicago Press.

Thapar, Romila

1966   *A History of India*, vol. 1. New Delhi: Penguin Books.

2005   *Somanatha: The Many Voices of a History*. London: Verso.

Thiranagama, Sharika

2011   *In My Mother's House: Civil War in Sri Lanka*. Philadelphia: University of Pennsylvania Press.

Thiruvalluvar

1990   *The Kural*. Trans. P. S. Sundaram. Delhi: Penguin Classics.

Tsing, Anna Lowenhaupt

1999   *In the Realm of the Diamond Queen*. Princeton, NJ: Princeton University Press.

Upadhya, Carol, and A. R. Vasavi

2008   "Outposts of the Global Information Economy: Work and Workers in India's Outsourcing Industry." In Upadhya and Vasavi, eds., *In an Outpost of the Global Economy: Work and Workers in India's Information Technology Industry*, 9–49. New Delhi: Routledge.

Vanaik, Achin

1990   *The Painful Transition: Bourgeois Democracy in India*. London: Verso.

van der Veer, Peter

1994   *Religious Nationalism: Hindus and Muslims in India.* Berkeley: University of California Press.

Vanmikanathan, G.

1985   *Periya Puranam.* English trans. and commentary by Sekkizhaar. Madras: Sri Ramakrishna Math.

Vasavi, A. R.

2007   "Political 'Darshan' as Development in Karnataka." *Economic and Political Weekly,* July 28, 2007: 3076–3079.

2009   *The Inner Mirror: Kannada Writings on Society and Culture.* New Delhi: Book Review Literary Trust.

2012   *Shadow Space: Suicides and the Predicament of Rural India.* Gurgaon, India: Three Essays Collective.

Venkatarayappa, K. N.

1957   *Bangalore: A Socio-Ecological Study.* Bombay: University of Bombay.

Wallerstein, Immanuel

1979   *The Capitalist World-Economy: Essays by Immanuel Wallerstein.* Cambridge: Cambridge University Press.

1995   "Culture as the Ideological Battleground of the Modern World-System." In Featherstone, ed., *Global Culture: Nationalism, Globalization and Modernity,* 31–56. London: Sage Publications.

1997   "The National and the Universal: Can There Be Such a Thing as World Culture?" In Anthony King, ed., *Culture, Globalization, and the World-System,* 91–106. Minneapolis: University of Minnesota Press.

Weber, Max

1947   *The Theory of Social and Economic Organization.* New York: Free Press.

1996   "The Origins of Ethnic Groups." In Hutchinson and Smith, eds., *Ethnicity,* 35–39. Oxford: Oxford University Press.

Whitehead, Henry

1921   *Village Gods of South India.* Calcutta: Association Press.

Willford, Andrew

1999   "Cage of Freedom: The Politics of Tamil and Hindu Identity in Malaysia and Bangalore, South India." PhD diss., University of California, San Diego.

2001   "Anthropology (and Nationalism)." In Alexander Motyl, ed., *Encyclopedia of Nationalism,* 1–24. San Diego: Academic Press.

2006   *Cage of Freedom: Tamil Identity and the Ethnic Fetish in Malaysia.* Ann Arbor: University of Michigan Press.

2014   *Tamils and the Haunting of Justice: History and Recognition in Malaysia's Plantations.* Honolulu: University of Hawai'i Press.

2015   "1956: Bangalore's Cosmopolitan Pasts and Monocultural Futures?" In Tagliacozzo, Siu, and Perdue, eds., *Asia Inside Out: Changing Times,* 250–280. Cambridge, MA: Harvard University Press.

Wolf, Eric R.

1982   *Europe and the People without History.* Berkeley: University of California Press.

Young, Allan

2007   "America's Transient Mental Illness: A Brief History of the Self-Traumatized Perpetrator." In Biehl, Good, and Kleinman, eds., *Subjectivity: Ethnographic Investigations,* 155–178. Berkeley: University of California Press.

Zizek, Slavoj

1989   *The Sublime Object of Ideology.* London: Verso.

1993   *Tarrying with the Negative.* Durham, NC: Duke University Press.

Index

About the Author

Andrew C. Willford is professor of anthropology and Asian studies at Cornell University. His research has focused on various forms of Tamil and Hindu displacement, revivalism, and identity politics in Malaysia. His publications include *Tamils and the Haunting of Justice: History and Recognition in Malaysia's Plantations* (2014), *Clio/Anthropos: Exploring the Boundaries between History and Anthropology*, coedited with Eric Tagliacozzo (2009); *Cage of Freedom: Tamil Identity and the Ethnic Fetish in Malaysia* (2006); and *Spirited Politics: Religion and Public Life in Contemporary Southeast Asia*, coedited with Kenneth George (2005). He received his PhD in anthropology from the University of California, San Diego.